Behavior Adjustment Training 2.0

New Practical Techniques for Fear, Frustration, and Aggression in Dogs

Grisha Stewart, M.A., CPDT-KA

Dogwise™ Publishing

Wenatchee, Washington U.S.A.

Behavior Adjustment Training 2.0
New Practical Techniques for Fear, Frustration, and Aggression in Dogs
Grisha Stewart, M.A., CPDT-KA

Dogwise Publishing
A Division of Direct Book Service, Inc.
403 South Mission Street, Wenatchee, Washington 98801
509-663-9115, 1-800-776-2665
www.dogwisepublishing.com / info@dogwisepublishing.com

Graphic design: Lindsay Peternell
Cover and interior illustrations: Lili Chin, www.doggiedrawings.net. Humane Hierarchy: Susan Friedman and James Fritzler.

Interior photographs: Animals Plus, Company of Animals, Dan Catchpole, Simon Conner, Dennis Fehling, Katrien Lismont, Dana Litt, Carly Loyer, Marie Legain, Stevie Mathre, Melissa McDaniel, Midwest Metal, Premier Pet Products, J. Nichole Smith, Smart Animal Training Systems, Thundershirt, Risë VanFleet.

Some text has appeared previously in: *The Official Ahimsa Dog Training Manual: A Practical, Force-free Guide to Problem Solving and Manners* by Grisha Stewart and *Behavior Adjustment Training: BAT for Fear, Frustration, and Aggression in Dogs* by Grisha Stewart.

Limits of Liability and Disclaimer of Warranty:
The author and publisher shall not be liable in the event of incidental or consequential damages in connection with, or arising out of, the furnishing, performance, or use of the instructions and suggestions contained in this book.

ISBN: 978-1-61-781174-6

Library of Congress Cataloging-in-Publication Data on file at http://www.loc.gov/publish/cip/

Printed in the U.S.A.

For my mother, who taught me that
humans aren't the only ones with feelings.

For Peanut, the first BAT dog:
my soulmate dog, teacher, and muse.

I keep learning to pay even more attention
to your choices.

What will you and little Bean teach me next?

TABLE OF CONTENTS

ACKNOWLEDGMENTS

I am grateful to many people in the creation of BAT in general and this book in particular. First, I have so much gratitude to Peanut and Boo Boo, for showing me that there is a wise dog underneath the bluster, and for being patient as I looked for what was under my nose.

Thank you to:

My husband, John, for understanding that sometimes I just have to go camping with Peanut in the wilds of Alaska to write.

My amazingly empowering BAT support team, both in front of and behind the scenes: Ellen Naumann, Kristin Burke, Joey Iversen, Carly Loyer, Jo Laurens, Lisa Walker, Viviane Arouzoumanian, Jennie Murphy. I couldn't do it all without your help.

Jill Olkoski, for your patience during the development of BAT 1.0, for trusting me to train your dog (who's featured on the cover), and for invaluable help getting me to focus on the essentials.

Artist extraordinaire, Lili Chin for her lovely illustrations throughout this book and her efficient, friendly attitude during the process.

All of the people who developed the many methods using functional reinforcers from which I drew inspiration for BAT plus Leslie McDevitt (for *Control Unleashed*) and Karen Pryor and all the great clicker trainers.

Guild Certified TTouch Practitioner Lori Stevens for engaging conversation and idea-bouncing during my initial brainstorm on BAT 1.0.

Alta Tawzer of Tawzer Dog for her unbelievable support. You helped me get BAT off the ground, and I will never forget that.

Trainers Kathy Sdao and Joey Iversen for your training wisdom and insight—with Peanut and in general. And now we can say, "We'll always have Paris."

Susan Friedman, for bringing scientific information to the dog community about many things, including the importance of empowerment for our learners. I'd also like to thank Susan for helping me keep my chin up and focus on the people who are ready to learn.

Certified BAT Instructors (CBATIs) around the world who have put time and energy into fully learning BAT and demonstrating their skill. Your effort makes the world a better place!

My seminar hosts around the world. I have learned from every experience and that information is all folded into BAT 2.0. Thank you for graciously welcoming me to your area and sharing BAT with the people there. You are part of the reason so many people have learned to do BAT.

From the first book: The trainers and dog lovers in the FunctionalRewards Yahoo! group around the world (including Sarah Owings, Jude Azaren, Donna Savoie, Irith Bloom, Dani Weinberg, David Smelzer, Barrie Lynn, Susan Mitchell, Danielle Theule, Rachel Bowman, Dennis Fehling, and many others), for your great ideas and for bringing BAT to the dogs in their lives. There are now about 10,000 people discussing BAT in various online discussion groups, so I'm afraid I can't begin to mention you all. There are 46 moderators of different BAT groups on Facebook alone! That said, I will highlight Liz Wyant and Chelsea Johnson for moderating the big high-traffic official Facebook group and Jude Azaren in Yahoo. Thank you!

The many helper dogs and people that have helped BAT dogs learn and change.

The volunteer proofreaders for this book, including Susan Friedman, Jo Laurens, Carly Loyer, Bree Mize, Kristen Thomas, and Matt White. Any remaining errors are still my own.

The lovely folks who submitted write-ups on their experiences with BAT: Your stories help people see the power of choice.

Dogwise for publishing this book, especially Charlene Woodward for contacting me to publish the first BAT book. Thanks to Larry Woodward, Lindsay Peternell, Jon Luke, and Nate Woodward for helping me pull everything together.

INTRODUCTION

I'm passionate about the emotional well-being of dogs. This book will teach you how to use the latest version of Behavior Adjustment Training, a tool that I developed to help dogs and people live better lives together. For those who read my original BAT book, released in 2011, you might remember that I called BAT a work in progress. I have continually strived to fine-tune the protocols I use. I've made so many changes that I no longer feel comfortable having clients read the older book. That means it was time to write a new one! The way I teach and use BAT now has simplified many of the procedures and makes them less stressful and more pleasant for the dogs.

You can use BAT to rehabilitate fear, aggression, and frustration in dogs and also to keep reactivity problems from developing in puppies. While BAT is not the only tool in my training toolbox, it is the foundation of how I relate to dogs and help clients with dog reactivity. I'm simply amazed at how much faster the dogs are progressing than they were before BAT, and even compared to BAT 1.0. Trainers around the world are seeing this with their clients, too.

If you have trained your dog before, you probably have techniques in your training toolbox that you really like. Most modern, force-free training is compatible with BAT in some way. That said, the BAT philosophy is less trainer-driven than you may be used to; it gives dogs maximal control of their desensitization experience. On the other hand, if you have trained by being the 'pack leader,' given corrections with a leash or electronic collar, or alpha rolled your dog, then reading about BAT is going feel sort of like switching from a flip phone to a smart phone. It may seem very different (or even uncomfortable) at first. The science of behavior change, called behavior analysis, is decades ahead of what is being shown on television, so you are not alone. It's very common for people to use correction-based techniques, even though we now have better alternatives. You may not be ready to get rid of that flip phone yet, and that's okay. Like the smart phone versus a flip phone, this style of training has very powerful possibilities that the old way does not have, but there is also a lot to learn, and it can be frustrating to switch technologies. I encourage you to put that old phone up on a shelf somewhere and try something new for a couple of months.

Mark your calendar. For the next three months, be consistent about sticking to the philosophy in this book. Change is hard. You may have some setbacks along the way that make you want to revert back to what is more comfortable for you. If you get stuck or aren't sure whether a particular training habit you have fits with the philosophy, ask me questions through the Animal Building Blocks Academy, my online school. When your three months have passed, take a look to compare what you did before to what you are doing now, and assess what style of training you prefer.

I am pretty sure that if you have picked up this book, you may be ready for change. You might be relieved to find that BAT is very different from a lot of other ways to work with aggression, frustration, and fear. BAT doesn't involve leash corrections, nor does it involve constantly feeding your dog. We use treats when needed, because treats are effective and better for the dog and our relationship than leash corrections. But in my experience, lessons on how to socially interact are best learned through actual social interactions. We don't need to choose between actively reinforcing or punishing. Dogs have minds of their own, and we can use that to create behavior change. With BAT, we set the stage, then step back and get out of the way so the dog can learn from interactions within a safe environment.

I wrote this book to help both people with their own dogs and for professional trainers who work with clients. Experienced trainers and shelter staff should be able to readily understand this book and use it to help dogs with reactivity issues. I highly recommend that trainers try BAT first with friends' or neighbors' dogs so you can experiment with the techniques more freely than you can with paying clients. For extra help along the way, join one of the discussion groups (see GrishaStewart.com). I also have a section at the end of this book for getting additional support.

If you are not well versed in training, but still want to work with a puppy or a dog with fear or aggression issues, this book, including the four appendices and the glossary, should be very helpful to you. However, getting personal support from someone who has experience is better than going it alone. In particular, if you have any safety concerns or any difficulty understanding your dog or predicting what your dog will do, I recommend reading this book and then hiring a Certified BAT Instructor (abbreviated as CBATI and pronounced "sea-batty"). I have a CBATI directory on GrishaStewart.com. If no CBATIs live near you, that's not necessarily a showstopper: many of them do private consultations by video, as do I. If working with a CBATI is not feasible, a professional dog trainer or behavior consultant familiar with the latest version of BAT can also help you learn how to apply these techniques to your dog. I also teach online courses on BAT and there is a thriving online community for people using BAT (see GrishaStewart.com). So support is out there!

If you can't find a trainer experienced with BAT in your area, look for a "positive" or "force-free" dog trainer who already works with dog reactivity and encourage your trainer to read this book. There are a lot of further resources for you or your trainer to learn more about BAT, including my online courses. Another option is that your trainer could hire a CBATI as a mentor to further improve specific BAT skills. When your trainer is willing to learn new techniques, that's a good sign. It speaks well for the trainer's intellectual curiosity, problem solving skills, and professionalism.

What this book contains

This book covers all of the essentials of the BAT technique, from basic body language to the tiny subtleties of BAT. For my readers who are already familiar with BAT, some sections of the new book contain the same material as was in the original, but most of the book has been revised significantly. Where needed I have included comparisons between the two so you can see how my thinking on the subject has evolved. But don't worry; you don't need any prior experience with BAT to understand the book in front of you.

If you have used BAT before, you may be hesitant to learn a whole new way to do it. I assure you, if you really learn BAT 2.0, you will like it better. Think of it as a "Stage 4," building on the tools that you already have. I've been eager to write a new book about BAT because I have made many improvements to BAT in the last few years. BAT will always be a work in progress, and I will undoubtedly make even more changes as time goes on. The changes I made in this book focus on reducing stress, saving time, simplifying instructions, and making the process more natural. By more natural, I mean that we arrange the environment so the learner has more control over his outcomes. When specifically comparing the new version to the older one, I will call it BAT 2.0; if something relates only to the original version, I will call it BAT 1.0. When I just mention BAT without a number, know that I am referring to BAT 2.0.

I will describe more of the process and inspiration of changing from BAT 1.0 to 2.0 in the main chapters of this book. Three main principles of the original BAT still form the cornerstone of the techniques and protocols you will read about in this book:

1. Give the dog a chance to move around and learn about the **trigger**.

2. Continually assess stress and strive to reduce it.

3. Use **management** tools to lower stress outside of training to reduce set-backs.

I now interpret those three points in a different way than I did when I wrote the original book. Over the years, BAT has increasingly shifted toward empowering dogs (and other animals) and emphasizing the need for a more natural way of learning. This book goes into the details of that evolution.

What's new in BAT 2.0:

- The techniques are easier to understand and explain.

- The dog directs when to approach the trigger and move on, as long as it's safe (under **threshold**). By contrast, in BAT 1.0, the handler led more, both on approach and retreat, and sometimes had a goal in mind of how close to get to the trigger.

- You will learn specific leash skills.

- The caregiver is not specifically reinforcing behavior in **set-ups**—but will do so in certain situations.

- The protocol reduces stress even more than in the original version.

- The focus is on arranging the environment (**antecedent arrangements**) for the learner's emotional safety so that desired behavior can occur and be reinforced naturally.

With this new simplified version, *BAT takes the core philosophy of* **empowerment** *and* **antecedent** *arrangements to the next level.* I know change is hard, and some of you are worried about the existence of BAT 2.0 because you really liked the old version of BAT.

It's going to be okay, I promise. ☺

What some of you may have learned about BAT 1.0 has not disappeared. I have reframed techniques you learned as Stages 1, 2, and 3 into **Mark and Move**, which is easier to understand. BAT set-ups are now carefully arranged so that behavior is reinforced by naturally occurring consequences, without us needing to mark, but we do use Mark and Move when the dogs need that level of help. Remember my standard BAT 1.0 advice to always use the highest stage the animal can do? Well, what I talk about in this book is kind of like a Stage 4, and it's how you do BAT whenever possible. Mark and Move is used in situations where the free-flowing advice to "follow your dog" in BAT 2.0 isn't a good fit (that will make more sense later). Be sure to read through the Mark and Move chapter. There are some critical, subtle differences to pay attention to relating to stress reduction, including the very important point of not leading your dog toward the trigger.

BAT for broader uses and for professionals

While I focus on a dog's reactivity to other dogs or to people, almost all of what I teach can be generalized to other objects of reactivity. In other words, pretty much all of the concepts or techniques also applies to dogs who are reactive to objects in their environment and can even be used with reactive animals of different species. If my example is about dogs who are reactive to humans and your dog is only reactive to dogs, please understand that the concepts are the same. Be creative and don't skip over a section thinking that it doesn't apply to your issue! For example, when I write something like, "let your dog go in to sniff the person" you can translate that into "let your dog go in to sniff the helper dog."

This book is meant for anyone who needs help with dog reactivity, but it also has several features that are especially helpful for professional dog trainers and behaviorists. These are included in "Tip for Pros" sidebars throughout the book with extra information on 'BATting' with clients. Chapter 14 is specifically designed to help professionals use BAT with clients. Appendix 2 is a history of other methods that rely on **functional reinforcers** (i.e., they use consequences that maintain the reactivity to reinforce better behavior), including BAT 1.0. Appendix 3 is a discussion of all things geeky, like which learning theory quadrants apply to BAT. Both of those appendices are aimed at dog reactivity specialists. My goal is to help you put BAT into context, in order to differentiate it from and integrate with other techniques and integrate it with your preferred training methods.

Once again, recognize that BAT as a constantly evolving process. Please enjoy this book for what it is: the most current version of BAT at the time it was written. Practice the techniques in this book, discuss what you've learned with other people, attend seminars, share videos for discussion online, and combine BAT with other training methods to fit the needs of the animals in your life. *Above all, always set up situations where animals have the ability to make choices and learn from them, without fear, pain, or aversive force.*

A couple of notes on style

Throughout this book, I swap dog genders back and forth, to avoid the awkward "s/he," "he or she," or referring to a dog impersonally as "that" or "it." Also, terms that may be unfamiliar to some readers are printed in **bold type** the first time they appear in the text and are fully defined in the Glossary at the end of the book. Italics are used for emphasis.

For more help

To give you more support as you do BAT 2.0, I created a special free coupon code for my online school. Use the code BATBOOK at:

http://grishastewart.com/coupon-trial/

CHAPTER 1

Understanding BAT:
Key Concepts

My mission is to help dogs have a voice in their care. **Behavior Adjustment Training** (BAT) reduces reactivity by giving dogs more control over their own safety. I know that can sound like crazy-talk, because it seems like that means the dog is in control of us. Entire television shows are devoted to creative ways to gain dominance, based on the idea that the only way to get control is to take it away from the dog. Decades of science tell us that it's not necessary. It's actually a lot more useful and healthy to let dogs have some control over their safety. Dogs need effective ways to meet their needs.

If you're reading this book, then you're here for some reason. Maybe your dog is barking, lunging, or running away. Maybe you are a professional who wants more strategies to help clients with reactivity. Perhaps you'd like to learn how to use BAT to socialize puppies or rescue dogs in your care, because you know how isolating and scary it can be to have a dog with reactivity.

Whatever your reason for reading, you probably have at least one connection to reactivity, as I did when I first developed Behavior Adjustment Training. My professional connection to reactivity was that I wanted a better way to help my clients. More importantly, I needed a way to help the dog under my own roof. You'll learn more about Peanut later, after I give you a quick overview of BAT, so that his story makes more sense.

With BAT, you create opportunities for your dog to interact with his environment in emotionally and physically safe ways. It is especially useful when the **triggers** for frustration, aggression, or fear are living beings, like other dogs or people. Whatever the trigger is:

- BAT gives dogs maximum control over their own safety and other significant events in their lives.

- BAT arranges safe scenarios where dogs can socialize naturally and interact with triggers in socially acceptable ways.

There are a number of other key concepts to grasp in BAT. This chapter will serve as a brief introduction to these concepts. The rest of the book will provide more details and examples, including the next chapter about how I began to use them when working with Peanut.

Control and empowerment

If your dog is exhibiting some behavior you don't want, you may have wondered, "Why is he doing it?" Does he not love you? Is he trying to dominate you? If he knows you don't like whatever it is he is doing, then why does he keep doing it? Is he not your best friend, after all?

My muse, Peanut.

Behavior exists to have some effect on a given situation faced by an animal. The applied behavior analysis (ABA) term for those situations is **setting events**: context clues from the internal and external physical environment that predict possible consequences of behavior. Your dog behaves the way he does simply because he has some goal that the behavior helps him meet, not that he doesn't love you. That's the whole point of behavior. He may not even find the behavior particularly fun to do, as is the case with most reactivity. *But if your dog has learned that a given behavior provides a way to get what he wants or needs then he is likely to repeat it.* You may think it's a problem behavior. Your dog just thinks, "It works." Well, he probably doesn't think that, in so many words. But on some level, he gets the contingency, the relationship between behavior and outcomes.

Controllability is how much effect the dog's behavior has on outcomes, especially the degree of behavioral control over stressors. Having one's behavior influence external events is a basic need of all living beings. That's the whole point of behavior.

Empowerment-based training maximizes controllability by creating opportunities for the animal to meet his own goals. There's a balance, of course; we can't just let our dogs run around doing whatever they want. We have to make sure our dogs and families are safe. Whenever possible, however, we must empower animals to control their own outcomes.

Unfortunately, most training, even training without pain, emphasizes the caregiver's control of the dog's behavior. Exerting too much control disempowers the learner, whether it is done via threats or treats. It makes sense that we do it: we are animals, too, and control is a basic need for us! We just have to be careful not to get that control at our dogs' expense. When I need to stop specific behavior, I prefer to manage the environment from behind the scenes, rather than stepping in to micromanage each behavior. This helps teach them to make good choices independent of human intervention. For example, you could start by having only appropriate chew items in the room. Over time, add items that are inappropriate for chewing, but make them less desirable for the dog to chew on: harder to reach, bitter taste, etc. On the other hand, you could follow the puppy around to take precious items out of his mouth. With the first option, he is empowered and has a high degree of controllability (albeit within a controlled environment). The puppy develops a habit of chewing the toys that are available for him to chew and learns from the consequences of his behavior. Chewing appropriate toys becomes his **default behavior**.

In the second option, his behavior is thwarted at every turn as you follow him around taking inappropriate things away from him. Your items are equally safe, but the dog's controllability is low. Even using positive **reinforcement** can disempower the puppy in this scenario. For example, if you are cueing "Drop it" or "Leave it" and reinforcing his behavior with a treat, he does have some controllability, but his behavior only leads to access to the treat, which doesn't address the real issue: sore puppy gums. He may be having fun, but he still has no clear way to get that need met. You also run the risk of creating a behavior chain of grab toy → drop toy to earn treats.

Reinforcement of a behavior is any consequence that makes that behavior more likely in the future. Reinforcers can include treats, toys, or relief from something unpleasant, like social pressure.

Behavior change using BAT

A behavior you want to change the frequency of through behavior modification is called the **target behavior**. In particular, the target behavior is behavior that you can measure, that you want to build up, to happen more frequently so that you can replace the behavior you are seeing now. For example, instead of barking and growling, you might like to see sniffing, turning away, etc. Those are target behaviors. They are our goals.

Think creatively about what your dog gets as a result of his current behavior. In other words, what is the functional reinforcer for his baseline response? Think of the **functional reinforce**r as a 'real life' consequence that is the purpose of your dog's reactive behavior. Has your dog learned that barking at strangers makes them move away? He may see strangers as a threat and increasing the distance creates a safety buffer. That is the functional reinforcer for his barking (I called this the functional reward in most of the first BAT book). When you ask the question, "Why is my dog doing this?" the most helpful thing to do is to look for functional reinforcers instead of looking for what's 'wrong' with your dog. He's not sick. He's doing this for a reason. *Why are functional reinforcers so important? They are the key to changing behavior.*

What is the function of your dog's barking? What is he trying to achieve?

Once you know the functional reinforcer(s) for your dog's current behavior, the next step is to find target behaviors that your dog can do that would reasonably lead to that same reinforcer for him. This is also called a **replacement behavior**. In other words, how can the dog earn that same reinforcer using behavior you can live with? What do you want to see more of instead of the reactivity? For example, you can reinforce your dog's choice to turn his head away from approaching strangers instead of barking at them. The reinforcer you'd use for head turns would be the same reinforcer as for the barking, i.e., increasing distance from the strangers. It's a win-win, because the dog gets what he needs and so do you.

Sniffing the ground, yawning, sitting, or looking at you are also appropriate possible replacement behaviors for reactivity. With BAT 1.0, we would reinforce the replacement behavior(s) by using the same functional reinforcer that the dog earned from his reactivity. For example, when he looks away (a replacement behavior), happily walk your dog away from the stranger, thereby increasing the distance between dog and stranger (the functional reinforcer). Any arbitrary consequences that the dog will work for can reinforce alternative behavior, but I prefer to use the functional reinforcer. Instead of feeding a treat when the dog does an alternative behavior, you can provide the functional reinforcer that's maintaining the behavior you're trying to reduce. That way, the dog can still achieve his goals. The functional reinforcer concept is one of the fundamental techniques of ABA and can be applied to a wide variety of behavior issues. For more details, please check out my general training book, *The Official Ahimsa Dog Training Manual* (see Resources).

But here's an important change in BAT 2.0: we don't have to provide the reinforcer ourselves in order to strengthen behavior. In fact, sometimes it's better when it doesn't come from you. In BAT 2.0, we still use the concept of functional assessment that was presented in the original version of BAT, but now the functional reinforcer is usually a naturally occurring reinforcer. A naturally occurring reinforcer comes from the environment; it isn't delivered by the trainer as a consequence for behavior. In most of BAT 2.0, the reinforcer for the dog's polite behavior doesn't come from the handler marking or prompting the dog to move away. The reinforcer is a natural consequence of the dog's own movement. Not being the provider of all information and reinforcement can be tough for most people at first. It feels like we should be helping more, doing more. But that turns out to be distracting and not as helpful as you'd think. It's better to set the situation up so that the dog can be comfortable and the 'right' behavior just happens.

With BAT 2.0, we provide a reinforcer only in certain situations, which I'll go into detail about when I discuss Mark and Move in Chapter 7. BAT is now a behind-the-scenes approach, focusing on naturally occurring reinforcement and **systematic desensitization**. I know this sounds a bit technical, but it's actually pretty simple. By letting the dog investigate from a safe distance, he is empowered to choose appropriate behavior and observe the natural outcome. This helps him gradually get used to situations that normally would have brought out reactivity. BAT 2.0 lets dogs learn much faster and more thoroughly than 1.0 or other techniques, plus it has made people better at observing behavior and keeping stress low.

Let's pause to visualize what a BAT session looks like. Someone watching from the outside would see a dog just wandering around sniffing bushes and such with his caregiver, who is skillfully using a long leash for freedom and safety. In the example of a dog with a history of barking at strangers, we get a **helper** to play the role of the stranger. (Also called a 'decoy' or 'stooge.' I use the term 'helper' when referring to a human, otherwise I add the species, as in 'helper dog'). We work at a distance from the helper where the dog will sniff around the area, show some interest in the helper, but then move on to whatever interests him next, providing his own functional reinforcer. Over time, he will work his way closer and closer, but you do not lead him to the stranger, nor would you usually need to cue him to go away. In BAT 2.0, you give the dog freedom to learn and are mostly there to save him in an emergency, like a parachute. Like the puppy-proofing example, our task is to arrange the environment to let the dog form new habits. Always try to work in such a way that your dog can learn about the stranger and develop confidence without needing to be rescued.

Left to their own devices, dogs will resort to behaviors that have been working for them, like barking. We could wait for the dog to bark and then go about correcting it. In fact, that's how people used to train all the time. But for more than half a century, behaviorist analyst have been looking into reinforcement and now we are all much smarter than that. A good ski coach doesn't start out with the child skiing from the top of the hill and 'train' by punishing her failures. A good coach sets things up for the learner to be maximally successful, so that reinforcement can build strong behavioral patterns. By setting dogs up for success, they get a lot of practice meeting their own needs by using behavior we like. It's win-win.

A dog may resort to aggression when his choices are limited.

Staying below threshold

To use BAT you will temporarily need to micro-manage your dog's environment. This means arranging his routine so that he is not faced with situations that trigger him to react with barking, growling, lunging, etc. Trainers call that "staying below threshold" or "working sub-threshold."

A "threshold" is the line segment that a closed door makes on the floor—it's what you step over you as you walk into a house. It's also used to mean the upper limit of something. Because threshold has various meanings and interpretations, depending on who you're talking to, I'll define how I use it. Unless otherwise specified, when I use the word threshold, I mean the line between being relaxed and freaking out. When working sub-threshold, it's easy to get your dog's attention if you want to: she has little to no distress. If she does begin to focus on the trigger, which is a sign that stress may be increasing, it doesn't go too far. She is able to use active coping strategies like offering non-threatening **cut-off signals** (turn away, sniff the ground, greeting, etc.) to maintain a low level of arousal/excitement. The trigger (an approaching stranger, for example) is just barely in the foreground for a dog who is sub-threshold, meaning that the trigger has just begun to stand out from the rest of the perceived environment. If you mess up and put her over-threshold, she'll react with aggression, panic, a bout of frustrated barking, some other display of **reactivity**, or a combination thereof.

> *Reactivity: fear, aggression, or frustration responses that are over the level that dog-savvy humans consider 'normal.'*

Here's a visual analogy as reflected in the illustration of a Reactivity Chart on the next page. Your dog is just inside the threshold of a doorway feeling safe and secure. If he ventures beyond that doorway he encounters a scary world, which causes him to bark, pace, drool, growl, or display some other 'freaked out' behavior—generally all of the things we want to avoid. If your dog stays within the bounds of the threshold, he can shut that door himself, metaphorically speaking, and recover calmness. As soon as he goes over-threshold, he gets sucked through the reactivity doorway. Without a heart monitor or other ways of determining stress, we can only rely on behaviors visible to the naked (human) eye.

With BAT, you will create situations in which your dog is in her comfort zone, where she can stay at a low level of arousal: loose body posture, soft muscles (ears, mouth, face, feet, etc.), responsive to handler, and able to send cut-off signals. The behavior that indicates you are over-threshold is different for each dog, because every dog has a different amount of arousal he or she can handle. That said, pupil dilation, focusing on the other dog or person, and a slightly increased rate of breathing are signs to watch for that indicate your dog is at, or potentially over-threshold. I'll go over some more body language to watch for in Chapter 4.

REACTIVITY CHART

WHEN DOG ENCOUNTERS A TRIGGER

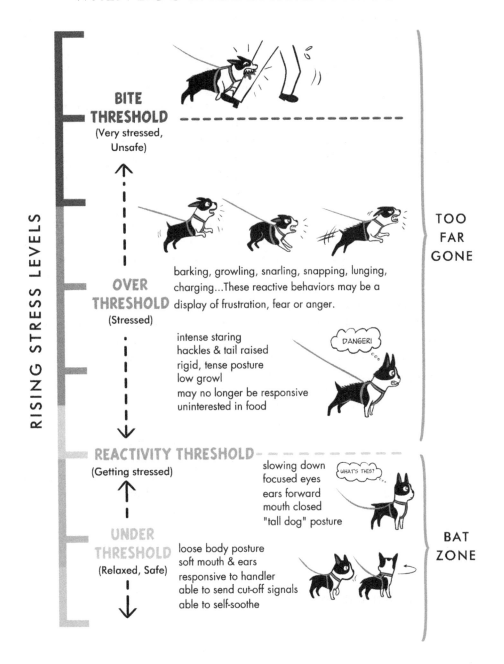

BITE THRESHOLD (Very stressed, Unsafe)

RISING STRESS LEVELS

TOO FAR GONE

barking, growling, snarling, snapping, lunging, charging...These reactive behaviors may be a display of frustration, fear or anger.

OVER THRESHOLD (Stressed)

intense staring
hackles & tail raised
rigid, tense posture
low growl
may no longer be responsive
uninterested in food

DANGER!

REACTIVITY THRESHOLD (Getting stressed)

slowing down
focused eyes
ears forward
mouth closed
"tall dog" posture

WHAT'S THIS?

UNDER THRESHOLD (Relaxed, Safe)

loose body posture
soft mouth & ears
responsive to handler
able to send cut-off signals
able to self-soothe

BAT ZONE

Set-ups

What most of us really want is for our dogs to be more boring around triggers. Right now, your dog may be way too interesting with that barking and lunging. People may-be even stare or point. In BAT, we use **set-ups** that are sub-threshold 'dress rehearsals' for your dog so that he can practice being boring around his triggers.

Notice I said bor-ing, not bor-ed. It's boring to watch, but not boring for your dog. The training area should be interesting, so that your dog is happy to hang out and do 'normal' dog stuff. The outcome of BAT is usually that the intensity of the reaction to the triggers drops significantly. Furthermore, fear often changes to curiosity and actually soliciting interaction with the former triggers. I have worked with dogs who used to bark at strangers who now nuzzle people's hands and lean into them for pet-ting. BAT builds the dog's confidence through positive experiences and the freedom to control exposure to stressors. As a result, if a BAT-trained dog does happen to become scared or startled in the future, he will likely just turn away. If the original reactivity is-sue was from frustration, he now has more self-control and can approach more slowly. Both options are a whole lot better than barking.

Be sure to *do lots of set-ups*. Meeting one example of a trigger is helpful, but repetition is what creates a new neural pathway in your dog's brain. It also brings fluency with the behavior we want to see and makes the older response less likely to return.

In theatre, actors rehearse the lines as they are written, even if it means that actors need to use the script along the way or have someone prompt them with their lines. To give your dog the chance to practice doing behaviors you like—and keep her stress very low—let her rehearse in a very watered-down version of whatever situation normally triggers the reactive behavior. All of your BAT set-ups are dress rehearsals for your dog's real-life performances in the future.

I will discuss set-ups in detail in Chapter 6, but here's a quick overview. Normally you will need helpers to play the role of the trigger. If your dog usually glances at men and easily moves on at 50 feet, then start your BAT set-up with the dog seeing a male helper at a distance of 75 feet or more, in an interesting location, just to be sure. Let her sniff around the area and choose whether or not to go any closer. It's very tempt-ing to push forward, because your dog will likely follow you. But let her lead. Having control of both approach and retreat teaches her that she can control the safety of her situation without resorting to biting; BAT empowers her to make safe decisions. Because she has learned that she can safely get away from the man, the end result is usually confident curiosity and trust.

Clicker/marker training

For close-up work and emergencies, we use something called Mark and Move, which I will discuss in detail in Chapter 7. Mark and Move is a technique of BAT that uses an event marker, such as an audible click sound, to tell your dog exactly which behavior has earned a reinforcer. An event marker pinpoints the behavior in time. It is also a double-edged sword, because it *brings attention back to you and away from the trigger.* In most of our work with BAT, we maximize learning by staying out of the way. Giving the dog the opportunity to look at or away from the trigger on his own can build confidence and self-reliance. Sometimes, however, we are working closer to the trigger and the dog needs a little extra motivation to turn around. That's where Mark and Move comes in.

If you are familiar with clicker training, you've got a good start. You'll see a lot of clicker training concepts in BAT, particularly the Mark and Move technique. During BAT set-ups, though, you will need to restrain yourself to let your dog have more control of the whole process. The laws of learning still apply even when you aren't administering the treats yourself. Focus on watching your dog and staying out of the way to empower him to make his own choices.

If you are new to clicker training, read Appendix 1 for ways to use this efficient way to train behaviors that can be done in situations that might otherwise cause reactivity like, growling, avoidance, or overly exuberant greetings. Clicker training is also very useful when doing BAT on walks.

There's a lot more to BAT, as you'll see in the chapters that follow. You'll get a lot of different examples of how BAT works in this book, especially barking, lunging, and other over-the-top reactions. Most of BAT is about setting up safe scenarios in which your dog can explore and collect information about triggers. Experiencing triggers from a new perspective can build confidence and change the habitual way your dog interacts with his environment.

CHAPTER 2

BAT Dog Returns:
Peanut's Lessons for Me

Before BAT, when I walked with Peanut and my students tried to say "hi," I couldn't hear them over the sound of my dog's barking. You can imagine that it was pretty embarrassing for me as a professional dog trainer! Peanut would not have the social skills he has today without Behavior Adjustment Training. Peanut was my muse and guinea pig for both versions of BAT. It may have not even been developed without him. Here is Peanut's story.

Peanut: 12-year-old, neutered herding dog mix
Presenting issue: Fear barking at humans

Peanut had a rough start. When he was eight weeks old, Peanut, his five littermates and their mother were taken to the shelter just after Christmas. The shelter staff separated Peanut's mother from the six puppies and assessed her to be too aggressive to place. She was put to sleep. They spayed and neutered the puppies, vaccinated them, and pronounced them ready to adopt when they were ten weeks old.

Unfortunately for Peanut, a puppy's defense system gets better at detecting threats between eight and ten weeks old, so he and his littermates were right in the middle of a sensitive developmental period during all of the stress involved with being moved to the shelter. This could explain why his basic response to something startling was always be to jump first and

Peanut in Autumn 2009

ask questions later. The other day, I accidentally dropped a shoe on the floor of the kitchen and Peanut, now a senior dog, bolted out of the room like he had a rocket strapped to his back.

But the good news is that he bounces back more quickly now. My work with him over the years has physically changed the response of his defense system, decreasing the amount of time it takes to recover from being startled. Before BAT, Peanut would have been terrified for hours and may have then started avoiding the kitchen. Instead, he immediately turned and walked back into the kitchen to receive my apologetic massage. Note: if I were in the habit of dropping shoes all the time, I could make him stop perceiving a shoe-dropping stop as a threat. I would use the sound desensitization techniques in the puppy section (Chapter 13) to get Peanut used to this trigger.

Peanut probably experienced the world as being full of threats during those two critical weeks of neurological development—he was taken from his mother, moved to a new location, neutered, and surrounded by the pheromones of frightened dogs just as his brain was very receptive to learning which stimuli in his environment should trigger his defense system. Peanut's whole litter probably wound up with a triple dose of sensitivity to danger: genetic (inherited predisposition from the mother); chemical (in utero stress from the mother); and environmental (stress of moving and being in the shelter during a sensitive period and lack of early socialization).

But Peanut was an adorable two-pound ball of fluff at ten weeks old, and I couldn't resist. I was volunteering at his shelter and was on the lookout for another dog. I looked at his litter and quickly fell in love. I chose Peanut because he was neither the most outgoing nor the shyest puppy in his litter, but I hadn't really thought through the fact that the whole litter was probably traumatized.

I took Peanut to two six-week puppy kindergarten classes and two six-week adolescent dog classes; I was intent on socializing the fear out of him. I primarily used systematic desensitization and classical **counter-conditioning** to help him overcome his fears, using the open-bar/closed-bar technique. I kept his stress level low and every time he saw a person, dog, or something else that was potentially scary, I immediately fed him tasty treats or played with toys. When the scary thing went away, the fun stopped. I also taught him a solid auto-watch through that process. That is, he learned to turn to automatically look at me to get a treat if he encountered one of his many triggers. If you're not familiar with those helpful techniques, you can learn about them in Patricia McConnell's *Feisty Fido*, Leslie McDevitt's *Control Unleashed*, Nicole Wilde's *Help for Your Fearful Dog*, and Ali Brown's *Focus Not Fear* (see Resources). Basic and advanced/ active counter-conditioning are also covered online at GrishaStewart.com and a little bit in Chapter 14 of this book.

There were a few bad incidents with a classmate in Peanut's puppy class. The other puppy bullied Peanut with behavior that was inappropriate in a socialization class for young puppies. He would consistently charge right at the other dogs, pin them to the ground, and growl in a serious way until the instructor pulled him off. That only took a few repetitions, with Peanut on the bottom with his throat in the other puppy's mouth, before he was sure that other dogs were a danger.

Peanut never played in puppy class and he barked at the children in the classroom. I have a very clear memory of three-month-old Peanut's muffled bark at a child who had tossed him a tennis ball from a chair. I wish I had realized that his puppy class was not a good fit for him. Even though Peanut was a rock star in the training exercises in puppy kindergarten, he entirely missed the socialization benefits. It could have been different if I had known about BAT then, but attending class backfired. It was too overwhelming, so interacting with other dogs and people was not a positive experience.

To make things worse, at four months old, he also was on the losing end of a two-on-one scuffle at the dog park. If I could turn back time, I would've been more careful in puppy class (spending more time on socialization, giving him more space). I also would have absolutely avoided the dog park, especially the park where people simply stood around drinking coffee as the dogs 'played.' I would also have made friends with my classmates and with parents with young children, to give him calmer experiences outside of the excitement of puppy class.

Peanut developed several phobias because of his genetic predisposition mentioned above and the early lapses in positive socialization that activated his amygdala. He was afraid of humans (any age and size), wheeled objects, dogs, basketballs, and a whole list of other things. One time, we were approached by a man with skis strapped to his back. Peanut jerked the leash out of my hands and ran like the devil himself was at his heels. Peanut was very sensitive to loud noises and fast motions.

Using classical counter-conditioning on walks, I was eventually able to get Peanut completely past many of his fears, including bicycles, Frisbees, and basketballs. He was able to compete and win in agility trials. He never barked in the ring and only very rarely in the whole trial. He and I could walk on a busy hiking trail or a city street, as long as I gave training cues, treats, toys, or even just my attention whenever he saw people and dogs. Even after five years of consistent classical counter-conditioning on walks, Peanut's threshold distance without my micro-managing was still about 80 feet (24 meters) for adults and over 100 feet (30 meters) for children. Any closer than that without me focusing on him, and he was in trouble. On the rare occasions when I wasn't paying enough attention and missed out on micro-managing, his tail and fur would go up and he'd tip his back his head to bark in alarm. Bark, bark, bark, shift away, bark, bark, bark, shift away.

Peanut didn't seem to remember people he had met and no one outside of our family could pet him. We would shower him with treats for being around strangers, but Peanut's list of Trusted Humans never went beyond the seven people with whom he had extended contact as a puppy. I think that was because he didn't actually pay that much attention to people, except for noticing that their presence cued him to turn to me to feed him. Like I said, he had a great auto-watch.

BATting with Peanut

The problems I had in reducing Peanut's threshold distance with both adults and kids led me to work on trying to get better results than I had with the other techniques. This is where BAT began. When Peanut was 8, I started with adult humans as the helpers for my first BAT sessions with Peanut. The goal was to work at enough of a distance that Peanut did not have a bad reaction, and having helpers and helper dogs that I could control was helpful for him.

> Tip for Pros: Canine and human helpers are critical to using BAT. They safely play the role of triggers that would normally cause over-reactivity in the student dog. Because you are coordinating their actions, the dog can rehearse being relaxed.

Like most dogs barking out of fear, Peanut felt safer when people were further away from him. He had learned that his barking was effective, because it led to a desired outcome: either people moving away from him or me leading him away from them. With BAT 1.0, I used an increase in distance as a reward to teach him replacement behaviors, like looking away from the approaching people, shaking off (as if wet), sniffing the ground, and other actions. Here's how that looked. In my set-ups, the helpers posed as 'scary people' loitering down the block and Peanut and I would approach them, just to the edge of his comfort zone so there was a very good chance he would not bark. If instead of barking, he looked away or sniffed the ground or did something I asked him to (like Sit), I said "Yes" (my event marker) and walked him away from the people (the functional reinforcer). We practiced this over and over in different locations.

Whenever I accidentally walked Peanut too close and he started barking, I helped him calm down by calling him away or using some smaller signal, like a kissy noise or even shifting my weight. From that new position, further away from the trigger, I would give him another chance to offer a replacement behavior and get the reward of walking away again. I didn't use food during Peanut's set-ups, so he paid more attention to the helpers than he had when we used counter-conditioning and clicker training. I recommend doing BAT without food or toys whenever you can, especially for set-ups. Working without these distractions allowed Peanut to focus more on the social situation and gather more information about the helpers or decoy dogs.

It quickly became obvious that Peanut didn't have a memory problem when he met people this way. My helpers acted in set-ups only a few times before they joined Peanut's quickly expanding Trusted Humans list. After twenty BAT 1.0 set-ups with ten different people, Peanut got to the point where he actually seemed to want adult strangers to pet him on walks! When he was ignored, he would go up to them and lean into their legs. He'd stay for petting and then walk away when he was done. Peanut progressed so much that he and I began volunteering as a therapy dog team at an assisted living facility. Children were still an issue for him at that point, but fortunately there weren't many around the nursing home that we visited. I grinned from ear to ear when residents commented that Peanut was the perfect dog! He made an excellent therapy dog—interested in them, welcoming their attention, but polite and not pushy. What a hugely positive difference in quality of life from before BAT: for him, for me, and even for the residents of the assisted living facility.

After the success with adults, I took about a year and half off of officially working with Peanut's issues before returning to training to help him get over his fear of children. Doing a single BAT 1.0 approach/retreat with the occasional children that we'd see on walks, I found that Peanut's comfort buffer (threshold distance) near children had shrunk, so that he could now be within twenty feet from them in a busy area. However, he still needed one hundred feet when a child was the only person in the area with us, unless I actively distracted him. If you have my older DVDs, you have seen how far away I started Peanut's first session with kids.

I wasn't sure how much Peanut would generalize his prior training with adults to the trigger of children. Dogs tend to be very good at discrimination—i.e., noticing that trigger X and trigger Y are different. In this situation, **generalization** is the process of learning that X and Y are similar enough that they do emit the same behavior in both situations. He clearly did not put children in the same category as adults at that point, because he barked and moved away from children and yet he solicited attention from adults. Would he need another twenty set-ups to see that what he learned before applied to children, too? It turned out that the answer was a resounding no. He learned to trust children in less than half of the number of set-ups that we had needed for adults.

The scientist in me has to note that I can't draw a lot of conclusions from this good result, for many reasons. For one thing, Peanut had experienced some Behavior Adjustment Training between the work with adults and the formal work with children, from chance encounters with children on walks. On the other hand, he didn't have the repetitions that he would get from staged BAT set-ups. Furthermore, I had refined the techniques of BAT in the year or so between Peanut's work with adults and his work with children. But anecdotally, his progress was a great sign!

The eight BAT 1.0 set-ups with children were spread out over five months and included a total of nine different children (some sessions had two kids). The first BAT set-up with a child started at one hundred feet and ended up with Peanut sniffing the girl as she sat in the lap of her mother, who was petting Peanut. During our first session, I got greedy and accidentally got him too close to the helper a lot, but I interrupted his barking and he recovered well each time. I think we would have made faster progress if I had been as careful with him as I am with my clients. I've seen several trainers work their own dogs and I think it's hard to be careful with your own dog's threshold! Fortunately, I filmed the session so that I was able to see some of my mistakes and fix them in the next session.

At the beginning of the second set-up, a month later with a different child, Peanut was able to begin just twenty feet from a seated child and fifty feet from her when the child was walking around. That session finished with the child petting Peanut with the child sitting beside her mother. The third set-up was with two children eating at an outdoor restaurant, so they were sitting the whole time. Peanut made pretty quick progress and finished by hanging out with them and getting some of their food. The food wasn't part of his BAT training, but it's always helpful to end on a pleasant note, one way or another. The fourth set-up began at twenty feet from a standing child and ended with the child and Peanut walking around together. In the fifth set-up, we added in some motion and also worked closer to home.

The last three BAT 1.0 set-ups (six through eight) were informal, more like a social gathering rather than the more formal approach/retreat training pattern we worked on in earlier sessions. Peanut and the children were allowed to interact naturally while I continued to watch for behaviors to reward. In the sixth and seventh set-up with kids, Peanut was off leash in a safely contained outdoor setting, walking around with two boys (one was new, one he had met before). He saw more realistic behavior from the boys, including some running, a few fits of frustrated crying, and lots of happy laughter. During the eighth set-up, Peanut was able to be off leash and calmly interact with two girls at their home, with no need for treats or micromanagement, and not a single bark. He had done BAT 1.0 with only one of the two girls before.

> Tip for Pros: Unlike most of the dogs that I use BAT with, Peanut has no history of biting or snapping and he has a great warning system, so I chose not to use a muzzle. If the dog you work with has any history of biting, or you are not sure of what might happen, train her to be comfortable wearing a muzzle, and use it during the session. See Chapter 3 on safety for more tips.

In the last BAT 1.0 set-up with children that I mentioned above, Peanut went up to the girls and leaned in for petting, but he still occasionally seemed to feel uncomfortable when the girls approached him. The good news is that instead of barking at them, as he would have done in the past, he just moved himself to a safer position. The children could have kept pestering him, but they didn't, because I was watching and asked them not to follow Peanut around.

Peanut went from barking at children from one hundred feet away to actual interaction. I was (and continue to be) thrilled. I still sometimes need to help children he meets reinforce Peanut's attempts to create safety. That is, if I notice that Peanut is trying to move away from children, I honor his need for distance by having the children turn away from him. The need for intervention became less necessary over time, but I think it's part of responsible caretaking for all dogs that we translate for them when people don't notice their need for space. I moved to Alaska a few years ago and then did not have him around children for a long time. As expected, we had to do a few more set-ups to help him be comfortable around children again, and they were effective.

BAT evolves

As I mentioned before, BAT is constantly evolving. Each year, I take a sabbatical from sessions with clients to really look at some aspect of my work. At the end of 2013, I focused on BAT and how I was teaching it. One change from the first version of this book was already in progress before the sabbatical: the introduction of specific leash handling skills for long leashes. The leash skills help you maintain safety while also giving your dog a sense of freedom. I have refined those even further and will go over them in Chapter 5.

In BAT 2.0, we give dogs a full chance to explore and learn.

The leash skills are designed to minimize stress and increase effectiveness of the protocol. There are other changes to BAT with the same goals in mind. After teaching trainers and families how to use BAT for several years, I noticed that it was still a challenge to keep people from letting their dog get too close to the trigger. Even professional trainers who had taken BAT coursework were still putting dogs in stressful situations. As a teacher, I know that if my students are making similar mistakes, then I need to change either what I am teaching or the way I'm teaching it. So I dug into research journals and carefully re-watched my BAT videos. I walked Peanut and observed his behavior with a different eye. Aside from a few set-ups, I hadn't really focused on Peanut's dog issues for many years, so working with dogs as a trigger for him was an opportunity for me to continue refining the BAT process.

During this time of intense reflection and research, I realized that dogs would benefit from more control over the process. In fact, I came to recognize that *BAT creates dogs who seem to have a better understanding of how the world really works, which in turn makes them feel safer.* Because of that, the set-up procedures from BAT 1.0 could be adjusted. In BAT 1.0, we had the dogs return to the trigger over and over. We didn't cajole or force, we just walked. If they didn't follow, we didn't push it. But that was still exerting more influence than I'd like: they usually just followed the handler. It wasn't what they would have done on their own, and it increased the risk of being over-threshold. With BAT 2.0, we now just follow the dog around the area, except for movement at the trigger. This way gives dogs a lot more options and doesn't put them in the position of being obligated to follow their handlers toward danger. One exception to the idea of just following the dog is that we bring dogs to a stop if they head toward a trigger and show signs of arousal. Otherwise, we just stay out of the way.

I realized that when working at the right distance, even the marker was unnecessary. In fact, using a marker got in the way of taking in information about the situation. One of the strengths of BAT 1.0 is that the dog finally has a chance to just learn about the trigger, without distractions from the human. BAT 2.0 takes that a step farther, by letting the student dog explore the area, including the trigger, from a safe distance. This also allowed me to simplify the instructions. There are no more stages, just two main principles—following your dog using the leash skills or using Mark and Move when up close. I'll give more instruction on this valuable tool later, especially in Chapter 7.

Peanut happy and free in the forest

Peanut continues to be my muse. When I was developing BAT 2.0, he was 11 and still had one trigger to experiment on: dogs. Instead of the approach-retreat of the first version of BAT, I began following Peanut as described above. Letting him "vote with his feet" gave me a clearer picture of his comfort level: he wanted to be much farther from the other dogs than I had previously thought. Throughout his life, if he was doing agility, obedience, or other cued behavior, he could work near dogs, but he actually preferred more space. In experimenting with other dogs, I have found that even the dogs who run in to attack or play benefit from a chance to clearly demonstrate their threshold distance in this way.

That was two years ago, and trainers and caregivers all around the world are using BAT 2.0. People have told me that they like it better, because even though you need to start farther away, it is faster, easier to explain, and more relaxing than BAT 1.0. When I met my new puppy, Bean, at four months old, he barked and snapped at Fiona, the dog we brought to test him. BAT 2.0 was essential in reducing his reactivity to dogs and socializing him with people.

When I work with clients, they are excited to get on with the business of fixing their dog's problems. I imagine you are, too. I want to make sure you get the BAT information that you need, but skilled trainers are kind of like trauma surgeons—first you need to save the patient, then you can work on the finer points of treatment. I want you to become a skilled trainer and successfully help your dog. That is why the next chapter goes through tips on how to make the dog's situation as safe as possible before getting into all of the details of BAT.

> Tip for Pros: If you're a professional trainer who is familiar with reactivity, you are probably already advising your clients on many of the management solutions in the next chapter, but it's still worth a read.

Peanut doing agility with human jumps and weave poles post-BAT.

CHAPTER 3

Quick Fixes:
Safety and Management Essentials

Management is the trainer buzzword for changing your dog's environment to make it impossible or unlikely that he'll be triggered to do the behavior that you're trying to stop. Behavior Adjustment Training and management go hand in hand; when using BAT to rehabilitate a reactive dog, you will also need to implement management to keep your dog out of trouble. Management is essential to keep your dog under threshold in relation to environmental triggers—that is, your dog's life should be set up to help him stay calm, relaxed, and safe. Behaviorist B.F. Skinner called it "environmental engineering" (see Appendix 2) and is referred to as **antecedent arrangements** in Susan Friedman's "Humane Hierarchy" (see Appendix 3). In this chapter, I'll talk about the management strategies that are especially helpful for reactivity.

Management solutions can create a safe situation right away, because they don't require actively training your dog. Rather, making some environmental changes can set the dog up for success. Generally, this means installing some piece of equipment or changing the way you expose your dog to the environment. Closing the door to your house or the gate in your yard is an example of management. A fence is a simple device that keeps dogs from leaving your property and it requires no training. Putting up a baby gate and giving the dog a Kong before visitors come over are also management techniques, as is walking your dog on a leash. Most cities have leash laws, so there will most likely always be some level of management in your dog's life.

If you find that your dog frequently barks, lunges, growls, or cowers, please read this chapter carefully. *Creating a safe environment is critical to successful reactivity rehabilitation.* Management solutions like baby gates and locked doors can feel restrictive, but they are immediate, effective, and not necessarily permanent. My goal with most management strategies is to put them into place right away to prevent trouble, and then change the dog's response to triggers using BAT and other techniques so that management can be reduced or stopped.

If BAT is going to help your dog, why do you even need to know about management solutions in the first place? Because the dog needs to feel safe as often as possible in order to thrive. Here's an analogy: in the HBO hit television series "The Sopranos," Mafioso Tony Soprano repeatedly visits a therapist to help stop his panic attacks. Meanwhile, opposing gangs try to kill him, he strangles his rivals, his marriage is in shambles, his children are in trouble, and he even has issues with his mistress. Even if his therapist were a genius, Tony's recovery would come slowly, if at all, because he is fully aware that there's more danger in his world than he can handle and he shows no real willingness to change his environment. Unfortunately, this is the sort of situation people put their dogs in all the time. *We want our dogs to change their behavior without changing our behavior or their environment.* We want them to feel safe while loose dogs run down the street, kids pop into elevators, and loud motorcycles whiz by. But, in the dog's mind, the mafia is out to get them, they are in way over their heads, and they know it.

For any training plan based on reinforcement to work, you have to tone down the environmental stimulation that sets up dogs to fail, like exposure to loud noises or windows with views. Just as you might use fencing to keep a toddler out of the pool, physical barriers can help keep dogs away from situations that they aren't yet trained to handle. If BAT and management are used properly, your dog will be given multiple chances to succeed and little or no chance to panic or rehearse unwanted behaviors.

If your dog can see triggers out the window, his baseline arousal stays high, setting you both up to fail.

Why is it so important to set dogs up for success? Whether you use them intentionally or not, consequences change behaviors. If your dog's reactivity is significant enough that you're reading this book, chances are that your dog has found that behavior to be effective. It's important to prevent your dog from being rewarded for unwanted behaviors with basic problems like jumping up or pulling on the leash, but *setting your dog up for success and preventing failure is even more critical for reactivity, because reactivity is emotionally driven and can have dangerous consequences.*

In this chapter I will discuss some management steps that increase safety and reduce your dog's overall stress level. These include:

- Reducing visual stimulation
- Preventing face-to-face encounters
- Avoiding problems while on walks
- Distractions
- Using muzzles and other safety equipment

Out of sight (and sound), out of mind—reducing visual stimulation

Starting at home, one simple solution to reducing visual triggers for your dog is to eliminate any perches from which your dog can spy on passing dogs or people. Dogs with lookout posts can successfully practice barking all day long, and the training time you put in is nothing compared to your dog's nine-hour shift of guarding the house! Dogs need entertainment, but working for Homeland Security all day is not fun, it's stressful. Chronically elevated cortisol levels can lead to a host of health issues that may shorten your dog's lifespan.

Guarding the home all day erases the good effects of a BAT set-up.

Let's look at just the training part from the dog's perspective. She barks, the boy or dog walking by goes out of sight, and she thinks her behavior has worked to protect the house—but then it happens again and again! Her barking becomes a stronger habit with each passing day.

Tip for Pros: A home with a perch is like a giant Skinner box (operant learning chamber); it automatically trains your dog to bark. If your clients aren't willing to make environmental changes to prevent the reinforcement and rehearsal of reactivity, they might as well just hand over your fee and send you on your way without even bothering to hear the rest of what you have to say. Don't just ditch them, of course, but to make any improvement, you must convince them to change their home and habits to prevent a build-up of stress and auto-training of unwanted behaviors. One way to do that is to have clients shoot a video of the dog's activity while home alone.

To get rid of perches, you can move furniture, use baby gates or exercise pens to block off an area, and/or install Roman shades that allow a human to see out of the top while the bottom is closed off. During our dark Alaskan winters, I find that Roman shades that let light in at the top are much better for my mood than fully closed top-down shades! Hardware stores carry a plastic film that will cover existing windows and make them look like stained or smoky glass, fluffy clouds, or other patterns. The fake snow that comes in a spray instantly removes distractions and is easy for renters to clean off of windows. This spray can also be gradually removed by wiping away little bits to make the outside world more visible. For a cheap solution, tape waxed paper to the window. Waxed paper is the squirrel-barking solution I used on the bottom half of my sliding glass doors. I only have so much time to train and turning off the 'backyard TV' was a quick fix for barking at my house.

Waxed paper is a quick fix to prevent barking at squirrels.

If you live in an apartment or condo, you may need to find ways to keep your alert-barking dogs from being able to hear (and bark at) people in the hallway or neighboring units. To keep dogs from noticing and barking at noises outside, leave the television on or play sound recordings that are mostly monotonous, with occasional changes—like ocean waves with high-pitched birdcalls. Because sudden changes are specifically what tend to grab a dog's attention and make him bark, variations in the sound recording are important, because then the dog gets used to the environment changing. Turn down the volume as weeks or months go on, so that the dog begins to hear more and more of the 'real' environment.

There is also a lot you may need to change outside as well. For example, I love dog doors, but they should be closed unless a human is home to supervise. Dog doors can lead to the same sort of reactivity rehearsal problem as perches. Fences should be sturdy and, ideally, not allow the dog to look through. Privacy fencing that completely encloses the dog's area is my favorite way to fence a yard. *The main criterion for a fence is that it actually prevents escapes and intrusions.* That may sound too basic to mention, but it is not. A student in my Growly Dog class complained that his dog kept getting out and chasing other dogs down the block. How did she get out, you might ask? There was a lovely fence around the house, but no gate! Another client complained of the same problem, except that his dog was jumping his three-foot fence. This was an athletic thirty-five pound dog, and I'm pretty sure even a five-foot fence would have not been a challenge.

Make sure your fence keeps your dog inside and triggers outside.

I have seen a surprising number of clients for aggression and fear issues whose fences were inadequate. They had holes under the fence, broken slats, areas only secured by bushes that the dog could get through, electronic fencing, you name it—somehow people just expect their dogs to understand the concept of a fence and respect it, even if it's not 100% secure. I always recommend clients install a real, physical fence. Aside from the ethics of electronic fences, an 'invisible' fence that you cannot even see does not keep people or other dogs or children from coming in and teasing, attacking, or getting bitten by your dog, nor does it help passersby feel safe.

A four foot fence is no match for an athletic dog.

Even if you have a solid fence, don't leave your dog alert-barking in the yard when you are not home. Although the dog may not be able to see through the fence, he can certainly hear what is going on beyond the fence. Extensive yard time is a privilege, not a right, and barking takes away that privilege until they have cooled off. Any benefit your dog may get from the chance to exercise is outweighed by the chance to practice unwanted behavior. Spending time in the yard alone, with no human at home to hear barking and do something about it, trains the dog to bark. As with the indoor perch where they can bark at passersby, the yard is like a giant auto-shaping machine for barking, with the functional reinforcer of getting the dog or person walking by to keep going. If your dog has this problem, be sure to read the Chapter 11 on Fence Fighting.

Tip for Pros: If you have an intake questionnaire, ask about the existence, state of repair, and visibility of their fence, as well as whether the dog is supervised while in the yard.

If you need proof that being left alone in a yard can lead to barking, just take a walk in the suburbs during a weekday. For example, on our first walk in a new neighborhood, Peanut and I passed by seven yards with unsupervised dogs. Every single one of the dogs barked at us, and they were reinforced for that barking as we walked away. That's just what's happening to your dog if you are leaving her in the yard (even if fenced) while you go to work. In one of the yards we passed by, a fight actually broke out. First, the Doberman and Corgi in the yard began barking at us. Then the Doberman quieted down, followed by the Corgi. When the Corgi started barking again, the Doberman redirected her aggression to the Corgi, pinning him to the ground with her mouth around his neck! The Corgi squealed. I yelled and threw a small rock at the Doberman. Fortunately, they broke apart before I felt compelled to use my Spray-Shield (citronella spray for breaking up dog fights) to stop the attack, but how many other times has this happened? Replacing their reactivity with better behaviors will take some practice and their training will go nowhere if the dogs continue to be left out in the yard during the day.

Legal tip: a sign like this may be admitting fault.
It's better to have a neutral "Dog Inside" sign.

Reducing the amount of stimulation your dog encounters will help her relax and keep the home quieter, which should drastically improve your family's quality of life. However, giving your dog downtime from her job as Chief of Security is more than just simply covering up the problem. *Setting up your dog's environment to prevent barking is essential for successful training.*

Preventing accidental close encounters

In addition to removing the rehearsal of stress and barking from a distance caused by poor fencing and perches, you need to protect your dog by making accidental run-ins with their triggers impossible. Well, anything's possible, *but opportunities to bite another dog or a person should be made extremely unlikely.* Your door probably opens over a thousand times per year, so even a one percent chance of escape through an open door would mean that, on average, your dog gets out over ten times per year. That's pretty scary.

One of the most effective solutions is to install some kind of airlock on all exits to unfenced areas, to help prevent escapes and reduce the opportunity for aggression. An airlock is a physical buffer that keeps your dog from escaping even if the door is left ajar. Even if one door is open, there is another that blocks the exit. The airlock can be a permanent bit of fencing or a portable exercise pen, like those available at pet stores. When traveling with your dog, bring an ex-pen with you to go inside of your hotel room or around the door of your camper.

Most daycares, dog parks, and training centers have airlocks for each exit, so dogs don't get loose. An airlock for the exterior doors of the home gives your family a place to welcome guests without dogs escaping from the property or coming face-to-face with guests. You can just open the door to your house, close the dogs in the house behind you, and then let the guest into your airlock. If you are getting a pizza, the delivery driver never comes into contact with your dogs. Because freedom is no longer just on the other side of the front door, dogs also make fewer mad dashes outside. Why bother, when it's just another room of the house?

Airlocks around exits prevent escapes.

If you really want to be safe and keep your dogs calmer, put a lock on the gate to prevent people from coming up to the door. Installing a wireless doorbell and mailbox on the gate are a must if the mailman and visitors are locked out, but even if the gate is unlocked, putting the mailbox out at the fence will prevent or reduce the once-daily rehearsal of aggression toward the mail carrier. Installing a doorbell along with instructions on the gate will further reduce unwanted encounters.

Tip for Pros: A nice side effect of a new doorbell is that it sounds different. It has no negative association, so you can easily do a cue transfer to teach the dog that the doorbell is a new cue for "Go to Bed." You save time by purchasing a doorbell (like the iChime) that lets you record your voice saying "Go to Bed."

Replacing your doorbell with a recording lets you cue behavior to reinforce.

Even children can understand safety concepts, like airlocks, with some training. I worked with a family whose dog, Roxy, had bitten a neighbor's son. The reason they first contacted me was that their daughter had opened the door and their barking dog charged out and bit the visiting child on the upper thigh, leaving a nasty bruise through layers of clothing. They have installed an airlock and a system of gates in their home, so that Roxy has to go through an internal gate, a door, and the gate on the porch to get to a visitor.

Instructions explain what to do with this locked gate.

I recommend putting in extra safety steps with children, because they can't always be relied upon to remember the rules. A system needs to be made childproof, or as much as any system can be. In the example above, Roxy is limited to the kitchen and living room. It's really helpful to have an area of the house that Roxy can be in that is away from the doorway. Her area was created with tall baby gates, but you can also do this with exercise pens. We found that Roxy was happiest when she could interact with the family, so the baby gates keep her with them but away from the front door.

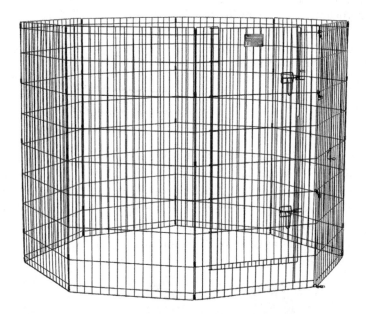

Exercise pens are flexible management tools.

When the doorbell rings, the children are supposed to ask mom or dad to open the door for them. The guest is still outside of the gate, not at the door, because their doorbell is outside of the airlock. Mom can then double-check that Roxy is in her pen, and then open the door, go out, open the gate, and let the guest in. If the child forgets the rules and opens the door herself, the visitor is still protected, because of the airlock. If the child opens the gate to Roxy's pen while mom is in the airlock with the guest, mom will hear barking and knows not to open the door. If the guest ignores the note on the airlock and walks in without an invitation, the guest is still safe, because Roxy is still penned up within the house. In order for Roxy to be set up to bite another guest, all three safety systems would have to fail at once, which is unlikely. Note: With the recordable doorbell that I mentioned above, the family could set "Put Roxy away" or "Is Roxy in her pen?" as the message that plays when a visitor presses the button outside.

These steps are a lot to go through, but the emergency room for a child and euthanasia for a dog are terrible possibilities. A bite is very unlikely, but the consequence is so bad that prevention is of the utmost importance. These extreme management measures are not something I would expect a family with children to do forever. Many families with young children simply cannot be expected to make enough changes to keep everyone safe, and the family dog must find a new home or be put to sleep. Contrary to popular belief, there are not a lot of homes (or farms) out there that are willing to take a dog with a bite history, and these steps can help keep your dog's record clean while you improve the dog's behavior with BAT and look for a new home. These steps can also give your dog a chance to relax until the training has time to change the dog's emotional response.

Putting your dog in a crate, behind a strong, tall baby gate, in a bedroom, or on a tether (short leash attached to a wall or heavy object) with a tasty bone or food-stuffed puzzle toy can work well if your dog's reactivity is mild. Having visitors is stressful and potentially unsafe when your dog is loose in the house. A spot that allows your dog to get used to the guests in the home is the best location for the crate or tether, unless there is just too much stimulation. You might have tried putting the dog away, but simply being put away is not enough. Without the proper (edible) distraction, your dog is likely to become more and more stressed by the visit, and your training may backslide. I have special food-stuffed toys in the freezer at all times, so I can instantly have them available when needed.

Coach guests and/or put your dog away to avoid unsafe situations.

If your dog would continue to bark regardless of the distraction of food puzzles, put her off-site in advance. Possible locations include: in the car in a temperature-controlled garage, with a friend, or some other location out of the home when people come over. Having her off site keeps her from making an even more negative association with visitors. Continue keeping her off-site until your BAT sessions and other training prepare her to handle visitors. Take separation anxiety issues into account, of course, and don't keep her in a location that would add even more distress or set her up to destroy anything.

Keep in mind that treats and toys that are high-value enough to distract a dog from a scary visitor are, by definition, valuable. This might cause fights in multiple dog households. If you have more than one dog, you may need to give your dogs their bones in crates, separate rooms, or otherwise safely separate them to keep the peace. To prevent crate guarding, close the crates when the bones are picked up. Do not allow visitors to greet or taunt the dogs while they are eating. Even when dogs are being quiet, they are still aroused by the visitor's presence, so it's a good idea to ask visitors to ignore them unless the dog specifically requests attention. See Chapter 12 for more tips on having guests.

Braving the great outdoors—avoiding problems on walks

As you know, your home is not the only place where training can be sabotaged by overexposure to triggers. Walks are a big challenge for dogs with reactivity issues. The most important aspect of keeping your walks safe is making sure you can physically keep your dog with you. I recommend using a leash that you can grip and slide over comfortably. That means no cord-type retractable leashes, chain leashes, or other leashes that might tear your skin.

The leash should be about 15 feet (5 meters) and attached to a harness so that your dog can feel free, but adjust the length as needed. Shorten the leash before blind corners, so you can check for safety. Use an actual leash, not a gadget. It's really hard to use a retractable leash without letting the dog get into trouble (think of the momentum a dog can build up in twenty feet!), so I usually recommend a soft, round leash from multi-filament polypropylene solid core roping. Some people prefer leather or pleather for comfort, but it doesn't vibrate in quite the same way when you slide your hand along it, and that vibration can be useful for communication. I find 15 feet to be about all people can handle well. Until you feel capable of handling a 15-foot leash safely, a standard-length leash is the safer option.

There are lots of good harnesses currently on the market. My current favorites are the PerfectFit (UK), XtraDog (Canada), the Balance Harness (US), Haqihana (Italy), and a lot of great German brands, like Camiro, Stake Out, and Anny•x. Avoid harnesses that choke the dog, hurt the armpits, or make it so that it's impossible to run normally. Every dog is unique, so what works for a friend's dog may be uncomfortable for your own dog. It's kind of like jeans. They all fit each individual differently and the exact fit changes with age!

I like harnesses that have an attachment in the front and back (use the front with PerfectFit only if also attaching to the back). Harnesses should not hinder the dog's natural movement, giving them the full range of leg and shoulder motion. The Balance Harness is light and easy to attach and sits well out of the armpits. The PerfectFit and

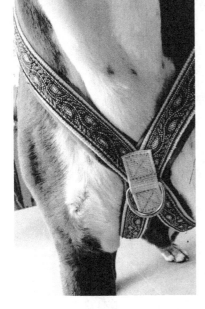

*A good harness allows
free range of motion.*

XtraDog can be fitted to be outside of the armpits as well and have fleece padding so they don't move around and rub the fur. PerfectFit comes in three separate pieces with their own sizes, so you can fit it exactly for your dog of any size. But that modularity also makes things slightly more complicated when you first purchase it. The German brands are really great for freedom of motion, with no pressure on the throat. They fall well behind the armpits and can be customized.

I prefer to use the back-attachment of harnesses whenever that is sufficient. Unlike head collars (with a nose loop), front-attachment harnesses give your dog the freedom to choose how to move his head, but they still get less control over the direction they can move than with back-attachment harnesses, so be careful of overusing the front attachment. A perk of the front-attachment harnesses for real life is that you have the leverage to pull your dog away if you accidentally put him into a stressful situation that makes him flee in panic or bark/ lunge. The BAT leash skills give you a lot of ways to communicate with your dog, so usually only a harness is required.

Symmetry Line attached to the front and back of the Perfect Fit harness.

The second clip is for safety, in case the front ring breaks off of the harness.

Whatever your dog wears, you want to maximize your dog's freedom and safety for all involved. I only recommend head collars for dogs that are much stronger than their humans, and only when paired together with a harness. Here's how: use two points of attachment, meaning you have one leash attached to both the harness and the head collar. You can attach the snap from one end of a European-style leash to the head collar and the snap on the other end to the harness. That way, you are primarily using the harness, but have the head collar if you really need more control. My Symmetry Line is a long line with multiple clips, so you can attach a fixed snap to back of the harness and the closest sliding snap to the head collar. Take time to get your dog used to wearing a head collar, using the same steps as for a muzzle (see page 55).

Note: Dogs often turn to bite the handler when given a leash correction. That style of handling is the opposite of what we use in BAT. If you are using a prong collar, shock collar, or other corrective device, please look into the gear recommendations above to find another option. Corrective devices can create a negative association, add more stress, and cause long-term physical pain in the neck and spine. We can avoid all of that and still get plenty of control using the BAT leash skills and a harness.

On urban dog walks, the first step out the door can be dangerous, especially if you live in a building with indoor corridors or elevators. The higher the building, the more likely it is that your dog will be trapped in a tight space with his trigger, unable to escape. You can help your dog avoid triggers in tight quarters in a number of different ways, balancing convenience and safety. For freedom of movement and fewer surprise encounters than the elevator, you can opt for the stairs with your dog. If you have a small dog, you can pick up your dog and face him away from the trigger. If your dog is only slightly uncomfortable about other dogs or people, you can have him sit and place yourself between him and the other people. Feeding your dog a constant stream of treats during this time can distract him even more and help elevator rides become more pleasant at the same time. To reduce visual cues, a Calming Cap may be worn. A Calming Cap is a semi-transparent hood that covers your dog's eyes to limit how clearly your dog can see the people or dogs in the elevator with them. Wearing the Calming Cap can allow some dogs to take the elevator without showing aggression. Another option, especially for small dogs, is to use a stroller, which protects their personal space and puts them up higher, out of reach of other dogs. A stroller can also be covered, with calming music inside to minimize outside stimulation. Like a crate, a stroller should be a safety zone. Do not let anyone reach inside to greet your dog.

A grass sod patch or some other way for your dog to eliminate indoors reduces the number of required walks, so that walks can be exclusively for training. Moving to a house with a securely fenced yard, or at least a first-floor apartment, is the ultimate environmental engineering for dog reactivity. When moving is impossible and other changes are insufficient, medication or other stress reducers may be necessary to allow apartment dogs to go through their days without freaking out every time they head out on a walk.

Suburban dogs may have more peaceful walks than their urban cousins because they are not trapped in elevators, hallways, and noisy sidewalks with other dogs and people. As I mentioned, they do tend to have a constant barrage of dogs barking at them from their yards. Imagine that your neighbors shouted obscenities at you whenever you went for a walk by their houses. How long would it be before you developed some reactivity?

If your canine neighbors go crazy when your dog walks by, note which homes have barking dogs and cross the street. Then change your route, if possible, so that your dog doesn't have to walk right past them. You can reduce the chances of being barked at by silencing your dog's jingling tags. This keeps the dogs who are napping inside their homes blissfully unaware of your dog's presence. Another option is to attach your dog's tags directly to the collar by drilling a second hole in the tag and sewing both ends to the fabric of the collar. Another option is to get some kind of tag silencer. A rubber band works fine for that and commercial tag silencers are available.

I have successfully trained most of the single yard dogs in my new neighborhood to stop barking at my dogs as we go by, and we avoid the rest. I train them using pure counter-conditioning. I just happily sing out "Treat Time," or the dog's name in an inviting voice as if I am calling the dog over to join us, and then toss in a few piece sof stinky treats. The treat I toss often hits the dogs in the ears so that they notice the flying food. I toss down some treats for my dogs to find, say "Treat Time" again, and tossed some more into the yard, followed by more treats for Bean and Peanut for putting up with all of this. If your dog can't get close enough to a barking dog to be able to feed it, you can either set aside time to train the neighbor dogs first without your dog or just focus on your own dog and let the dogs in the yard keep barking. Talking about the barking dogs in a normal tone seemed to help my dogs think that everything's ok. "That's just Ginger," I say to them, making up the name on the fly, "She has a fence." I use the same sort of tone that I would use if I were pointing out something mildly interesting to a friend on a walk, as in, "Looks like Sally has a new pool man" or "Max is such a good gardener! Look at those buds."

Sometimes when I toss treats to yard dogs, they immediately stop barking and start scarfing up the treats, or even offer Sits. Other dogs ignore the treats and bark like mad, but then eat the treats after we walk away. But each time I show up and sing out, "Treats," most of the dogs are less and less likely to bark. Eventually, once they hear the word "treats" they just quietly (if excitedly) await their cookies. I gradually start weaning off of the treats once the dogs are quiet, over the course of a few weeks to a month.

I have to throw in some words of warning about training other people's dogs on your walk. First, it's a good idea to get permission beforehand, as doing so without permission may be illegal or annoying to your neighbors. If you don't get permission, that's your choice, but for your dog's sake, be ready to just walk away or have a short explanation ready if someone comes up to yell at you. Everybody I've ever encountered has been fine with it, but Seattle, where I lived previously, and Alaska, where I live now, are pretty friendly places. Second, use simple treats without chicken, grains, or nuts, because the dog or family at that home may have allergies. Third, the neighbor's dog may be on a diet, so try to use low-fat treats, but not at the expense of taste or smell. Fourth, if there is more than one dog, the treats may cause a fight, so I only use this for dogs who are alone in their yards. (My Corgi-Doberman story earlier did not involve any treats.) Finally, be careful about hand-feeding treats through the fence. A dog may decide to bite your hand instead of the treats! I tend to toss the treats over (or through) until I'm really sure about the dog. A few dogs on my walk lean into the fence for petting, but that's not where we started!

Even if other dogs are not barking at your dog from behind fences, she may be overwhelmed by the proximity or intensity of her triggers on walks. For example, an off-leash dog running full-tilt toward your dog is like a tarantula falling on an arachnophobic person's head. It doesn't help you one bit to hear a happy reassurance that their loose dog (the spider) is "friendly." If I had a dollar for every time I have heard that shouted as a dog came bounding up to mine, that money would buy a lot of dog training books!

Off-leash dogs are a big hazard on walks. If you routinely encounter loose dogs, you should consider changing your route, unless you can manage to convince all of the humans there to keep their dogs on leash. I had some clients who lived next to a lovely forest park within Seattle. They delighted in walking through the park with their dog, but they encountered off-leash dogs several times per week. Progress in training had been slow, and we tracked the problem down to over-the-top meetings with loose dogs at the park. Imagine going for a daily walk in a place where you get mugged at knifepoint a few times a week. Would those walks help you relax? Fortunately, they realized what their 'peaceful' walks in the forest were doing to their dog and began taking their daily walks through their neighborhood, instead. Eliminating encounters with off-leash dogs helped this client's dog gain confidence and by doing BAT, the dog is now able to meet dogs on his neighborhood walks. To avoid off-leash dogs, some of my other clients exercise their dogs indoors or drive their dogs to walking paths by busy roads.

Here are a few indoor exercise ideas:

- Hide and seek games where the dog finds you or toys/treats/objects (my personal favorite). For example, you can hide pieces or small dishes of your dog's dinner all over the house, so he has to go hunt for it.

- Sprinkles: basically just finding treats, but you use something very tiny, like parmesan cheese crumbs. Your dog sniffs around and gets tired. For full details on this great technique by Sally Hopkins, see the Resources.

- Clicker training new useful physically or mentally demanding tricks, including Touch from a distance or between two targets, cooperative nail trimming/filing, Heel, or loose leash walking (see Appendix 1).

- Food puzzles.

Food puzzles are great for relieving pent-up energy and exercising your dog's brain. You can make your own as well as get official ones, like these Nina Ottoson puzzles.

- Treadmill: regular human treadmill or a dog treadmill (off leash only, using well-placed treats to reinforce staying on the treadmill and walking in balance).

- Puppy pushups: alternating Sit, Down, and/or Stand.

Dogs were born to search!

When off-leash dogs are a possibility on a walk, I recommend carrying something like SprayShield citronella spray, a water bottle that will squirt out, or Silly String (also known as aerosol string, which comes in a can). I don't recommend using aversives like this for training, but I pull out all the stops when breaking up fights. As I mentioned earlier, I had a can of SprayShield when the Doberman went after the Corgi. To break up a dog fight with SprayShield, spray it directly at the nose of the more intense dog(s), which usually results in sneezing. A trainer friend of mine accidentally sprayed his own face with SprayShield and he said that while it does sting, it's not as bad as pepper spray and a lot better than a dogfight. I have successfully broken up five fights with SprayShield—real fights, in which one dog had latched onto the other and would not let go. Trainers have different rules about citronella spray. I reserve it for fights where other methods of keeping the peace have failed; others use it as their first line of defense.

SprayShield is a safer way to break up dog fights.

Triggering a reflex that is incompatible with biting is an effective way to get dogs to let go of each other. I have used water to break up attachment fights in the street and it has worked well for me. Toss the water down the throat of the dog who is holding onto the other to elicit a coughing reflex. Water on top of them tends not to do much, but if you can get a dog to cough, she has to let go for a moment. Immediately move the dogs away from each other and secure them in separate locations.

Silly String is for kids' parties. It sprays out a fast non-toxic dissolving colored string. There's no a guarantee that it will work, but it's an idea—I've only used it once and not in a real fight. It did scare the loose dog and kept him from coming all the way up to Peanut, but he still followed us from a distance. Other possible options for repelling oncoming dogs are a squirt bottle or a Pet Corrector, which makes a hissing noise. I don't generally recommend either of those to clients because I'm afraid they may get the wrong idea and start trying to use them to train their dog. Suppressing behavior leads to all sorts of other issues that are best avoided.

Most loose dogs are not looking to start a fight, they are just coming over to sniff your dog, but because of your dog's reactions, that's still dangerous. Here's my hierarchy for repelling loose dogs and dogs on unlocked retractable leashes. If one step doesn't work, move on to the next. Some of these ways are not always safe, but I mention them because they can work although they should be used at your own risk:

1. When you see a loose dog far ahead of you, do an emergency U-turn (see Appendix 1) and cross the street or turn and walk the other way.

2. If the off-leash dog is too close to just walk away without causing a scene, then shout, "Call your dog" with a hand out, like a traffic cop, toward the dog. Do your U-turn. Repeat that statement in response to whatever the person says. Negotiation wastes time. Adding "my dog is sick" can be helpful, though!

3. If the dog is alone or the caregiver is not helping, toss a big handful of treats at the other dog. If you can just do it with treats, that's best, because the dog is happy to stay behind and you haven't added stress or risk.

4. If treats aren't enough, and there is nobody helping to move the other dog away, you can toss small rocks or spray Silly String toward the loose dog. This isn't ideal, but it's better than a fight.

5. If the loose dog follows, body block by quickly moving between the loose dog and your dog and stepping toward the loose dog to back him up. If your dog will do a Sit-Stay behind you, do it! Authoritatively tell the loose dog to Sit and use a big hand signal. He may not sit, but the tone might make him back off. If your dog is sitting, be sure to reinforce that!

6. While holding the leash to keep your dog's face away from the oncoming dog, use your foot to move the loose dog away (can also be dangerous to you, so only do this at your own risk).

7. If a fight breaks out, use SprayShield, water, etc. If that doesn't work and it's not just slobber and sound, use other ways to break it up: grab at the waist from behind and pull the dogs apart as soon as possible, etc. Wait to pull until the dogs are not attached, like when they are re-gripping or taking a breath. Otherwise they will just bite harder and may tear something. Grabbing this way can be risky, but it's way safer than grabbing the collar. Try to stay away from the teeth.

I prefer to save SprayShield for times when other tools don't work, because it is pretty aversive. But it is also safer, so if you have a dog who redirects (bites you when you try to interfere) then you may opt to use that sooner, rather than later. That said, if your dog redirects, you probably want to have him wear a muzzle during your walks, so that everybody is safer.

You could also pick up your dog and rotate away. Note that this could put you in danger from your own dog and the loose dog. I once read a horror story about a woman losing a finger this way, so now you have been warned, too. But it may help keep your dog safe from harm. Avoiding loose dogs is much safer than any of the steps given above, so I'll say it again here: *if you commonly run into loose dogs on your walk, be proactive and change your walking route!*

Even encountering a leashed dog up close can be trouble, but it's much easier to get away. The first thing to do is avoid head-on meetings by having your dog wait for you to check for dogs (or people) at corners, blind alleys, at curbs, in and out of cars, and in and out of the house. Practice short stays with a release word at the end, like "Free," and gradually build up time of the stay. The reward can be a treat, praise, or simply permission to move again. For times when you do get surprised by a trigger, it's helpful to teach the emergency U-turn that I mentioned before. That helps with off-leash dogs, children popping out of SUVs, and anything else that might suddenly put your dog out of her comfort zone. The emergency U-turn is like a flotation device tossed to get a drowning child out of the deep end of the pool. This book covers the U-turn in detail in Appendix I.

Scan for trouble as you walk, but don't dart your head and eyes around, because it will probably freak out your dog. Dogs will pick up on your nervousness if you are constantly looking about, so make sure that you are relaxed, breathe calmly, and look around without appearing nervous to your dog. The easiest way to do this is to have a friend who can scan for you. Have pre-arranged cues so that you can quickly get the information from him/her that a loose dog, child, or object is coming, and from where. If you are on your own during a walk, then feed your dog for polite walking and look around while your dog is busy with the treat.

Take a walk on your usual walking route without your dog. Notice your stress level and think about whether your dog's issues have influenced that. Take some time to learn about breathing techniques for relaxation via a yoga course, meditation class or books on breathing. I like the audiobook *Breathing—the Master Key to Self-Healing* by Andrew Weil (see Resources). It has suggestions for breathing for health and relaxation.

Another helpful way to avoid danger on a walk is to know where you are walking—where the yards with dogs are, where the lady who usually lets her dog out lives, etc. Take short walks on paths that you know, but gradually push the envelope and take slightly different walks each time, to keep things interesting. If you want to take a route, walk it without your dog first, keeping track of the triggers that you see along the way. Be aware of the various triggers that might be present on a particular walking path. Many dogs are very sensitive to noises, so walking along a busy street with cars may make them more likely to react to other triggers along that route.

Many dogs seem to handle noisy locations better if they are wearing some kind of body wrap, like the Anxiety Wrap or Thundershirt. The wraps physically calm dogs in the same way that swaddling helps calm a baby. To handle the city, some dogs may need medication, supplements, or better yet, moving to a quieter neighborhood. I worked with a human-reactive bulldog mix that lived in downtown Seattle. I felt terribly for this poor dog. A loud cacophony hit our ears as soon as we walked out of her apartment building: giant duck-shaped tour buses with loudspeakers, three fire trucks, hundreds of pedestrians talking, cars honking, and a dog barking. I can only imagine the smells that went along with that for a dog. She would walk about half of a block to eliminate and then would pull like mad on her prong collar (!) to get back inside the apartment. She was fine with dogs at daycare or walks on quiet streets, but with so much going on downtown, she also began to react aggressively to other dogs on walks. She was treated with a combination of anti-anxiety medications, the Thundershirt, BAT, and switching from the prong collar to a front-attachment harness. She also eventually moved somewhere quieter, where the caregiver and the dog could both relax.

Thundershirt

Some dogs do better on walks close to home, some need to be further away to avoid territoriality, and some dogs are so reactive to everything that their walks need to be indoors, just around the house. For those walks, you can put out interesting smells or do training along the indoor route. You can also hide treats around the home for your dog to find, activating the seeker circuit in the brain. Many dogs do well if they have a constant stream of dogs and people versus one or two strangers on their entire walk. For dogs who react to sudden changes in their environment, a walk on a busy urban walking path may actually be easier than a walk in the neighborhood, especially if your neighborhood is full of off-leash greeters and front-yard barkers who startle your dog.

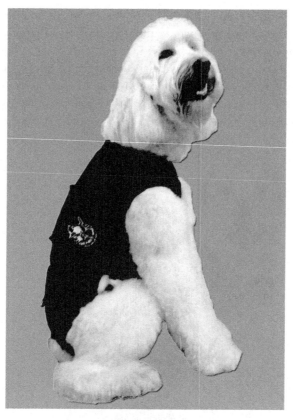

Anxiety Wrap

Speaking of barking, talking to people that you see on a walk may cause your dog to start barking. Why? I don't know, but one good reason is that your dog thinks you are barking at the other person. Think about it from a dog's perspective: you are facing directly at the person, staring, and you've suddenly stopped walking and started making noise on an otherwise quiet walk. Sometimes you even start wrestling (known to humans as a 'hug' or a 'handshake'). What's a dog to do? So I find it helpful to normalize the concept of talking on a walk by saying a quiet hello to everyone we meet, plus several hellos just out of the blue, to nobody at all. If this is a problem for your dog, keep that in mind as a trigger for when you are actually doing BAT set-ups.

Pay close attention to your dog when you walk her. If your dog is not responsive if you change direction or say her name, it might be because you've been ignoring her. Give her a reason to pay more attention to you. Leave the cell phone in your pocket. If you need to walk or run for exercise and can't focus on your dog, then don't bring her for the whole thing! You can use the walk as a warm-up and go for a serious run outside or on a treadmill afterwards.

When I say that your dog should pay attention to you, I don't mean that he should stare at you during the whole walk or walk precisely in Heel position. If that's what you want some of the time, fine, but I like to let dogs be dogs. Half the fun of going on a walk with Bean and Peanut is watching what they see or smell on walks, watching them prance along in doggie bliss. Being able to sniff on walks is important for enrichment and it also allows dogs to gather information about their world. I think letting them sniff is very helpful for confidence. Dogs also often have to sniff after they've encountered something scary; it can be self-soothing and it gives them information.

If your dog sometimes acts like you don't exist, reinforce the times that you do get focus on your everyday walks. Notice that the emphasis is on what you want her to do. Build that up and you won't have a problem with her disconnecting from you. Watch your dog and when you see her attention about to cut out, call her name and/or walk the other way, and treat when she notices you. That will help her learn to always keep at least a little of her focus on you. Having her use a treadmill before the walk can help tire her out so that she's ready to walk at your slow human pace. There are treadmills made just for dogs, but you can use clicker training to teach a dog to run on a regular treadmill.

When walking a dog with reactivity issues, leave your other dog(s) at home so that you can pay attention and avoid triggering one dog with your other dog's behavior. Reactivity can be contagious, so if you have one dog who does well with dogs and people, keep it that way by walking him alone, away from the influence of your other dog. Walking your dogs separately also prevents any redirection, where your dog sees a trigger and goes after your other dog because he can't reach the real target.

Having said that, there are benefits from social facilitation. If your dog sees and smells a dog who he is familiar with having a good time meeting other dogs or people, then it may make him more comfortable. If you have two people on your walk, one can handle the dog with issues and the other can handle the dog with better social skills. If arousal is kept low, the dog who is more comfortable in the situation can serve as a role model for the other dog. Keep your dog at a good distance from the trigger to allow him to stay relaxed.

Every dog is unique: walking your dogs separately lets you pay attention to space needs.

I met with a family who had two Rat Terriers with a host of self-control issues. Sophia, the dog who I was there to see, was very reactive to other dogs. Sophia would scream her little head off when she caught a glimpse of another dog, even from several blocks away. People thought her humans were torturing her! Being humans, the owners were convinced that they needed to walk both dogs together, out of fairness, even though the other dog had some reactivity issues as well. One dog shouldn't get a walk without the other, right? When we walked the dogs separately, Sophia's reactivity dropped to about thirty percent of what it had been, so we first did BAT with her alone, and then together with her littermate after the reactivity improved. Because of this, their other dog's reactivity immediately dropped down to almost nothing and they could all enjoy an easy walk without even training her at all!

Distraction

Distraction isn't a part of BAT, nor is it necessarily educational, but I'm mentioning it here in the Quick Fixes because sometimes you just get into a situation where you can't do BAT. This would include a situation where you can't walk away and your dog isn't yet ready to just wait until the trigger leaves. In cases like this, feed your dog super-delicious treats, one right after the other—distracting your dog—until the trigger goes away. Stand in between your dog and the trigger, if needed. Ideally, your dog will perceive the trigger and then you'll reach for the food. That way, you are doing counter-conditioning in the most efficient way and your dog has a chance to build some positive association with the appearance of the trigger.

With counter-conditioning, the idea is to associate a negatively charged trigger with one that has a positive association, or is inherently positive, like food. If you do present the stimuli in reverse order, i.e., you give your dog a hot dog or rustle with your treat pouch before your dog becomes aware of the trigger, then your dog may become afraid of hot dogs! This is all too easy to do, because people tend to reach inside of their treat bags as soon as they see the trigger, before the dog has perceived it. Counter-conditioning with desensitization could be your entire treatment plan, but I have found BAT to be more effective for teaching social skills. I recommend distractions as more of a way to keep the dog from freaking out when there's no escape. You can use food as a distraction to keep the dog from exploding, but do all that you can to avoid a trap like that in the future. If you live in a condo with an elevator and need to use distraction on a daily basis, then watch your timing!

If even stuffing your dog's face full of treats is not enough to prevent an outburst, then take some time after the incident to figure out how to keep that from happening again. Get creative to figure out how avoid encountering the trigger in that way. Until you have had a chance to do BAT set-ups that prepare your dog for that situation, avoidance is your best bet. Sometimes, the answer is just to use stinkier, meatier treats or to walk your dog before dinner, when she's hungrier. Sometimes it's better management. You may have to take the stairs instead of the elevator, or put your dog in a back room with a frozen stuffed Kong when company comes over. There is only so much responsibility you can put on your dog at this point. It's like a toddler who keeps falling into a swimming pool. To keep it from happening again, you could yell or explain the concept of death, but neither of those solutions is likely to be effective. For an instant fix, parents put up a barrier around the pool so that they just don't have a problem until the swimming lessons have started working and the brain has matured. The same is true for dogs. Sometimes, they just need some environmental engineering to prevent overexposure to the trigger.

Muzzles can be effective safety tools

Muzzles are like a safety barrier around the pool, except they go around your dog's sharp teeth. Muzzles may look scary, but they are a fairly easy way to reliably prevent bites. I think a lot of people are afraid to use them, because doing so forces them to admit that their dog has a problem. It also just 'looks bad' and there's the stigma that a dog in a muzzle is worse than a dog not in a muzzle. It's ironic, really, because you know that a dog in a well-fitted muzzle can't bite you! If you have muzzle phobia, I'd like you to ponder this. Imagine I had a magic wand that would make it so that your dog would never bite another person or dog. Picture a greeting and how much more comfortable you would feel, knowing that, even she did explode, your dog would not bite anybody. A muzzle is that magic wand, because biting becomes impossible.

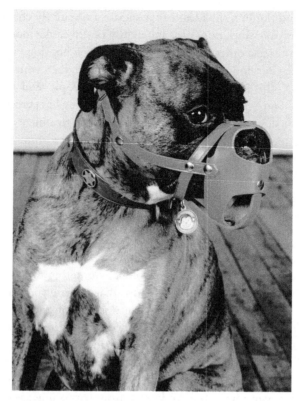

Hot Dogs All Dressed has cute muzzles with optional bling.

If that's not enough, go ahead and do a quick counter-conditioning exercise. I'm not kidding. Get about 30 to 50 of your favorite 'human treats,' like a candy bar chopped into little pieces. Over the course of a day, visualize your dog wearing a muzzle, and then eat a piece of candy. Relax and repeat.

I recently moved and the new vet has a blanket policy that all dogs need to be restrained by vet technicians, for liability reasons. Apparently people have been bitten by their own dogs somewhere in the US and then sued the veterinarian, and this vet wasn't taking any chances. I canceled the blood draw because I have worked too hard to get Peanut used to people to have it ruined by this vet. I have trained Peanut to actively participate in a blood draw, so he holds his own head in position (chin targeting) and I have my hands there as a back-up.

But this new facility refused to let me restrain him and I knew he would feel more comfortable doing it with me. I didn't want to violate his trust and, fortunately, I later had an idea that would reduce his stress. Peanut has never bitten, but I had conditioned a muzzle anyway. When I asked the vet techs whether they would let me do the restraint if he was wearing a muzzle, they were happy to oblige. In fact, given his complete lack of bite history, they were happy to just have him target into the muzzle, without even strapping on the straps. Problem solved!

(There's actually a bit more to this story: I have not returned to that new facility. I found a mobile veterinarian who came to our house to do the blood draw, with Peanut actively participating, without needing the muzzle. We will still go to the other clinic if the need arises, and now we have the option to do so without needing to be restrained by a vet technician, but my financial support goes to veterinarians who put a priority on reducing an animal's stress.)

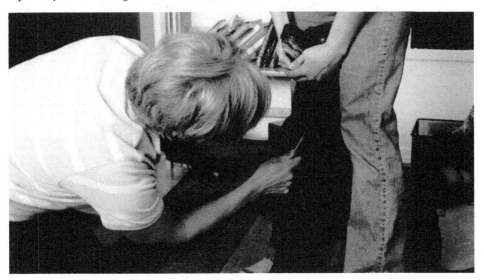

Peanut moved his body into position for this blood draw.
This is better than just being okay with us restraining him.

Tip for Pros: Make it easy for your clients to find the right kind of muzzle by referring them to specific places to purchase it. It's hard enough to get over muzzle phobia, much less have to drive around to ten different stores to find the right one.

In terms of which type of muzzle to use, I like the plastic Italian basket muzzles and the Baskerville Ultra because they allow the dog to pant, breathe, move their whiskers, drink, and eat treats (put the treats between the bars or use squeeze cheese). They don't allow ears from another dog to slip in, as the nylon grooming muzzles do. Here's a grizzly example of why I never use the grooming muzzles. I know a dog who was wearing a grooming muzzle during an on-leash introduction. A fight broke out and the other dog's ear somehow made it inside of the dog's muzzle. Grooming muzzles fit fairly tightly, so after biting down on the ear, the dog didn't have much choice but to tear it off and swallow. Ick! So basket muzzles are the way to go. The rubber Baskerville Ultra muzzles are softer than the hard plastic and metal ones, so if they run into you or punch into one of their triggers, it won't hurt as much.

An Italian basket muzzle with a K9 Bridle head collar underneath.

I have three rules for muzzles: 1) train your dog to get used to wearing a muzzle rather than just putting it on your dog; 2) always set up your dog to be below threshold; and 3) always supervise a dog in a muzzle to avoid accidents. You may make an exception to the first two rules only when it's an urgent safety issue and there's no way to avoid the stress. For example, if a dog who is reactive toward people injures herself and must be inspected by a veterinarian, that's an appropriate time to muzzle the dog.

For up-close work, when there is even the tiniest bit of doubt, put a fence between your dog and the trigger or use the muzzle. Keep in mind that your dog can still 'muzzle punch,' i.e., run into the target at top speed, which can hurt a child or smaller dog. Make sure the muzzle fits well, so that neither the dog nor their opponent can slip it off.

Never just put a muzzle on your dog without proper training. Imagine that you are a dog who has never worn a muzzle before, and you find yourself wearing a muzzle at the veterinarian's office. For one thing, this unfamiliar piece of plastic is suddenly stuck to your face. But it gets worse: once you have this thing on your face, the vet proceeds to be much ruder to you than ever before; poking, prodding, and generally wreaking havoc on your nervous system. Now something that started as just uncomfortable is a big contextual clue that bad things will happen to you. If you've already put a muzzle on your dog and had a bad response, it'll take more time to get her comfortable wearing it, but please persist, because it's worth it.

There are many ways to get a dog used to a muzzle, but using clicker training to teach your dog to put her own snout into the muzzle is an elegant solution. You can start by treating your dog for just looking at the muzzle and gradually raise criteria (get pickier about which behavior earns a treat). Soon your dog will be actively seeking out the muzzle to target, and then eventually holding her snout inside the muzzle. It becomes a sort of game to your dog. Here is a suggested way to train. You may need to add more steps or be able to skip some of this for your own dog.

1. With the muzzle in one hand and treats in the other, present the muzzle to your dog. As soon as she looks at it, say "Yes" and feed a treat. Just as she finishes the treat, hide the remaining treats and the muzzle behind your back. Repeat until your dog happily looks at the muzzle. Note: Note: you can also mark with an i-Click with your foot—just don't use a box clicker right in the dog's face.

2. Cup your hand around the front of the muzzle so that you can put treats in the muzzle (on your hand) without the treats falling out and tuck the straps out of the way. Repeat the step above (marking for looking at the muzzle), but put each treat reward in the muzzle for your dog to eat, and then step back after your dog gets the treat, so you relieve any pressure of being around the muzzle, and so your dog has to follow you to get to the muzzle. Repeat ten times.

3. Raise criteria by waiting for your dog to move toward the muzzle before you mark and reward in the muzzle (continue stepping away after your dog eats the treat). Repeat until your dog is moving toward the muzzle eight times out of ten.

4. Raise criteria by waiting for your dog to put her nose into the muzzle before you mark and reward in the muzzle. Repeat until your dog is touching the muzzle eight times out of ten.

5. Working in blocks of ten touches, start marking only if your dog holds her nose in the muzzle for at least one second. Repeat until she is able to stay there for one second at least eight times out of ten, then change criteria to 2, 4, 8, 10, 15, 20, 25, and 30 seconds. If this is a challenge for your dog, I recommend targeting a Post-It note or other target and teaching her to hold her nose to it for longer and longer periods of time. The paper target can then be put into the basket of the muzzle to help her learn to put her nose in there for a long time.

6. Now start to work from farther away, so she has to come further to the muzzle to target. She's already had to move a little because you have been retreating away from her after she eats each treat. Start stepping three feet away after she eats each treat, then raise criteria to six feet once she's doing well. When you change the distance, you may need lower criteria. For example reinforce just touching the muzzle for ten times and then raise your criteria back to putting her nose all the way in for ten times. If

that's going well, build up duration again by doing ten trials each of 2, 8, 15, and 30 seconds.

7. Now that your dog is diving into the muzzle when you bring it out, you can pretend to put the straps on (just holding them in your hand), for half a second. Mark and reward in the muzzle. Repeat about ten times.

8. Gradually increase the duration of how long you have the straps over the back of her neck, and then start attaching the clips. Continue marking and rewarding duration. If she starts to paw at it, it means you have probably asked for too much, too soon. Just ask her to do something, like a Sit, and then reward by treating through the muzzle and use the time that she's chewing to take it off.

9. Practice in different locations and with different amount of distractions. You can also attach the collar part of the muzzle, with the basket just hanging down, and play fetch with a ball or do a Find it session with treats.

10. Continue rewarding your dog every time you put the muzzle on—either with food, toys, attention, or something else that she loves.

Always remember that dogs are fabulous at learning what predicts danger or safety, so never do something 'mean' to your dog in the thirty seconds after you first put the muzzle on. That might mean toenail trimming, a vet examination, greeting another dog if they're afraid of that, or walking outside for those who are scared to go outside. Even though the muzzle is for bite prevention, put it on at some other times when you are just hanging out and loving on your dog, so that it becomes a very normal piece of equipment. For the visual learners, I've got a streaming video on how to do muzzle training on my YouTube channel. Chirag Patel and Emily Larlham also have their own techniques with videos on YouTube (DomesticatedManners and Kikopup, respectively).

One way I've thought of to help make the muzzle a great thing is to make a "Muzzle-cicle." Tightly wrap the nose-end of the muzzle with plastic wrap. Put about a half an inch of wet dog food in and mush it into the end, so the muzzle is basically like a bowl with some dog food at the bottom. Put that in the freezer. Once it is frozen, remove the plastic wrap and put it on your muzzle-trained dog. This is a great way to have visitors over, too. Again, your dog should be 99.99% fine with visitors, but the muzzle is there as a just-in-case. The Muzzle-cicle helps distract your dog when visitors first come in and makes that 99.99% into 99.999999%. Either put the Muzzle-cicle on at least thirty seconds before your dog notices the visitors, or put it on just after she (safely) notices that you have company. I would only do the latter if your dog truly loved her Muzzle-cicle!

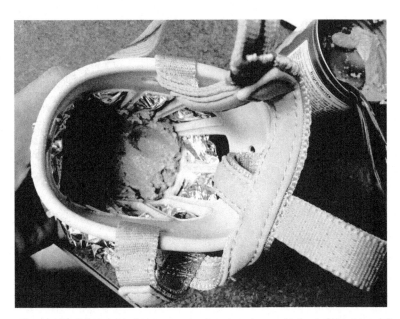

Muzzle-cicle fresh from the freezer. Turn the muzzle into a food dish in your hand.

In case you can't tell by now, I think that bites must be strictly prevented. As Yoda sagely said in *Star Wars,* "Do, or do not. There is no try." Engineering your dog's environment for safety is essential when you choose to keep a dog with a bite history in your home, and it's still important even if your dog hasn't bitten yet. Any dog will bite, with enough provocation. Many jurisdictions allow "one free bite," but even a single bite can be enough to have the dog euthanized, depending on local laws and the severity of the bite. For example, a dog in Seattle that inflicts an injury requiring two or more stitches to a person would be immediately considered "dangerous" and must be euthanized or removed from the city (see Resources). Given the severity of the consequences of a bite, preventing bites is critical. Training takes time, and good management gives dogs an opportunity to change their behavior patterns.

Checklist of useful products for dog reactivity

- **Calming Cap:** Worn over the eyes to calm the dog, especially useful for reducing visual stimuli, as when the dog is riding in the car or elevator. Developed by Trish King.

- **Clicker:** Little hand-held box that makes a sound, which the trainer always follows with a reinforcer. I use the clicker only with tangible reinforcers, like food and toys.

Box clicker

- **Exercise Pen:** An "ex-pen" is a portable fence, like a baby gate with multiple panels. Used to block off areas that you want to keep the dog in or out of, as well as a barrier for greetings between dogs and decoys. Comes in metal and plastic.

- **Front-attachment harness:** Harnesses where the leash clips to a ring at the dog's chest to give you leverage if your dog lunges or pulls (visualize the physics). Whenever safe and possible, use a rear-attachment harness, instead, for the dog's balance and freedom of movement.

- **Head Halter:** These are collars with a loop around the nose and around the neck, like a horse bridle. They come in various brands and designs like K9 Bridle, Comfort Trainer, Halti, and Gentle Leader. Head halters help you control the movement of your dog's head, which can be useful in emergencies, but are restricting for BAT set-ups. Acclimate to head collar before using, as you would with a muzzle. These are not the most humane walking tools, but are better than a prong collar, and should be used only if other leash walking devices with the leash skills are insufficient. Use a double-ended leash attached to a harness or other point of contact.

- **Leash:** Use 15 feet (5 meters) with good leash skills for BAT set-ups. All dogs should be under control when out in public, and definitely on leash if your dog may scare, bite, or overwhelm someone with over-friendliness. In areas that are tempting to let your dog off of the leash, a 15 to 50 foot leash attached to the back of a harness provides plenty of exercise without completely compromising safety.

- **Phone:** Bringing your phone lets you call for help, if necessary. Focus on your dog, instead of chatting while you're walking, but have a phone for safety and to take video.

- **Muzzle:** Having your dog wear a basket muzzle drastically increases the safety of working up close. Use with supervision and train in advance.

- **SprayShield:** Citronella spray that can repel oncoming dogs and break up most fights. Illegal in some countries because it is an aversive. Water or silly string can also work.

- **Thundershirt and Anxiety Wrap:** Body wraps that reduce anxiety by swaddling the dog. Especially useful for sound-sensitive dogs.

- **Treat Pouch:** Convenient access for treats, especially helpful on walks.

Treat pouches are essential for quick access to reinforcers. Look for features like easy open, secure close, washability, and extra pockets.

- **Yellow Ribbon/Leash/Harness/Vest:** Having something yellow on your dog signifies that he needs space for emotional or physical reasons. This is not universally known, though, so a vest with big letters works best. Just don't get yourself in legal trouble: "I need space" is better than "I bite," for example.

I imagine that you're ready to get working on BAT! Let's start with an in-depth discussion of body language.

CHAPTER 4

How to See Trouble Before It Starts

Most dogs who bark, lunge, or bite aren't chemically imbalanced killers, out to injure other dogs or people for sport. If we could translate what their barking or lunging at some trigger means, it would generally be either "Go away!" (anger), "Get over here and play with me!" (frustration), or "Let me get out of here safely!" (fear). When the behaviors become over-the-top or obnoxious, we call that "reactivity." The point of barking, lunging, etc. usually seems to boil down to increasing or decreasing distance between the dog and the trigger. When we work at the right distance, the dog is able to move more freely and gather information. He can be interested in the environment and doesn't need to run away from or toward the trigger. While I tend to talk most about dogs who are afraid of the trigger, BAT also works for dogs who run toward the trigger like a bullet to fight and for the ones who just want to play.

Where is the reaction coming from?

In a way, it doesn't matter. We should be watching each moment to assess what the dog needs at

This dog is clearly trying to avoid something.

that time, and to keep him far enough away that he can learn naturally. There are some subtle differences in what to do if you look at which consequences are most reinforcing. Remember, we mostly want the dog providing his own consequences with BAT, but there will be times when we step in to help.

- **Fear/Avoidance.** "I want to get away." Walking away from trigger is the best functional reinforcer and the trigger leaving is also reinforcing. Visual clues: the dog's center of gravity is low and away from the trigger (rear end tucked under, legs bent) or the dog alternates between lunging forward and bouncing away.

- **Anger.** "I want you to go away." The trigger leaving is most reinforcing. However, I usually have the student dog walk away anyway as the functional reinforcer, because it's a good pattern for the dog and owner and it's still helpful because it reduces stress by increasing distance to the trigger. Visual clues: the dog is standing up high and stiff on his toes, squarely facing the trigger.

- **Frustration.** "I want to get closer to you." Ironically, both walking toward the trigger and away from the trigger seem to be reinforcing. Visual clues: the dog is fairly bouncy, vocal, and greets without fighting when allowed to get up close, although the dog's rude greeting may cause the other dog to start a fight.

GO! Leaning forward with bared teeth is a distance-increasing behavior.

Dogs may have a combination of the above emotions. For example, a dog who normally avoids people may also show territorial aggression near her home, so her behavior indicates both fear and anger. Anger is a reaction to a response to the violation of rules, for example "this is mine, that is yours," so territoriality and resource guarding are both examples of anger. While science has traditionally avoided using anthropomorphic terms like fear and anger, recent research seems to indicate that dogs definitely do have these primal emotions. Read Patricia McConnell's excellent book, *For the Love of a Dog* and Alexandra Horowitz's *Inside of a Dog* for more information about recent research on dog emotions and cognition (see Resources).

This "go away kid, you're bothering me" tooth display reflects a combination of fear and anger.

Magnetic power

In a social situation, the trigger itself has some 'magnetic power' for dogs who show aggressive displays, no matter what emotion is driving the behavior. I call this the **magnet effect**. What I mean by that is that once the dog gets too close, it's like she's sucked in and can't seem to help herself. She might prefer to put a lot of distance between herself and the scary monster, but first she just has to bark, growl, or even bite. That probably serves the purpose of making sure the scary monster will let her get away, or will stay away from her next time. Whenever barking, growling, or biting work to make a dog feel safe, she's just gotten a functional reinforcer and she is even more likely to repeat those behaviors next time. That's why I spent so much time discussing management in the Chapter 3—you need to help your dog avoid rehearsing reactivity, because it's a lose-lose proposition.

Triggers may draw your dog in like a magnet.
Keep your dog at a distance when triggers have a strong pull..

During an initial consultation once, I explained the concept of functional reinforcers to a couple with Gigi, a Cattle Dog mix with fear and territorial issues. My clients said that they didn't think Gigi would want to put distance between herself and other dogs, because she always ran toward other dogs. She had escaped from the yard once and chased a dog way down the alley before attacking him, inflicting wounds that required veterinary attention. I asked whether they thought she wanted the other dog to be close to her, as though the purpose of chasing the other dog down was to keep him around. They laughed and said, of course not, she wanted to get rid of this dog! I think Gigi was explaining, in no uncertain terms, that she didn't want the other dog anywhere near her house. A good offense is the best defense, right?

They still weren't entirely convinced that Gigi would find walking away reinforcing until we took her outside to work. There is always some distance, outside of the threshold boundary where the dogs are not 'magnetically' drawn in, at which they are happy to create space by moving their own bodies away from the trigger. We quickly found that spot for Gigi. She would briefly stare at the helper dog and then look away. This was back when I taught BAT 1.0, so my client said "Yes" and walked her away from the other dog. Gigi's body language was relaxed and happy as she left. The couple commented that Gigi looked so proud of herself and that she seemed to be paying more attention to them than usual. If we had walked Gigi too close to the helper dog, we definitely would have gotten barking and lunging, and they probably would have had to pull her away instead of her happily trotting away with them. Note: with BAT 2.0, I would have started farther away with Gigi, at a point where she was not likely to stare, but could explore the environment and gather information about the other dog with softer looks.

When training begins, the magnet is too strong up close, but there's still some distance at which dogs are happy to gather information from the trigger without running away or launching toward it. In Chapter 6, I will give you some ways to do set-ups, i.e., how to arrange environments for your dog to be interested in the trigger, but still remain comfortable. Using BAT, the distance from the trigger at which your dog can be relaxed and boring will eventually shrink to nothing.

Setting boundaries with cut-off signals

Dogs have many ways to say that they need space, ranging from the canine version of "you make me uncomfortable, please step back" to the more threatening "go away or I will kill you!" These are called **cut-off signals** or **distance increasing behavior.** Dogs often escalate to growling, lunging, or biting when the more subtle signals they engage in are not enough to get the job done. Looking, turning, or fully walking away from the trigger are less threatening cut-off signals. When those are respected, the dog doesn't need to resort to the behavior most people classify as "aggression."

Barbara Handelman defines cut-off signals as being used to "interrupt behavior coming at them from another animal. Cut-off displays unequivocally signal that further interaction is not desired" (see Resources). Learning to recognize *polite or acceptable* cut-off signals and setting up situations in which they are effective will help you honor your dog's need for safety and distance.

My training goal is to help dogs with reactivity issues rely on the more polite cut-off signals instead of behaviors that look like aggression. I use the term "polite"cut-off signals (or "good choices") to mean the non-confrontational cut-off signals which, while more subtle, are also understood by most dogs. I should probably use something that sounds less judgmental than "good" choices, because the opposite would be a "bad"choice and it's not a far stretch to a "bad dog," a phrase I never use. But clients seem to understand the phrase "good choices" a lot faster than "replacement behaviors" or even "polite cut-off signals," so I use it, with a small inner twinge each time.

In this section I'll be referring mostly to dogs who show fear or aggression, but if your dog is frustrated, then the problem is not that other dogs are ignoring his cut-off signals, but that he isn't honoring their requests for space. BAT will help your dog learn to approach slowly and take the time to give and receive cut-off signals. It's important to deal with frustration in a way that teaches dogs that there is nothing to fear or get mad about. Use BAT to help your dogs understand that they will be able to greet, but that they can do it without the high energy they normally bring to the situation.

For many dogs who show fear or aggression, their reactivity may have started with frustration, but a lifetime of leash corrections and disastrous on-leash greetings have led to a fear of what happens when they are on leash around other dogs. With confrontational training techniques, polite (and more direct) cut-off signals are ignored or even punished. Dogs are forced to either use really obvious cut-off signals, like barking and growling, may forego them altogether and go straight to biting when they finally can't take it anymore.

Polite cut-off signals are pretty much the same set of behaviors that you, as a human, might do when a somewhat creepy stranger tries to make eye contact with you in an elevator. These are subtle ways of setting boundaries, which say "you are crossing a line that makes me uncomfortable." Boundary violations can be about physical space; for example, the person is too close. But boundary violations can also be about what the person is doing, versus where they are at: staring, saying rude things about you, moving toward you, or making you uncomfortable in other ways.

Take a moment to picture what you do in the elevator situation. Personally, I break eye contact, turn my head or body away, avoid sudden movements, and maybe do some out-of-place **displacement behavior** like looking at my fingernails or phone. If the creepy stranger doesn't respect my boundary setting and steps in too close for comfort,

I may become more assertive in a way that people might label "reactive" in a dog—stand tall, square off my shoulders, make direct eye contact, lean or move forward, deepen my voice, scowl, and tell him to back off.

Dogs also have boundaries and they use many of those same cut-off signals. Meeting another dog on leash on a narrow sidewalk may feel a little bit like being stuck in that elevator with a creepy stranger. If you see a polite cut-off signal from your dog, make sure that it is respected by the other dog or person or that your dog has room to move away. If she seems stuck, help her out. If your dog is the 'friendly' one who doesn't notice the other dog setting boundaries, call your dog away.

Here are some examples of what typical polite cut-off signals look like in dogs:

- Look away from the trigger
- Head turns away from the trigger
- Lip lick
- Turn body away from the trigger
- Ground sniff
- Sigh
- Shake off (as if wet).

Lip lick can indicate anticipation or a polite cut-off signal indicating stress.

GOOD CHOICES

POLITE CUT-OFF SIGNALS

HEAD TURN
or look away from trigger

SNIFF GROUND

BODY TURN
loose spine

SCRATCH

LIP-LICK
or nose-lick

YAWN
somewhat stressed

SHAKE-OFF
stress release

INTEREST

BLINK
BLINK

SOFTEN EYES
"I'm friendly"

EARS TO NEUTRAL
relaxed

BOW
"I'm friendly"

SNIFF PREVIOUS LOCATION
where the other dog just was

SNIFF REAR

Polite cut-off signals, like look-aways and body turns, make excellent replacement behaviors for reactivity, because they are friendlier ways to achieve the same goal as the barking, biting, fleeing, etc. All of the above behaviors help the dog set boundaries and protect himself. If your dog is afraid of the trigger, this indicates that an increase in distance and safety is the whole point of doing the cut-off signal, be it a polite or an aggressive display. BAT set-ups can teach him that he can efficiently get what he wants by doing an easier, more polite behavior.

Head turns and other polite cut-off signals are probably already in your dog's repertoire when he encounters something slightly stressful, but he just doesn't use them persistently or he tries to use them and they don't work, so he switches to the more extreme form of those behaviors: reactivity. BAT sets up situations in which the dog is comfortable exploring and when the dog does happen to need more space, the polite cut-off signals are effective. This builds a new habit so that your dog begins to use them automatically, instead of resorting to aggression or panic. Good news: if the emotion is really more about frustration than aggression or fear, BAT still works to give self-control.

If your dog sees another dog from far enough away, he will check out the situation for a little bit and then move on. The level of interest or fear is minimal at the right distance. Your dog will do polite cut-off signals spontaneously without any prompting from you. That's where we practice with BAT set-ups. Up close or in other times when your dog needs help, you can specifically reinforce the cut-off signals and help your dog move away as a functional reinforcer and to relax. *BAT works well because you pick replacement behaviors that your dog is naturally disposed to, meaning that your dog's brain already links the replacement behaviors to the same functional reinforcer when the trigger is mild enough.*

> Tip for Pros: Replacement behaviors are species-specific, but can also vary within the species. When you do BAT with other species, like birds, horses, or humans, reinforce replacement behaviors that 'normal' animals of that species naturally do.

Giving the dog a chance to practice replacement behavior that is naturally linked with the functional reinforcer has a great side effect: automatic training. Once your dog understands the link between his behavior and the consequences, the environment will begin to train your dog for you. For example, if you've taught your dog to walk away from a person if she wants some distance, that should work in real life, too. Most adults will leave your dog alone if your dog walks away from them. I've seen that happen time and again with client dogs and with Bean and Peanut.

Trouble is coming!

When small cut-off signals aren't enough to get the dog some space from a trigger, his next attempt is often a more pronounced version of the same request, like moving away from it. If the polite signals don't work or the dog is too close to the trigger to offer them, then he may escalate to a threat, as I did in my elevator example. When most people think of a dog as reactive, the problem is not that the behavior exists, but that the dog is not persistent enough with the more polite ways to ask for space. This is usually due to a lack of reinforcement for those behaviors (i.e., nobody has been listening) in that context.

If you see any cut-off signals, be aware of the situation and ready to intervene if necessary. When the cut-off signals are polite and the other animal or person responds to the dog's request for space, just stay out of the way. If not, you can help your dog by moving the trigger away, calling your dog away (if safe), or by reducing the intensity of the trigger. If your dog is starting to use a threat and/or the excitement level is likely to get worse, then help your dog choose better behavior immediately by prompting with something like a weight shift away or even giving a trained cue. Try not to over-prompt; use the least intrusive prompt that you think will work, so that it's mostly the dog making her own decision. That said, if you see trouble coming, don't be afraid to call your dog back to you or have her do the Touch cue (see Appendix 1).

Only prompt when you have to, and if you do need to urge the dog to move away, then change something about the situation so that you are less likely to need to prompt again. The goal is to arrange the scenario so that your dog can practice making decisions without your help. But sometimes you have to prompt, especially out in the real world. In surprise situations that you know will push your dog over-threshold, just immediately call your dog. If you have more time, use **graduated prompting**.

Graduated prompts

Here is a graduated list of prompts to help tip the scale toward calmness if your dog is looking at the trigger and arousal is going up. This list starts with the least intrusive and builds up to the most assertive. Try to use the ones higher up on the list, because they give your dog more of a chance to learn without relying on your signals. You won't have time to use all of them, just use the least intrusive prompt that you think will work. If your dog is having a hard time turning away from the trigger, mark any sign of disengagement, move away, and reinforce (see Mark and Move in Chapter 7). Dogs will have varying responses to these prompts, so the order may be different for your dog:

- Relax your shoulders
- Shift your weight
- Calmly praise dog for looking
- Shuffle your feet
- Sigh or yawn
- Cough
- Move your hand or body in the dog's peripheral vision (it's 270 degrees, unlike our 180 degree vision)

Behaviors that indicate
YOU SHOULD PROMPT *

Your dog may have a full-blown reaction unless you quickly prompt or reduce the trigger intensity.

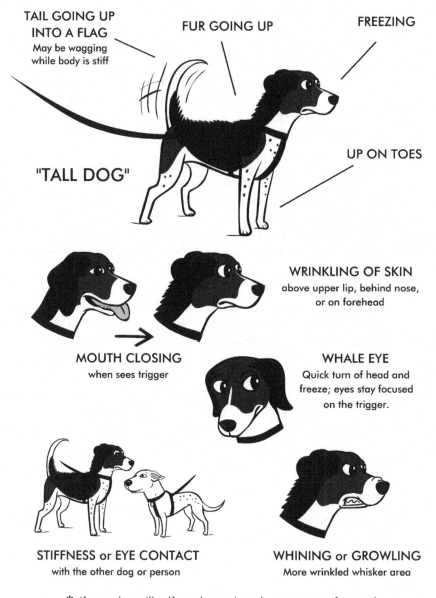

TAIL GOING UP INTO A FLAG
May be wagging while body is stiff

FUR GOING UP

FREEZING

UP ON TOES

"TALL DOG"

MOUTH CLOSING
when sees trigger

WRINKLING OF SKIN
above upper lip, behind nose, or on forehead

WHALE EYE
Quick turn of head and freeze; eyes stay focused on the trigger.

STIFFNESS or EYE CONTACT
with the other dog or person

WHINING or GROWLING
More wrinkled whisker area

* If your dog will self-soothe, wait and move away afterwards

- Kissy noise

- Name

- "Leave it" cue

- "Come" or "Let's go" cue

- **Mime Pulling** (see Leash Skills in Chapter 5)

- Pull dog away (can trigger an outburst)

The following five photos show an example of using graduated prompts to encourage a dog who is over-threshold to walk away instead of barking.

Tail began to rise, so handler made a kissy noise to prompt dog to turn.

Bigger prompt: Kissy noise plus finger lightly touching dog.

The touch worked!

Marked the turn with "Yes!"

Reinforce turn by walking away and treating.

I developed a stress chart shown on the next page to help people understand the various behavior dogs show when encountering a trigger. Some dogs get taller/larger, as shown here, and some get shorter and more 'invisible' (see page 117). Either way, a significant change from a neutral position is important and tells you that the dog may need your help.

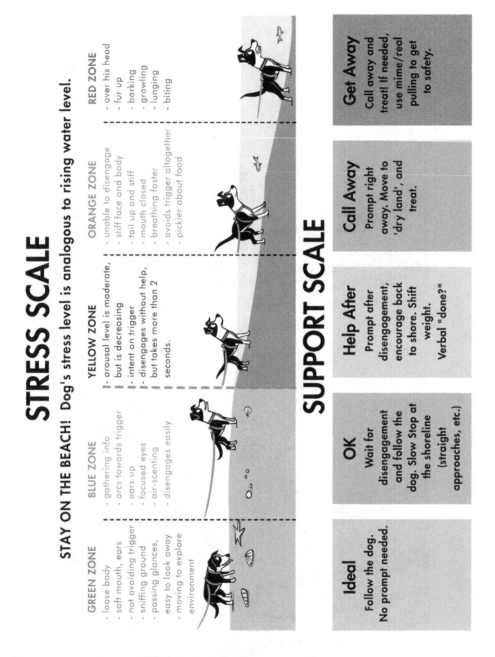

STRESS SCALE

STAY ON THE BEACH! Dog's stress level is analogous to rising water level.

GREEN ZONE
- loose body
- soft mouth, ears
- not avoiding trigger
- sniffing ground
- passing glances,
  easy to look away
- moving to explore
  environment

BLUE ZONE
- gathering info
- arcs towards trigger
- ears up
- focused eyes
- air-scenting
- disengages easily

YELLOW ZONE
- arousal level is moderate,
  but is decreasing
- intent on trigger
- disengages without help,
  but takes more than 2
  seconds.

ORANGE ZONE
- unable to disengage
- stiff face and body
- tail up and stiff
- mouth closed
- breathing faster
- avoids trigger altogether
- pickier about food

RED ZONE
- over his head
- fur up
- barking
- growling
- lunging
- biting

SUPPORT SCALE

Ideal
Follow the dog.
No prompt needed.

OK
Wait for
disengagement
and follow the
dog. Slow Stop at
the shoreline
(straight
approaches, etc.)

Help After
Prompt after
disengagement,
encourage back
to shore. Shift
weight.
Verbal "done?"

Call Away
Prompt right
away. Move to
'dry land', and
treat.

Get Away
Call away and
treat! If needed,
use mime/real
pulling to get
to safety.

Trigger stacking: "What?! Another one?!"

The phenomenon of **trigger stacking** is one reason why your dog's behavior may seem unpredictable. Events that trigger a reaction from your dog that occur too close together in time can pile up and put your dog over-threshold.

The various stimuli that concern your dog have an additive property in each context, so that if your dog is stressed 5% by hats and 10% by strangers, the total stress is not 10% (the larger of the two) but 15% or more, because your dog is now concerned

TRIGGER-STACKING

Example: Some triggers and their intensities

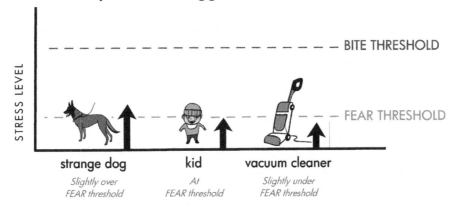

Each time a dog is exposed to a trigger, stress hormones are
dumped into the brain and they build up over time.

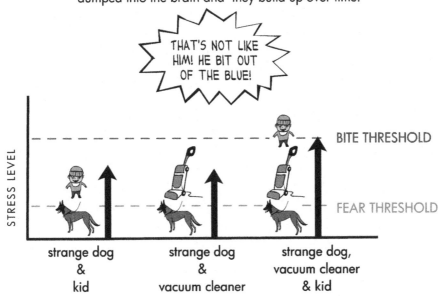

Regardless of where each dog's "Fear Threshold" or "Bite Threshold" is,
THE STRESS OF TRIGGERS IS ADDITIVE.

Dogs don't bite out of the blue.

about both scary things (those are both made up numbers). Let's say that a dog named Charlie bites someone when he reaches a 30% stress level. If it happens to be a hat-wearing stranger, he is well on his way to getting bitten by Charlie. If he is also stressed 10% by someone at the door and 10% by the sound of the doorbell, then a hat-wearing stranger who rings the doorbell and comes inside will push Charlie past his bite threshold and get bitten.

The graphs on the previous page illustrate how trigger stacking works. The top graph shows how much stress a dog experiences when he encounters his triggers one at a time. The bottom graph shows how that stress is additive when two or more triggers happen close together in time or simultaneously. By being prepared for trigger stacking and avoiding it when possible, you can reduce your dog's overall stress level and make your training more successful.

Stress signs–move away, take a break, or stop for the day

BAT set-ups (see Chapter 6 for more details) should ideally be low-stress, certainly not more stressful than the dog's everyday life. If you were to ask the dog "do you want to do that again?" the answer should be yes. We can't always create a totally stress-free situation, but we can certainly set something up that is better than usual. If you see indications that stress is actually higher than your dog's regular baseline, change something about the scenario. Take a break, remove the helper, move farther away, etc. I have more ways to fix things in the Troubleshooting section, but I know that some of you are going to want to train your dog right away, without finishing this book. So I put the stress illustrations here because I want you to have an image in your mind of behavior that indicates that something is wrong. But please read the whole book!

If there is a physical issue leading to temporary pain or discomfort, wait until that is fixed before doing BAT set-ups with a trigger. If your dog's baseline stress is high, I recommend that you wait to do BAT set-ups until you can reduce the overall arousal level. You can do an anti-stress program of nutrition (possibly including vitamin B supplementation), brain games, massage, management, relaxation training, routine changes, etc. You may need to cut out classes that your dog attends or routes that you walk that bring her in close proximity to the trigger. I highly recommend Anders Hallgren's excellent book *Stress, Anxiety, and Aggression in Dogs* and Nan Arthur's *Chill Out Fido* and Jo-Rosie Haffenden's *Real Dog Yoga* (see Resources). I would still recommend that you learn to do the BAT leash skills and that you do Mark and Move if your dog is around any triggers. As always, respect your dog's need for space and freedom whenever possible, and help others do the same.

I have included a number of stress signs to watch for during set-ups in the chart on the next two pages.

SIGNS OF STRESS

There's always an emotional lesson. If your dog is stressed, do something, like take a break, stop for the day, enrich the area, and/or SLOW STOP sooner.

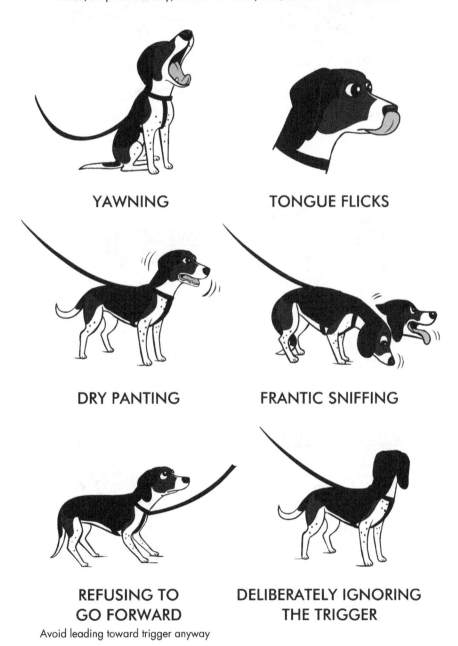

YAWNING

TONGUE FLICKS

DRY PANTING

FRANTIC SNIFFING

REFUSING TO
GO FORWARD

Avoid leading toward trigger anyway

DELIBERATELY IGNORING
THE TRIGGER

CROUCHED, SHIVERING, WORRIED FACE

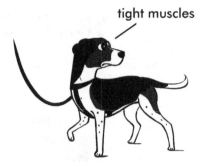

tight muscles

STARING AT TRIGGER AFTER MOVING AWAY

SWEATY FEET, DANDRUFF & SHEDDING

FLEEING FROM TRIGGER

SCANNING AROUND FOR DANGER

BARKING, LUNGING

CHAPTER 5

Leash Skills for Freedom and Safety

You can do BAT off leash with a barrier to maintain enough distance between the dog and the trigger. However, most of the time we begin with a harness and long line (15 feet / 5 meters) and then work up to off-leash sessions. Using the leash handling skills in this chapter, you can give your dog a sense of freedom while still maintaining safety. The sense of freedom helps him to have a more positive emotional experience and make better decisions. It also makes it easier to transition away from the leash.

> Tip for Pros: Practice the leash skills before your BAT set-up, in a separate session. You might even want two sessions to work on leash skills; teach the skills in the first session and use the second session to give the dog and handler a chance to get used to using the leash skills in the area with your BAT set-up, without a trigger. People need time to get used to this new way of handling the leash. When teaching, use the names below for each skill (or something similar that's easy for the client to remember). Then you can use those names as cues to remind the client of specific skills during the set-up.

Feel free to adapt the leash skills to fit your situation or physical abilities. You can even work with the dog off leash, using fencing instead of a long line to keep the dog from getting too close to the trigger. Just make sure that whatever you do is in the same spirit of BAT and addresses the "why" of each item. I have noted what each skill was designed to help with: Safety; Freedom; and/or Control.

- **Safety**: Useful for handling the long line without injury to anyone

- **Freedom**: Allows the dog to choose his own direction for movement

- **Control**: Prompts a change in how the dog is moving

The Safety and Freedom skills should be used at all times. The skills that are exclusively for Control should not be used very often in set-ups, if at all. If you need the leash to control the dog's behavior, you can probably change something else about your set-up to allow the dog to control himself, instead.

Body Bubble / Follow Your Dog (Freedom)

Why: Lets your dog make decisions and keeps you from accidentally pushing the dog over-threshold. Getting in your dog's way changes her natural behavior and may accidentally move her too close to the trigger. We all need personal space.

How: Observe how your movements influence your dog. Stay slightly behind her and off to the side, so that you can watch her, but you are not pushing or pulling her anywhere with your presence. Move in such a way that if she were tracking an odor, for example, you wouldn't pull her off of the scent trail.

Practice: Find a small, trigger-free area where she can be safely off leash. The idea is to let her sniff around without influencing which way she goes. Toss a bunch of treats onto the grass so that your dog will sniff around to get them (if this is a no-no for you, get creative). Stay within about five to eight feet of your dog (1.5 to 2.5 meters) without accidentally 'herding' or drawing her anywhere. If she moves quickly, just let her get ahead of you and then casually catch up the next time she stops to sniff. Anticipate when she will change direction and step out of the way. When she's stopped, stand behind her and off to the side. Pay close attention to the movement of her head. If you have no fenced in area to practice, you can do this indoors. After you learn all of the leash skills below, practice Body Bubble again with a long leash attached to your dog's harness.

Handle (Safety)

Why: Letting go of the leash is a safety risk.

How: Have a good grip on a loose leash. Choose which hand will hold the handle. I use my stronger hand for the **handle hand**. Put that hand through the handle on the leash and grab the base of the handle. The handle forms a tight bracelet. The leash crosses your palm and is clasped by the "V" between your thumb and forefinger. If you open your hand as if shaking hands, as shown in the illustration, the leash should be able to slide right off. I recommend practicing that. If you are wearing gloves, you may want to have the handle loop off of your wrist, closer to your palm, so you can let go if you really want to.

Practice: Keep your hand soft. The base of your thumb pins the leash in place when you need your other fingers for other things, like Mime Pulling.

LEASH SKILLS

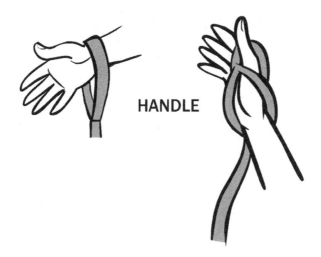

HANDLE

Braking distance (Freedom, Safety, Control)

Why: Allows you to stop the dog slowly to avoid pain/pressure to you or the dog.

How: The **braking hand** is the one that is not holding the handle (although you will sometimes use the handle hand for braking). The braking hand is the one closest to the dog. It controls the direction of the leash and keeps it out of the dog's way. Whenever possible, keep both hands on the leash.

Practice: Put your *braking hand under the leash*. You should be able to hold both of your palms up easily and the leash will go from your handle hand, drop down in front of you in a U-shape, then drape across the palm of your braking hand, and past your thumb to the dog. Holding it from underneath puts your joints more in alignment and gives you more fine movements of the leash with your thumb.

The amount of leash between your hands is your braking distance: the length you can let out as you slow down. When you have your hands relaxed at your side, with one hand in Handle position and the other loosely holding the leash, the bottom of the leash should be at about your knees. This is called Basic Position.

LEASH SKILLS

BRAKING DISTANCE

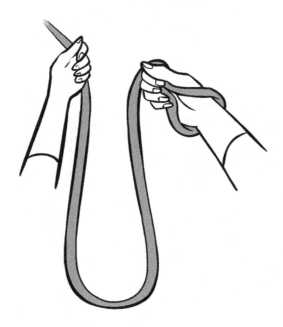

2-3 feet of leash

Shorter (Safety, Control)

Why: It's safer to keep the leash off of the ground to avoid tripping and tangling.

How: Shorten the leash so that it is still loose but above the dog's knees. If the dog moves closer to you or you move closer to the dog, gather the extra leash into your handle hand. Keep your braking hand stationary so the dog doesn't feel the leash jerking around.

- **Bow (preferred)**: Make a figure 8 with the leash with the center of the 8's in your handle hand.

- **Loops**: This is how you'd gather up a garden hose, just loops of leash. It is easier, but a little less safe. If your dog sprints away from you, the loops may tighten on your fingers.

In the following series of four photos, notice how I shorten the leash by gathering into it into a figure 8 shape in my handle hand.

Whenever your dog stops to sniff, go closer and shorten the line.

Keep your braking hand steady as you draw the leash out with your handle hand.

Notice my braking hand has not moved, so the leash isn't bouncy for my dog.

In basic position near the dog, with relaxed arms and braking distance, I can easily keep up with Bean's next move.

LEASH SKILLS

SHORTEN THE LEASH

Shorten the line whenever your dog stops to sniff or when your dog comes to you.

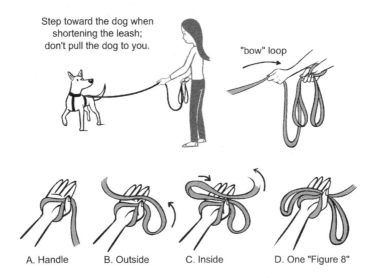

Step toward the dog when shortening the leash; don't pull the dog to you.

"bow" loop

A. Handle   B. Outside   C. Inside   D. One "Figure 8"

Longer (Freedom)

Why: In my experience, a restrained dog is more likely to overreact with aggression, frustration, or fear. A longer leash gives him more options and allows him to make better choices. Unless you are using the leash to stop your dog, the leash should be in a smile shape. If you have a shorter dog, it will be more like a smirk (think Mona Lisa smile), so it still has a bend in it but is less likely to be stepped over.

How: If the dog moves away from you, you can let out line instead of stopping the dog or running to keep up:

- The Noisy way (most common when the dog is moving away from you): Let the leash slip through your braking hand. As you use up the braking distance, use your handle hand to release another bow or loop of leash.

- The Quiet way (useful for times when you are trying to move away from the dog without prompting movement, as during elimination): Bring your handle hand to your braking hand. Use your braking hand to grab one bow or loop from the handle hand. Back away and lower your braking hand while lifting your handle hand, until the leash goes from a "W" to a "U." Repeat.

LEASH SKILLS

LENGTHEN THE LEASH

Use when the dog is moving more quickly than you can go
or when you want to encourage movement

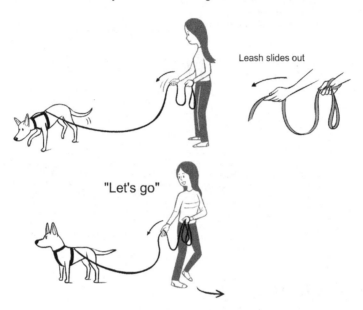

Leash slides out

"Let's go"

Use the quiet way to lengthen the leash when you don't want to distract your dog.

To minimize vibration, lower your braking hand and lift your handle hand.

Make the line straight each time before letting go with the braking hand.

Slide (Control)

Why: Allows you to communicate that you are stopping or that you need the dog's attention. Use when you want to get the dog's attention with the leash or as you slow the dog down.

How: Hand over hand. Grip the leash with one hand. Softly slide your other hand along the leash toward you, without actually pulling the leash. (Repeat, switching hands). This is the TTouch technique of "feathering."

> Tip for Pros: To avoid creating a loop around your handle hand, make an outside bow (as seen in Step B on page 89) before doing Slide.

LEASH SKILLS

SLIDE

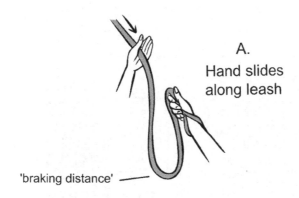

A.
Hand slides
along leash

'braking distance' ———

B.
Reach past with
other hand, from below

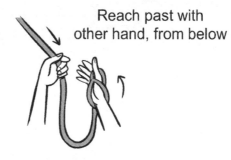

C.
Other hand
slides along
leash...

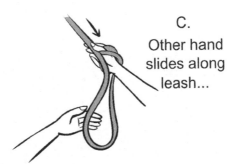

Left hand is sliding along leash.

Right hand reaches under and slides along leash. Note the outside bow in my right hand.

Slow Stop (Control)

Why: Your dog is less likely to bark when you come to a stop more slowly. It is also easier on your body and on the dog's, too.

How: Let the leash slide through your fingers for about one foot (30 cm) as you stop the dog. Your movement acts as a shock absorber when you slowly bring yourself to a stop and sit back a little. Stay in balance with your feet just over shoulder width apart. Point only the front foot directly at the dog to help your balance. Have the back foot at about 45 degrees, with your weight balanced more on that back foot so that you are in a strong position. Experiment with positions by having a friend hold the dog's end of the leash and try to pull you over.

LEASH SKILLS

SLOW STOP

A. Leash with braking distance

B. Leash slides out through hand

C. Slowly stop your dog

D. Step back towards dog to gather braking distance. Rebalance dog, center yourself, breathe.

Relax the Leash (Freedom)

Why: When you stop your dog with the leash, he is often out of balance because he is leaning into the leash. If you relax the pressure of the leash after stopping, he will be able to get into balance and make better choices than generalize well to off-leash situations. When the leash is in a U-shape, that's a "smile."

How: Keep a smile in the leash or put one back into the leash after you stop the dog. Very slowly bend your knee forward or extend your arm until the leash is loose and the dog is back in balance.

LEASH SKILLS

RELAX THE LEASH

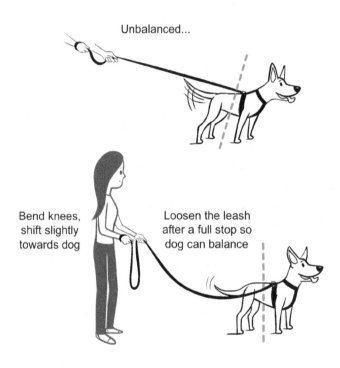

Unbalanced...

Bend knees, shift slightly towards dog

Loosen the leash after a full stop so dog can balance

Center Yourself (Safety)

Why: The leash also puts *you* out of balance. If you are off-balance when your dog pulls, you may fall. Standing with tension may also encourage your dog to go over-threshold.

How: Stand with your body softly balanced above your feet, knees relaxed, and hands at your side. You will be vertically centered, but still keep one foot slightly back, as in the Slow Stop, so that you will be harder to tip over if the dog suddenly pulls.

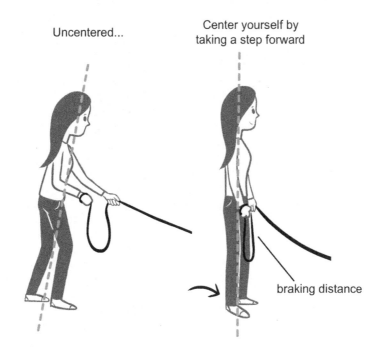

LEASH SKILLS

CENTER YOURSELF

Uncentered...

Center yourself by taking a step forward

braking distance

Mime Pulling (Control)

Why: Gets the dog's attention more quickly than Slide. Used for times when the dog is too focused on something and/or you want him to go a different way.

How: Do Slide where the dog can see you (they have 270 degree peripheral vision). Make inviting eye contact (flirt!) and keep eye contact as you bend your knees and pivot your body *away from the dog* in the direction that you want to go. You are sort of doing a 'play' bow to invite chase.

LEASH SKILLS

MIME PULLING

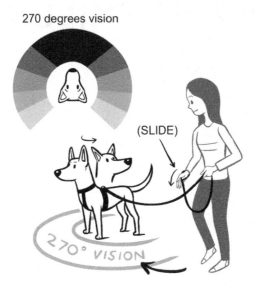

A. Move into vision to catch eye contact

B. Bend knees & rotate away

Here's a photo series of me doing Mime Pulling with Peanut. Thanks to Carly Loyer for being such a good distraction with those treats!

Slide as you step into the dog's peripheral vision. Don't really pull!

Twist away once you have eye contact. You may need to let some leash out as you go to avoid actually pulling your dog.

Walk away and keep your dog's focus.

Toss a treat for your dog to find. If your dog still lunges at the trigger, keep both hands on the leash.

CHAPTER 6

BAT Set-ups for Reactivity

This chapter walks you through the details of using Behavior Adjustment Training to help reduce a dog's reactivity. As I mentioned before, all training with BAT is done below threshold, meaning that stress levels are kept low in order to create a positive experience. Your dog should be able to react well, without going back to barking or fleeing, thus rehearsing the behavior that you are trying to change. Keeping your dog below threshold is easiest to do when you have a carefully arranged situation with human helpers and/or dogs to practice with, but it can usually be done on walks, too. Keep thresholds in mind at all times as you work with your dog.

In order for BAT to work, you must be able to recognize when your dog is at or below threshold versus when he is over-threshold.

Dog is at threshold: mouth open, tail wag slower, center of gravity fairly neutral, but facial muscles are tense, spine is oriented toward trigger, and tail is slightly raised. This could go either way.

Prompt! Dog is over-threshold: mouth closed, forehead wrinkled, tail moving fast, body coiled and ready for action.

Choice points

A **choice point** is a situation in which a dog has a decision to make, like choosing between two paths in a maze. As your dog walks around, he has a lot of choice points—from "do I follow this deliciously stinky odor?" to "Do I bark at that dog?" BAT set-ups create situations where your dog has a really high chance of choosing to sniff around and explore the area, gathering information about the trigger at a distance. So when your dog notices the trigger, that's not any old choice point—the deck is stacked so that he is very likely to do a polite cut-off signal instead of panicking or being aggressive. I suppose I could coin a new term for that, like a "favorable choice point," because the odds of your dog offering the desired behavior are in your favor. But as an empowerment trainer, any choice point I set up would be a favorable one. Let's stick with the simpler term: whenever I use the term "choice point," please take that to mean "favorable choice point." We always want to set the dog up for success.

In BAT, your dog practices the act of choosing the new behavior. If your dog hasn't noticed the trigger, you can just wait, do something to attract your dog's attention to the trigger, or zigzag closer. Starting too far away is better than starting too close. If you are too close, the dog has a negative experience and you need to micro-manage, taking away the dog's chance to choose.

One obvious sign that your dog may too close to the trigger is walking directly at the trigger. Straight approaches are a predictable sign that your dog is headed over-threshold, so when that happens, do a Slow Stop or subtly change direction. Your dog will gradually be interested in meandering closer to the trigger, but don't let him go straight there unless you are sure he is below threshold. Keep the odds at each choice point in your favor, so your dog is choosing what you want, over and over.

The choice point is not a set spot: it's an event whose location moves closer and farther from the trigger during your set-up as your dog moves around and as you keep an eye on your dog's arousal level. This is in contrast to BAT 1.0 when sometimes the choice point was pre-determined, and the handler would proceed as long as the dog was still not too aroused. The training environment becomes more and more realistic over time and you will gradually let the dog move closer to the trigger when he is ready for it. Let's use the analogy of rehearsing a theatrical play again. The first set-ups are like reading the script in a quiet coffee shop; the middle set-ups are rehearsing with other actors; dress rehearsals get the actors used to the distraction of costumes and sets; and the final choice points are like performing on Broadway. For example, in Peanut's first BAT session with a child, he was on leash, with a single child sitting on an adult's lap behind a barrier, far, far away. In the final sessions, Peanut was off leash and two children were running around a room with him. You wouldn't perform on Broadway without a lot of rehearsal. The same is true for training—performing well takes lots of rehearsal, at the right difficulty level. In all of your dog's encounters with their triggers, especially the riskier ones in which your dog is off leash, the chance of a successful 'performance' should be very high.

Here's another example of a choice point, from Kathy Sdao's *I-Cue* seminar, which is where I first heard the term applied to dog training (see Resources). Kathy played a video of her teaching puppy raisers at Guide Dogs for the Blind in which she demonstrated how to set up choice points to train polite walking around distractions. The puppy was to walk in a straight path that was marked on the ground, with a distraction off to the side. The distraction was close enough to get the puppy's attention, but far enough that the puppy was likely to turn away from it and keep walking. The choice point began the instant the puppy noticed the distraction. Just as the puppy chose to look away from the distraction, the handler clicked and rewarded with a treat, praise, and continuation of the walk. Genius!

Note: In BAT 1.0, we used to always mark all replacement behaviors at the choice point and provide a functional reinforcer of moving away from or toward the trigger. We still have that option (see Mark and Move in Chapter 7), but with BAT 2.0 set-ups I prefer to do something different. Unlike training a service dog to focus and heel, we don't want working mode in BAT. We let the dog choose the best reinforcer at that instant by simply following him, as long as he's not going directly toward the trigger. Because we are working a bit farther away than we used to, the dog is likely to just move on after disengaging from the trigger. We don't have to move him away—in fact, he may not want to leave.

When your dog takes that first step after a choice point, he can be moving away from the trigger or toward something interesting, but we don't necessarily know which one. By just letting the scenario play out, the dog gets the functional reinforcer that he wants. The consequence of moving in that direction is exactly what the dog was trying to make happen in that moment, so it is a naturally occurring reinforcer that makes the behavior more likely. The trainer doesn't have to provide the reinforcer, it just happens. Since we don't prompt the dog to move anywhere after his good choice, we avoid the possibility of giving him the wrong functional reinforcer and distracting him from processing what he's just learned about the trigger. It's a much more natural, empowering interaction with the trigger and the environment.

What success looks like

Many factors will influence the success of your BAT set-up, including whether the dog stays below threshold. I'll cover that next, but first let's discuss what success means.

My clients all have slightly different pictures in their mind about what overall success should look like. If they didn't take reality into account, their goals would all be about the same, something like, "I want my dog to be a normal dog." Actually, that's not quite true. What they really want is a dog that's better than normal, and I don't blame them—that's what I want, too! They want a bombproof dog, who never shows aggression, no matter what happens. If children pull his tail or fall on him, they want him to wag happily and enjoy himself. If another dog growls in his face, they want him to peacefully diffuse the situation. And by the way, could we have that at the end of just one session?

This may seem like a simple situation, but it's tough for the dogs!

Fortunately, most of my clients (and hopefully you) understand that rehabilitation of reactivity—like physical therapy, psychotherapy, and learning a new sport—takes time and effort. But there should be some progress in each successful BAT session. Knowing what to look for and having a realistic goal for the training session makes it more likely that you'll get there.

Your dog should be below threshold for all or most of a successful session. I'll explain how to collect data on your set-ups so that you can tell whether this really happens. If you have any outbursts, they should be few and far between. They should be dealt with calmly and your dog should be given the chance to relax. Your dog should be allowed to take breaks whenever he wants to and he should seem comfortable with the training.

In an ideal session, you have picked a location to work with where there are minimal intrusions, or a location where intrusions still allow your dog to remain sub-threshold. For example, if your dog (over)reacts to other dogs, and a neighborhood dog comes walking by with his human, you could call your dog away from the sidewalk, cross the street, put her in a car, feed her a bunch of hot dogs, toss a tennis ball, or whatever else it takes to keep her in a good mood.

To consider a training session a success, your dog should make progress in one or more dimensions, such as average distance to the trigger, unless the session is very short, like two minutes. Session length can vary from a minute to about 45 minutes, however the latter only works if there are lots of breaks and the dog is having fun exploring the environment. Usually it's more like 20 minutes. In a lot of my sessions, the dog actually sniffs or meets the helper or helper dog by the end. This often can't happen in the first few set-ups, but it's great when you can. I think progress is accelerated when the dog has a chance to learn that the trigger is not scary after all and he leaves the session with a positive feeling. This positive feeling can be created by winding your session down with easier work, like following the trigger from far away, or for milder issues, actually letting your dog spend time relaxing around the trigger. Even if you only get to within ten feet of the trigger as your closest approach point during the session, you can spend some time at the end of the session just chatting from fifteen to twenty feet away, a distance at which the dog is more comfortable. Then encourage your dog to move away first, so that the sudden motion of the trigger doesn't startle him.

Ending well is important. I confused a client once by saying she should get as much use out of each helper as she could, meaning that you could dress them up, have them change their gait, and do all sorts of other things. Once the dog realizes the helper is friendly and not scary, you can't really do BAT with him as the trigger without being creative. So she did session after session, careful to not let her dog get to know the person, so she could re-use him as a trigger. Unfortunately, that slowed down her dog's progress. Having her become fully acquainted with one nice person after another would've helped her become comfortable with humans more quickly. Not only does a positive ending to the session speed up progress, it also helps you see that progress more clearly. So she could have gone all the way to friendly interactions with the person and still varied the situation by dressing the person up in later sessions. These would probably go quite quickly from "odd stranger" to "my friend Sam in an outfit," but they'd be useful.

The amount of working time between the beginning of a session and 'first contact' is a good data point to record. You might define first contact as the point where you had to put a muzzle on, a certain distance from the trigger, the first time your dog touched the trigger, or the first time the trigger could touch your dog.

Keep in mind that if your dog starts out a football field away from the trigger, it's unlikely your dog will get close enough to greet in your first few set-ups. Getting to know the trigger can take a while, and you should always take the dog's stress level, interest, and stamina into account.

That process does start to move quickly. After each successful BAT set-up, the dog can usually begin closer to the trigger than in the previous set-up, even with a new person or dog as the trigger, unless there is something more challenging about the trigger or the set-up. But dogs are individuals. Your dog may take a different route to success. Always let your dog work farther away from the trigger when she needs to.

How to make your set-up a success

As trainers and caregivers, our main task is to set up situations in which the dog is empowered. This means we arrange scenarios in which we don't have to micro-manage the dog's behavior. He is just likely to get it 'right,' because it's similar enough to a context with which he is familiar and comfortable. All animals, including dogs and humans, learn through the consequences of their behavior. They learn that certain behavior works in certain situations. The situation doesn't cause the behavior, but certain things in the environment are cues that certain behavior will be reinforced. Other aspects of the environment bring about emotional states that make certain behaviors more likely.

For example, being close to the trigger may make your dog scared and being on leash may signal that barking is a better option than trying to escape. So we work far away and use the BAT leash skills for a sense of freedom. That way, you create a situation where your dog is able to see a trigger and feel empowered to just check it out and move on, or even show interest in interacting with the trigger in a pro-social way.

Set up situations in which your dog can behave in a way that you like, then gradually change the scenarios to be more realistic. Sessions that maximize learning and minimize stress take careful planning. The more experience you have, the more easily you can avoid or deal with issues. For trainers new to BAT or reactivity, the most ethical way to learn on the job is to follow the case supervision model that psychologists use: work with a mentor to help apply the theory to individual clients.

> Tip for Pros: Antecedents create the context that sets the occasion for behavior. They can be distant antecedents, like health, nutrition, state of arousal before the session, etc. They can also be proximal antecedents, like motivating operations (emotions, hunger, etc.) or cues from us and the environment that predict certain behavior → consequence contingencies. The strength of the

dog's reactivity depends on her reinforcement history, but also on the context in which this history occurred. Reinforcement selects behavior in context. See Appendix 3 for more explanation.

Choose the location. Do BAT set-ups in many different locations to help your dog generalize. Pick locations that balance out safety and enrichment. Find large, interesting areas without random triggers popping by. We usually work outside. Here are a few safety considerations:

- Room for student dog to move away from the helper/trigger.

- Large and wide enough for student dog to move around; ideal if helper/trigger could be moving at the same time, like a big walking path.

- No glass, poison, thorns, or other hazards.

- Look for obstacles that might snag the leash or trip the handler.

- Visually diverse (bushes, trees, elevation change, versus one big open field); this gives the dog objects to move behind and more to investigate.

- Quiet at dog height—particularly for dogs who are sound sensitive.

- Mild distractions, but not extreme (squirrels running around may be too much).

- Wide entrance/exit—ideally the student can enter the area and zigzag instead walking straight at the helper through a narrow entry.

- You or an assistant can see unplanned triggers enter the space from a position where you will have time to change something to help your dog stay under threshold (move away, step behind a visual barrier, etc.).

Look for (or create) an enriched location that your dog can explore comfortably. A more sterile, boring environment will likely increase excitement when your dog sees the trigger, because there's nothing else to do. Each dog is different. Individual dogs may need more or less enrichment, based on how excited or relaxed they get by the stimuli in their environment. Here are some aspects to keep in mind, and a few examples of ways you can add those in when you can't find a naturally interesting location:

- Smell (primary sense for the dog): grated/powdered cheese, powdered peanut butter, drizzled chicken fat, other dogs walking through, sheep dung in a box with holes for odor to escape, cat fur on a towel, used gloves, etc.

- Sight: trees, bushes, boxes, cars, crates, hills (things for dog to move around or behind).

- Touch: different surfaces, things to step over or on.

- Hearing: I don't usually add extra sounds, although I may include calming music or brown noise if we are in smaller areas; sense of hearing mostly comes into play when the dog is distracted by something outside of the set-up area.

- Taste: I sometimes hide a few treats around the area for the dog to eat, but be careful because this may be too distracting.

Keep in mind that your dog uses contextual clues from the environment to figure out what's happening. Any stimulus that reliably precedes a certain situation can accidentally turn into a safety signal that tells the dog that he's only safe with that stimulus around. By varying the context, you can help your dog learn that his new BAT skills work everywhere. If you have parmesan cheese at every set-up, then your dog may end up only being comfortable around the trigger when the smell of parmesan is in the air. So mix it up!

Work in an area where your dog will be relaxed.
For most dogs, this involves sniffing around.

Avoid doing BAT set-ups in areas that you normally do sports or competition training unless you are specifically working on reactivity in those contexts. Dogs tend to go into working mode in places they are used to being trained. When dogs are in working mode, they are distracted and show more trained behavior and fewer natural communication signals. They are so busy staring at you that you can easily miss the moment between 'fine' and 'explosive.' In my experience, dogs learn less about the helper when they're busy focusing on the handler, so it's more efficient to arrange the situation to let dogs explore and stay out of working mode.

Plan the session in advance and communicate throughout. When you discuss your plan with the helpers, keep your dog and the trigger 100% separate, so they can't notice each other before the session. Take odor and wind into account. Choreograph the environment session very carefully, from the first opportunity to notice the helper down to the end of the session. Note that your focus is on micro-managing the environment, so your dog can freely choose her own movement within it.

- What should the dog do on the day of the set-up? Focus on low-arousal mental and physical exercise, healthy meals—but not so much that food is not motivating, and minimal stressors—so no vet visits.

- What happens when the student dog and helper or helper dog arrive at the site (parking separately, enrichment of the space, check area for new triggers, on leash before getting out of the car, walking around to sniff and explore, out of sight or far away until training begins).

- Who is bringing the water bowl and water? Is there a dog bed? Parked car with a door open? Open crate? Where do those go?

- Who is going where and in what order?

- When does the student dog first move to a position from which she can see the helper? How does she move there (usually a zigzag)?

- If the helper is the one moving, when does the helper come into view? Who decides (trainer, caregiver, helper dog handler, etc.)?

- How do you efficiently communicate:

  ◦ Break time (dog asks for a break, accidentally too close to trigger, temporary trigger stacking, helper having trouble, etc.).

  ◦ Stop the session (pain, fatigue, general stress, too hot/cold, etc.).

  ◦ Loose dog or other unplanned trigger.

- Who is watching the stress of the dog(s)?

Check in frequently with the helper and any assistants. You can do this as a running commentary during the session or by stopping to take breaks and putting the dog(s) away so you can talk. The first option has the benefit of getting your dog used to conversation with strangers if your dog has issues with people. The second option has the benefit of being able to concentrate on the dog(s) instead of chatting. Two-way radios or a hands-free mobile phone can be used to communicate to helpers who are far away.

Pay attention to talking. Any talking, or lack thereof, will be part of the stimulus conditions, i.e., the context that your dog is noticing and taking in as part of the training. I have had some client dogs who only lunge and bark when their handler starts to talk to the stranger, and the reverse has also happened—the dog only barks when the handler does not talk to the stranger in a friendly way.

Keep sessions upbeat. Make the sessions pleasant for the sake of all involved: dogs and people. Take multiple breaks, especially if any of the dogs ask for one by moving out of sight or avoiding the helper. Most of the time, dogs just like to explore and sniff, but they can also sniff to displace their stress. In that case, you will notice that the dog is sniffing a bit frantically and can basically look everywhere but at the helper. If something has stressed your dog, or his behavior seems to be getting worse instead of better, take a break to discuss it. For breaks, keep your dog and the helper out of sight from each other and give them something relaxing to do (stuffed Kong in the car, off leash time in a safe space, etc.).

Breathe, but keep your breathing calm and steady. Do your best to breathe normally, to help the dog relax. If the dog gets a bit stuck looking at a trigger, people commonly hold their breath while they wait for their dogs to disengage. When I was starting out as a trainer, I hired the fabulous Associate Certified Applied Animal Behaviorist and author Kathy Sdao to consult on cases I wasn't yet ready to tackle on my own. I got a lot of great advice from her, including the idea to sing happy birthday to bring one's breathing back to normal for the sake of the dog. I made up a little song for Peanut, too, to the tune of "I'm a Little Teapot." It works.

I have also had some success with relaxing Peanut just by thinking of things that make my own mouth water, like a bowl of ice cream or Thai food from a certain restaurant in Seattle that I adore. He is a mama's boy and even though I'm pretty sure he can't read my mind, you can bet that he's paying attention to my stress level by smell or some other sense. Conversely, I have accidentally caused him to pace around the house in a stressed-out state by practicing a certain kind of energetic yoga breathing. If you find that you aren't breathing well, or your dog looks stressed, start by breathing out slowly. Inhaling first seems to make them more likely to bark. I figure that's because they figure you are taking in a deep breath so you can bark, too.

Watch for intruders. If dogs are a trigger, be ready for off-leash dogs who can intrude on your set-ups; it can be disastrous if they run up to your dog. It's critical for training and safety that the dog stays sub-threshold as much as possible.

Designate one of the people in your set-up as the loose dog wrangler, so if there's a loose dog in the neighborhood, you and your dog can disappear into a car, behind a fence, down the street, or elsewhere while the wrangler intercepts the off-leash dog and returns him to his owner. If you have one student dog, her human, and a helper dog with his person, then the latter are the designated dog wranglers. Helper dogs make excellent dog wranglers if they don't have dog issues, since they are drawn to their own species like a magnet. This is less necessary when you are working with a dog who only has issues with people, but it's still a good idea to designate someone to intercept curious bystanders or running children chanting "Doggy!!!"

When I do set-ups with clients, we often **park a car nearby**, unlocked, so that my client and the dog can pop inside in case there's a loose dog. Another option is to have the set-up on the sidewalk or road just outside of your home, so it's easy to quickly run back inside.

If you can't park a car near the set-up, **put an open, blanket covered exercise pen around an open, covered crate**, so student dog's handler can quickly send the dog to the crate, close the crate door, and seal up the ex-pen. Then if the off-leash dog comes over, it still can't run right up to the crate. The handler can drop treats in for the student dog and toss another handful for the loose dog to eat until the situation can be brought under control. By having the dog in the crate/ex-pen combo, it's less likely that he'll even see the loose dog, plus the caregiver knows everything is safe and can be more relaxed. Be sure to rehearse the whole process at least once in every session.

If you're working indoors, you don't have to be as careful about random triggers just showing up, but it's usually more stressful for the dog because of the smaller space. I've had a few dogs who were lovely and friendly up close inside of a building (any building) and very loud and snarky at a distance outside, but those are the exception, not the rule. I tend to do outdoor work on fairly neutral territory first, like down the street or even in a different neighborhood, unless the dog is able to stay below threshold at her house. You don't want to stress a dog out, but you don't want to waste your time in a situation where the dog is 100% fine, either. A good general rule is that you should work at the most challenging location at which the dog can handle well. BAT sessions should be pleasant.

Film your sessions. For one thing, filming your training set-up seems to discourage random intruders—somehow people are more hesitant to interrupt a video shoot than a training session. You and the other handler will be looking very intensely at your own dogs, so you may have trouble scanning the neighborhood. I'm speaking from experience here. I like to think of myself as being pretty aware of my surroundings as I work, but unfortunately, that's not one hundred percent true. I know this because I have a video of myself being completely unaware of danger.

I often film my sessions and go over them later. When I review the video, I see things I completely missed during the session. In the session that I mentioned above, a client and I were doing a BAT session with her dog and mine. Two dogs were being walked along the sidewalk across the street from our session. The client and I were doing an up-close introduction, but stopped doing so as we focused on our dogs' reactions to the dogs across the street. Then a third dog and handler came walking down the sidewalk toward us. Fortunately, they saw the camera and tripod and crossed the street when they were about fifteen feet away. Disaster averted, no thanks to us! Neither of us even saw them during the session. Eek! That's why I recommend having a third person there, if you can manage it.

Engineer an environment that keeps your dog below threshold. If a dog, person, or noise interrupts your session, watch for trigger stacking, i.e., the stress from different environmental triggers piling up and putting your dog over-threshold. When you notice that your dog has been stressed by something in the environment, decrease the stress of his exposure to the trigger by encouraging him to work farther away, having the trigger behave more calmly, or even take a break. I once worked with a Chihuahua who had gotten to the point where she'd come up and I could briefly pet her under the chin. The upstairs neighbor made a noise and she barked once, and we got back to work. The next time she approached me, I attempted to pet her without thinking, just like before, and she air snapped a warning at me. Trigger stacking can sneak up on you if you aren't paying attention!

Bring fight break-up equipment. Have SprayShield, Silly String, water, or some other way to safely break up fights, as mentioned in Chapter 3. There's always the possibility that the loose dog wrangler cannot keep other dogs away from your dog, that someone accidentally slips and drops a leash, or that a greeting goes completely awry. While I've never had to use SprayShield during a set-up (knock on wood), I plan for the worst-case scenario. Have it accessible during the session, and if you have a helper, both of you should have a can of it. You might even want to have a blanket handy, in case the SprayShield fails.

Pretty much all ways to break up a fight have some level of danger to them, so use these tips at your own risk. If a dog is latched on and won't let go, you can use a blanket to cover up the attacker's head and eventually get her to open her mouth, while minimizing the possibility of a bite to you. Wrap the blanket over the eyes and mouth and either just wait and pull the dog back when he lets go, or if the other dog is in danger of further injury or death, twist the biting dog's collar to cut off the air supply. Having safe gear, working below threshold, and wearing muzzles during set-ups in which the dogs may come into contact will make this highly unlikely, but it is good to know what to do, just in case everything goes wrong. Then consult with a professional trainer (even if you are a trainer yourself) to see if there was any way you could have prevented the situation.

> Tip for Pros: Rehearse breaking up a dog fight in advance. If you run a training facility, vet office, daycare, or are otherwise responsible for multiple dogs, have a specific, written plan for all staff on breaking up fights.

It helps to rehearse. You can do an actual reenactment or at least mentally rehearse having a fight break out. I give this advice because I have forgotten to use the SprayShield before. I have such a history of reaching into rough puppy play and grabbing the upper part of the back legs (a safe-ish place to grab if you need to separate scuffling dogs) that I automatically did that, even in real fights where the dogs were latched onto each other, rather than grabbing for the SprayShield. So now I rehearse using the spray by grabbing it every time I see an off-leash dog. Even though I don't use it on them, my brain is getting ready, and I was able to remember to use it when I saw a bite-and-hold fight break out at the park.

Check leash connections and gear. Do a safety check on your dog and the helper before each session. Look for chewed or frayed leashes, loose collars, harnesses, muzzles, unsafe footwear, and leashes that are painful to grip. For example, the chest strap of the EasyWalk harness (which I don't like using anyway, because it restricts shoulder movement) tends to loosen while the dog is wearing it. In our regular training classes, I have seen several dogs slip right out of the front of the EasyWalk harness. The chest straps had gotten so loose that the neck holes were bigger than the dogs, and the harnesses just slipped over their bodies! To prevent that, you can attach the snap to both the collar and the front ring of the harness at the same time. Or better yet, get one of the harnesses I mentioned in Chapter 3 which allow free movement of all joints and doesn't loosen without your help. Make sure the leash is attached in a safe way and the ring to which it is attached is secure. If you use a head collar, attach the other end of the leash to a harness so that you really only use the head collar as a back-up. If you really must attach the leash only to the head collar, make sure it has a safety strap, because they can slip off.

If your helper dog shows up with an extendible or bungee leash, replace that leash with a regular leash that is safe and comfortable to hold. The same goes for the thin puppy leashes that can easily tear through someone's hand. Look for anything that is unsafe and fix issues right away.

Use physical barriers. For close up work with a student dog with a bite history or even a possibility of biting, I highly recommend a physical barrier between the student dog and the helper dog or person. We are human and we make mistakes in judgment, observation, and physical coordination. It's not worth risking the safety of your dog and the helper by assuming that you can observe and act quickly enough. Teach your dog to be comfortable wearing a muzzle or choose a location where a fence can stand between your dog and the helper. I use muzzles for close-up greetings whenever the dog either has a damaging bite history, I don't know the bite history, or I just want to be extra safe with the helper (especially children). Muzzles must be properly fitted, so check the fit of the muzzle before allowing any greetings.

Use barriers to provide for safe, protected contact if need be. Note: This child is facing front and staring, which could be really scary for a dog.

Have a back-up plan. In case of emergency, it's most efficient to tell people what to do, by name. In order to do that, *you must learn your human helpers' names!* Use them from time to time during the session, to keep yourself fresh. Besides, people prefer being known by their own names instead of just, "Hey you" or "Fifi's mom." Your back-up plan should have a back-up plan. Know the closest open veterinarian's office and save their contact information on your phone. Most helpers seem to be available for set-ups only on evenings and weekends, so that limits the possible vets to go to.

Empower all participants. Make sure to give everyone *"veto power"* as Kathy Sdao says. Our dogs can stop the set-up at any time with their behavior. That is also true for the people who are there: if any person at the session feels the slightest bit uncomfortable about the safety or wisdom of a particular set-up, they should feel comfortable speaking up. Take a break, discuss the situation, and make any necessary changes before moving on.

> Tip for Pros: Veto power is especially important to point out in set-ups with your clients, because people are socialized to respect authority figures and tend not to question a trainer's judgment, especially in the moment. They need your explicit permission to speak up for safety, at anytime, even if it's just a hunch.

Keep records on how the session went. This allows you to see what needs to be changed, what your dog did well, and gives you a very clear picture of your dog's progress. That progress is what will motivate you to do another session, and another, so it's helpful to collect at least a little data. I find it helpful to aim to minimize the number of times that the dog needed to be slow stopped and the number of times the dog goes into yellow and beyond. Your number of Slow Stops may never go all the way to zero, but ideally you do end up with zero instances of yellow, orange, and red. Also minimize the average distance to the trigger during the session. With each helper, the average distance to the trigger will decrease. I've also included other possible data to collect.

I have included an example of a record-keeping sheet on the following page. Some of these are more complicated than others, so feel free to leave out the ones that you don't want to use. The form should be simple enough for you that you will do it consistently.

Whatever data you end up collecting, just be consistent in how you measure it. Write out what you mean by each item and what units you are measuring in, so you can refer back to it later or share with me or another trainer.

Date			
Trigger (People, dogs, etc.)			
Helper (Name or description)			
Duration (not including breaks)			
Duration of breaks			
Number of breaks			
Break Activity			
Filmed (yes/no)			
Description: (Following, stationary trigger, parallel walking, "parallel play," etc.)			
Start Distance to Helper			
End Distance to Helper			
Average Distance*			
Slow Stops (number of times)			
Yellow (number of times)			
Orange (number of times)			
Red (number of times)			
Total Over-threshold (number of times past shoreline)			
Number of unpredicted triggers**			
Better (1) or worse than (0) last time***			

* *The average distance is complicated to calculate but what you can do is look at your videos and then take something like 10 or 20 samples during the working part of your session. To do that, pause it every 2 minutes of working time and estimate the distance to the trigger. Add those up and divide by the number of data points. Another way is to calculate the average distance for a choice point: look at the distance the dog was at each time he looked at the trigger (each choice point). Add those all up and divide by the number of choice points.*

** *The number of unpredicted triggers helps you know whether you should change something about how you do your set-ups, and also feel a little bit better about instances where your dog got into the 'water.' Your dog could be improving, in general, but if there were a lot of triggers, you'd expect more over-threshold instances. If you had a lot of unpredicted triggers, then the number of over-threshold instances doesn't reflect the overall trend of whether or not the way you are doing*

*BAT is helping your dog. You may choose to consider any unexpected stimulus to be an unpre-
dicted trigger, or you can only count the number of unpredicted triggers that your dog couldn't
handle. Or you can keep both numbers, as a measure of how well your dog is handling real life.*

**** I do this either as a gut feeling about how things went, overall, or I look at some specific
metric, like number of times over-threshold (or do this for each of those items). You can average the better/worse for all of your sessions. If you are over 0.5, then things are improving.*

> Tip for Pros: Feel free to add your own data fields and remove some of mine.
> You could even just record the date, helper name, and number of times the
> dog went into the water. The most important number here is that you keep the
> number of over-threshold instances low. If you focus too much on decreasing
> the average distance, you'll be tempted to lead the dog forward.

BAT set-ups

Now that you're prepared, let's take a good look at how to actually do the set-ups. Remember from the overview that you are facilitating a situation in which the dog can
wander around and explore the area, with a little help from you to stay out of trouble.

Choose the trigger after analyzing the variables

Choose the trigger you'll be working with for your dog (people, dogs, a slippery floor,
etc.). That will determine your location and get you started on how to do the session.
Think about the variables for the helper/trigger that you want to focus on. Each variable can adjust the amount of stress and not taking them into account can lead to
trigger stacking. It's kind of like having a lot of difficulty settings on a video game and
you want to only have them up as high as the player can easily handle.

Look at the variables that your dog may encounter in real life. When your dog is ready
for variation, make some other aspect of the situation easier and adjust one variable
to generalize the context cues and make your dog's responses more reliable. Gradually make your set-ups more realistic. Go through different variations to ensure that
your dog has had a chance to be relaxed in lots of situations. The lists below give some
important dimensions to consider for each variable. For example, one dog may not
distinguish between an intact male and a neutered female dog, but another dog may
think that's a huge difference.

These variables should be thoughtfully combined. When making one thing more difficult, make others easier at first. Start with an approach that is successful and build very
gradually from there. For example, when you consider the entrance order, you still
need to take the motion variables into account. For example, walking rudely directly
toward the trigger is more likely to lead to trouble than if you help your dog politely
zigzag in until he notices the trigger. Speed also matters since walking into the area
directly toward the trigger is different than running into the area directly toward the
trigger. The second one would be harder for both the student and helper dog.

Location of trigger (see above on choosing the overall setting):

- Distance to trigger
- Direction of trigger—ahead / behind.

Entrance order:

- Trigger in area, then student dog enters
- Student in area, then trigger enters
- Both student dog and trigger enter area at same time (from opposite ends).

Motion:

- Amount of trigger movement (or lack thereof)
- Trigger's speed
- Student dog's speed
- Direction of motion (parallel / opposite / angle/ arc)
- Erratic motion / gait of trigger
- Excitement level of trigger (directed at handler or toy / directed at student)
- Significant motions (reaching to pet / kneeling / leaning over / dog bowing / other).

Sounds:

- Environmental sounds
- Trigger making noise (talking / jingling tags / barking / whining)
- Handler talking to student dog (happy narration, silence, fake phone call)
- Handler talking to trigger (in person or via 2-way radio)
- Other sounds in the environment
- Meaning of sound
- Volume, pitch, or other quality of sound.

Timing:

- How long a session lasts (or in real life, how long is your dog expected to be around the trigger?)
- Amount of time since last break

Other dimensions to vary:

- **Actors and Stage Crew:** Who is at the session? In what role? If Mom is always there and always the one doing the leash work, she may become part of the context for the rehabilitation. Same thing for the trainer, camera person, helper, etc. Just as you must vary the location, you should also change who is in the scene and how far they are from the dog so that the dog learns that these rules apply in all scenarios. This is especially important for dogs at shelters or in foster care.

- **Presence/location of treats:** Remember, don't always do Sprinkles or have treats! Handler for student or helper dog having treats could cause resource guarding.

- **Disposition of trigger:** (wants to play, avoids, also has reactivity issues, etc.)

- **Objects:** (hats, hoods, umbrellas, boxes, agility equipment, rally cones, backpacks, crates, canes, crutches, wheelchairs, scooters, bicycles, skateboards, etc.)

- **Odors:** (smoke, alcohol, perfume, etc.)

- **Eye contact from trigger:** (none, soft/blinking, staring)

- **On-leash / Off leash:** (student dog and helper)

- **Barrier / No Barrier:** (careful!)

- **Helper dog:** size / age / breed / color / coat type / neuter status / sex / heat status (for the sake of the helper dog, avoid using helper dogs under 2 years until your dog is great with mature adults).

- **Helper human:** size / sex / gender expression / age / voice pitch / hair color / ethnicity (yes, dogs can be racist: they are great at figuring out differences in the context).

Obviously there are many variables that one could choose to work on, and you can't work on all of them in a given session. I recommend that you introduce just a few variables, one at a time, into a session. If you introduce more than one at a time, your dog may not attend to them both, or your dog may have a negative experience and generalize to the other new stimulus. It's also just more scientific to introduce one change at a time, so you know which variable is having an effect.

In the early sessions, you might just work on the dog being able to be around people at all. In an advanced session with the same helper a week later, you might start out with the helper having no props, then take a break to move farther away, then have the helper wear a hat, then later trade the hat for a walker or a cane, then use crutches, then switch back to no props.

Your main set-up for letting your dog learn about the trigger can be arranged in different ways, but however you do it, your dog should be sub-threshold. Varying the set-up is an essential part of the game, so be sure to read the end of the chapter for more variations.

More on choosing a helper

If the handler is new to BAT, I like to start with a fake dog as the helper, or have the helper behind a barrier, so that the handler can gain confidence in the activity. If the handler is experienced, you can start with a real live trigger that is walking away from the student dog. The trigger is far away, but is usually still allowed to interact with the dog, as in real life. Use whatever safety precautions you feel are best (and then add a little more). For example, if the dog has injured other dogs, you might want to use a fence between the dog and helper or use a muzzle the whole time, even far away, in case the handler drops the leash.

Follow your dog

In a BAT set-up, you basically just keep the leash loose and stay out of your dog's way, unless there's some reason to not let her continue walking in that direction. At first you will work without a trigger at all, to get used to following and being aware of your own movements. Most set-ups with a semi-stationary trigger have this general flow:

1. Stay out of the way as your dog freely explores.

2. Slow Stop if focus on the trigger gets moderately intense.

3. Call the dog away if she can't handle the situation on her own.

Getting occasional check-ins is normal and good. Respond by asking your dog where he wants to go: rotate your body slightly away to offer a change of direction.

How do you know that your dog is focused on the trigger? Dogs usually walk in curves unless they are pretty focused on something. So if your dog walks directly at the trigger, that's a sign that arousal is starting to go up and there's a higher risk of a reaction. I would say the dog is at the shoreline in our beach analogy, i.e., the dog is at the threshold of what she can handle on her own.

Let's take another look at the beach analogy for stress that I introduced in Chapter 4 on the illustration on the next page. In the green and blue zones, your dog is able to fully handle the situation herself. That corresponds to step one under "Follow Your Dog" above. If your dog is at the shoreline shown in the illustration (at threshold), do a Slow Stop or reduce the intensity of the trigger to keep things from getting too challenging. If you let your dog get closer to the trigger, it would be too difficult. Once your dog's "toes are in the water" or your dog is even deeper in, the arousal is too high and your dog may end up barking, growling, or lunging on the leash.

More importantly, if your dog goes over the working threshold for BAT, there may be a negative emotional take-away of the experience for both of you. The whole point of BAT is to create positive, empowering experiences. If you mess up once in a while, that's okay, but the goal is to stay out of the proverbial deep water

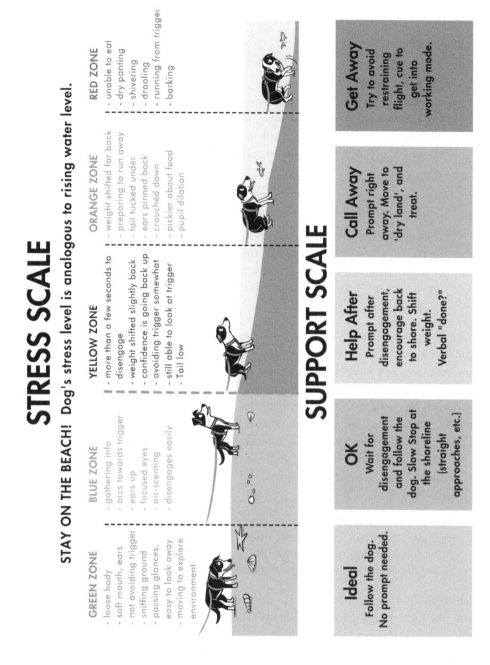

STRESS SCALE

STAY ON THE BEACH! Dog's stress level is analogous to rising water level.

GREEN ZONE
- loose body
- soft mouth, ears
- not avoiding trigger
- sniffing ground
- passing glances,
- easy to look away
- moving to explore environment

BLUE ZONE
- gathering info
- arcs towards trigger
- ears up
- focused eyes
- air-scenting
- disengages easily

YELLOW ZONE
- more than a few seconds to disengage
- weight shifted slightly back
- confidence is going back up
- avoiding trigger somewhat
- still able to look at trigger
- Tail low

ORANGE ZONE
- weight shifted for back
- preparing to run away
- tail tucked under
- ears pinned back
- crouched down
- pickier about food
- pupil dilation

RED ZONE
- unable to eat
- dry panting
- shivering
- drooling
- running from trigger
- barking

SUPPORT SCALE

Ideal
Follow the dog. No prompt needed.

OK
Wait for disengagement and follow the dog. Slow Stop at the shoreline (straight approaches, etc.)

Help After
Prompt after disengagement, encourage back to shore. Shift weight. Verbal "done?"

Call Away
Prompt right away. Move to 'dry land', and treat.

Get Away
Try to avoid restraining flight, cue to get into working mode.

If your dog walks directly toward the trigger, she is probably somewhere between blue and yellow on the stress chart. Do a Slow Stop to prevent her from going "in the water," and then remember to always relax the leash after a Slow Stop. Now just wait for her to disengage from the trigger. Give her a chance to gather information and then relax her body, turn away and move on. If you stopped her in time, she can easily do these things on her own. If not, you'll need to help her and then not go so close next time.

Use this logic to decide what to do after a Slow Stop:

- **Green:** If your dog disengages within a few seconds, great: you're in the blue zone! Just relax and follow her as she explores.

- **Blue:** If your dog takes more time to look away from the trigger, but arousal is steady or going down, just wait. She is a little too close, but she can handle looking and turning away on her own. Your help will come AFTER she disengages. After you see her relax and turn her head, use subtle prompt to get her to walk about 15 feet (5 meters) away to regroup. Stop her sooner next time.

- **Yellow:** If your dog looks away from the trigger, but immediately walks straight toward the trigger again, she hasn't really disengaged. She is a little too close to handle this on her own. Call her away and feed a treat.

- **Orange or Red:** If arousal goes up as you wait, instead of down, your dog needs help. Use a prompt to get her to disengage. Use the smallest of the graduated prompts that you think will work (something between a slight weight shift, recall cue, mime pulling, or physically moving her). When in doubt, just call your dog.

Note: You usually do a Slow Stop when your dog is walking toward the trigger, but sometimes you don't need to. The point of doing a Slow Stop for direct movement toward the trigger is because it's a sign that your dog's arousal is going up. If your helper is walking away, and your dog is following behind, it's perfectly normal to walk on a path toward the helper, but there should be some side-to-side exploration and ground sniffing, too. When you are doing a set-up where you follow the helper, take the whole picture into account, like the amount of movement of your dog's body or head. Do a Slow Stop if your dog seems too focused; when your dog starts to pull or go faster; or when you see other signs of increased excitement, like muscle tension or a height increase.

> Tip for Pros: Try not to micro-manage your dog. If you work at the right distance, she can do great on her own. That said, you always have permission to rescue your dog if you see arousal going up. If you think your dog is in a situation where she can't self-soothe, call her and move away from the trigger.

I've created a flowchart for BAT set-ups, shown on the next page, for those of you who like such things. Note that you are trying to stay in the green or blue areas. The yellow and orange boxes here mean that the dog has gone over the working threshold for BAT. When the dog can't handle things on his own, you do some sort of prompt to move away, either after disengagement (yellow) or before disengagement (orange).

Explore the space in advance

If you really want to be careful, visit the training area without your dog on the day of the week and time of day that you would be doing your set-up. This is especially important for your very first BAT set-up. Walk through the area or have a seat and see what your dog might encounter during that time. Do people visit the area with their

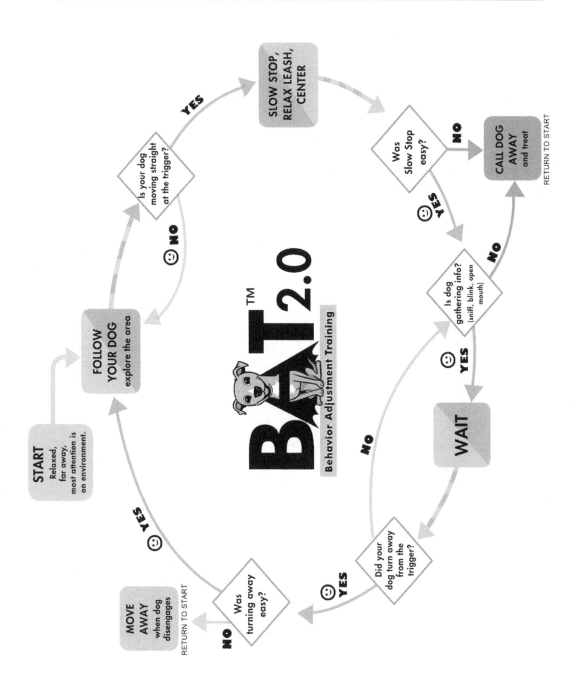

START
Relaxed, far away, most attention is on environment.

FOLLOW YOUR DOG
explore the area

Is your dog moving straight at the trigger?

YES

NO

SLOW STOP, RELAX LEASH, CENTER

Was Slow Stop easy?

NO

YES

CALL DOG AWAY and treat
RETURN TO START

Is dog gathering info? (sniff, blink, open mouth)

YES

NO

WAIT

NO

Did your dog turn away from the trigger?

YES

Was turning away easy?

NO

YES

MOVE AWAY
when dog disengages
RETURN TO START

BAT™ 2.0
Behavior Adjustment Training

dogs off leash? Do children run through after school? Are there loud sirens? Squirrels? Helicopters? Screaming peacocks? These are all real-life examples from my own training sessions with clients. Unexpected triggers can mess up your session, so the more you know about the sights, sounds, and smells of a space, the better. By going to the area in advance, you can come up with a plan to deal with the various triggers or choose another location.

Have a full session to explore the space with your dog without the helper. Follow your dog and observe behavior as she explores the area, so you have a baseline of her behavior without the helper being there. This session gives you and your dog a chance to practice leash skills, including the very crucial skill of staying out of your dog's way. Spend most of your time giving your dog freedom, but for safety, also do some practice with the control skills of Slide, Slow Stop, and Mime Pulling (toss a treat for coming with you after Mime Pulling).

Let's begin!

As I mentioned above, keep things low-key for your dog on BAT set-up days. Get sufficient exercise, but avoid high-arousal activities like intense fetching (search is much better). When you arrive for each set-up, let your dog explore the area for a bit at the beginning, even if you have been there before, but especially if you are working in a new place. If your dog is sensitive to environmental changes, then for each new location, you should also do at least one session first without the helper.

Carefully orchestrate the first time your dog notices the trigger. Depending on how sensitive the student dog is and how early you are in the training process, you may take this even more slowly. As a general rule, I assume the dog is sensitive until I learn otherwise. The steps listed below and the illustration which follows presents an example of how to gradually let the dog become aware of the trigger.

1. Student dog explores area for five to ten minutes and then is encouraged to move out of sight of the training area. For example, the dog can go explore another area or go into the car with a tasty food puzzle, if that is not stressful and it's not hot or freezing. Note: If the dog is already stressed walking around the environment alone, don't move on to Step 2. Instead, stop to figure out how to reduce stress and promote exploration.

2. Helper/trigger moves onto the area and explores or walks around for several minutes. This puts some odor in the area for the student dog to smell later, and is also good for the helper. If the helper is a dog, leave a dog bed and bowl on the helper's side of the area. If the helper is a person, they can leave an unwashed shirt or something else with odor. You can also put multiple scent articles around the training area. Feel free to put some treats on the items in some (but not all) of your sessions. When the area has been explored, the helper moves out of sight. If you are using a fake dog, you can still have the scent articles, to make the situation more realistic.

3. Student dog explores the area again for a few minutes, including helper's item(s). Watch out for marking or over-arousal. When the student dog is no longer interested in the helper's objects and is relaxed, encourage the student dog to move out of sight. Keep exploring.

4. Helper moves onto the area at a far distance from where the student dog will enter. The helper should walk even farther away from the student dog as the student comes back into the area. That way, the first view is the backside and the posture is not threatening. It seems to be less stressful if you first have the helper in place and then let the student dog enter the scene. If you're specifically working on dealing with sudden appearances of the trigger and you have already done basic set-ups, then you could keep the student dog in the area at Step 1 or 3 and then bring in the helper, at enough distance so that the reaction is just to notice and go back to exploring.

5. Bring in the student dog and casually zigzag into the space until the student dog sees the helper. Now the student dog decides where to go, for the most part. Follow the student dog, stay out of the way, and Slow Stop for signs of arousal going slightly up, like straight-line approaches toward the helper. Use the logic above about when to prompt.

6. If you have a big enough area, continue having the helper walk away and the student dog can follow the helper throughout the session. Otherwise, have the helper stay in one general area. If the helper is a dog, let him explore. You may need to hide some treats or enrich the helper's side of the area to make that happen.

7. Your dog gets to take breaks. Watch body language for avoidance or movement away from the trigger. If your dog walks entirely away from the trigger, follow there as well. You can take a break or end the session entirely. People often create training set-ups that are too close to the trigger. When you are at the right distance, most dogs will start to show some curiosity, rather than avoidance.

8. After the session, move the helper out of the area and let the student dog sniff and investigate that spot. If the helper had a dog bed, leave it there to be sniffed again.

BAT Set-Up
With Semi-Stationery Helper

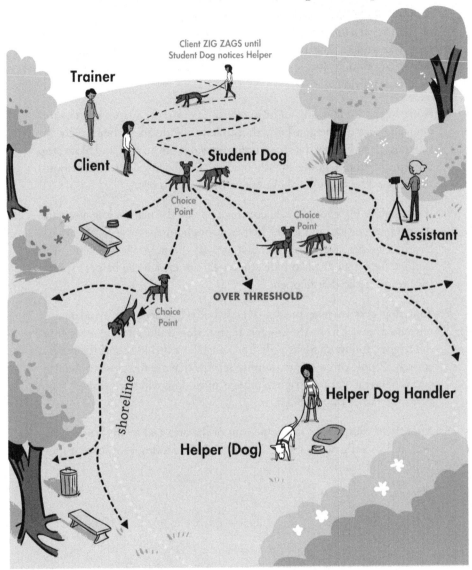

Remember to vary the way you make the training space more interesting and make your environment as natural as possible. Otherwise, you might accidentally train your dog to only be comfortable if a certain stimulus, like food, is present, or only in a specific location. Even with the dog beds and other scent articles, change things up. I like using them fairly consistently at first, but don't have scent articles out every time.

Tip for Pros: If arousal is already high at Step 1 or 3, then your dog isn't ready for a set-up with the helper in view. Slow and steady progress is actually faster than rushing things. Tell your helper thanks and have them put their dog away or go home. Practice your BAT leash skills and wander around the space. Let your dog self-soothe without the trigger even being in view. If even that is too much, put your dog away with a stuffed food puzzle and brainstorm how to reduce arousal even more. See the troubleshooting section for more info.

Parallel walking

Parallel walking is a core component of most dog trainers' toolboxes and can be used in BAT set-ups. With BAT, parallel walking is sort of a misnomer, because you aren't just walking on two parallel paths. The dog should still decide where to go, to a large extent. You might start out with parallel walking, but it may turn into following the helper or exploring the bushes on the other side of the training area.

Set-ups are more natural when the dog is on the move. Dogs don't normally just go outside and stand around. I like to have both dogs walk, with the helper in the front and the student dog following at her own pace. For a parallel version of this, we have the helper dog walking on a straight path with the student dog veering off of the path, away from the helper dog, as desired. You may start off with some Mark and Move to reinforce good choices, too, which would involve going off of the path as well. So you aren't walking in a straight parallel line, but more like a squiggly repeated S.

With parallel walking, your dog and the helper can walk toward each other (with some curves) or walk in the same direction. Always take the closest approach distance into account. The dog and helper can be even with one another, or with one following behind. Moving in the same direction with your dog following the trigger is much easier than walking toward the trigger. Moving directly at one another, as on a sidewalk, is usually the most challenging. Even then, you can add a little curvature to your path to make things easier for your dog. It's always important to watch that your own body isn't limiting your dog's ability to move away from the trigger, but it is easy to forget that when doing parallel walking.

Done right, parallel walking is great for giving the dog a chance to get comfortable with the movement of other dogs and people. It also keeps your dog calmer because he is in balance and focused on his own motion. Dogs tend to be less explosive when moving, versus holding still, which is why we include motion in every version of BAT. Dogs also learn to offer appropriate behaviors while still moving, versus only doing them as a response to you stopping or tightening the leash. If you are doing parallel work close up, I recommend a fence in between your dog and the helper or using a muzzle if your dog has been trained to wear one comfortably.

When walking in the same direction, it's a good idea to start far away and only allow your dog to slowly merge with the path of the helper, as you would on a freeway, rather than walking directly at each other and then heading off together. So if you and your dog are following the helper, have the helper walk ahead and then arc in to follow them, slowly allowing your dog to catch up. Note that you're not leading your dog to merge, but rather, when your dog does want to approach, you guide into a merging rather than a direct approach.

I really like doing parallel walking, especially following. But I find that with parallel walking, people get focused on staying with the other person. That makes them more likely to lead the dog toward the trigger or prevent retreats. I have seen it in my own videos, as well. Watch for any cut-off signal and make sure you aren't blocking your dog's retreat. Film your session and watch your own behavior, as well.

> Tip for Pros: When I do a private session at the home of dogs who guard their homes or are afraid of strangers, I start out by going for a walk using the merging concept mentioned above. I walk around their block and then the client and her dog come outside and gradually catch up to me, over the course of a block or so. I ignore the dog at first and he will naturally just approach to gather info and then retreat. Some will still bark at me, but most dogs feel brave enough to check out a person who is walking ahead and ignoring them while dropping treats. Note that I only do this after teaching leash skills to the client and: 1. the dog has no history of biting; 2. the bite history clearly only resulted from resource guarding or a perceived threat from a human; or 3. the dog is wearing a muzzle.

For parallel walking in the same direction, *the dog is at a choice point the whole time that he is walking near the helper*. When you get within about ten feet, start using Mark and Move: i.e., mark any replacement behaviors, then move away and reinforce. In this case, you'd continue walking in the same general direction, but move about ten to fifteen feet further away from the trigger, treat, then go back to following your dog.

When walking toward each other, set it up so that your dog and the helper are offset by some minimum distance, say twenty feet. If your dog moves farther away from the helper, that is definitely her choice, so follow her. Do not try to stay on parallel lines. Also allow the helper dog to move away at any time. The humans' job is just to keep the dogs from getting closer than the distance you want. If you see any cut-off signals, you can encourage your dog to move away (perpendicular to the parallel lines or reversing course). The closest distance that you get to (in this case, twenty feet) should be bigger than distances you've already rehearsed with other versions of BAT, since having the helper moving toward you is more challenging.

When you get to the point where your dog is close to the trigger, there's a strong pull to get even closer. When they are within leash range of one another, dogs are drawn in more quickly, even when they were below threshold just an instant before. You may need to prompt more, at first, to keep your dog from getting sucked in like a magnet. In the next chapter, I will go through that up-close work in more detail.

CHAPTER 7

Mark and Move:
Up Close and Tight Spaces

BAT is designed to help dogs make their own choices. When that's not possible, we still do our best to influence the dog's decision without being too distracting. The list below goes from the least to most intrusive ways to change the dog's behavior at a choice point:

1. **Empower:** Arrange situation in advance so the dog can freely explore (green, blue)

2. **Manage space:** Prompt retreat behavior *after* the cut-off signal (yellow)

3. **Redirect:** Prompt cut-off signal *before* the dog makes a choice (orange)

4. **Interrupt Reactivity:** Remove the dog's choice altogether (red, pull away, remove trigger, or use sci-fi teleportation to move dog to a better location)

Ideally we want to empower the dog throughout the set-up (#1 above). We never really want to be in the situation where we need to interrupt reactivity (#4). When the student dog is close to the trigger, the arousal level may rise suddenly if the dog is left on his own to choose. For that reason, I tend to use a physical barrier as well as graduated prompting to ensure that the dog does not get himself into trouble (#2 and #3). If the dog cannot stay relaxed, I will prompt in an obvious way, using a recall cue or a marker signal like a clicker. I move the dog away and reinforce. I call this technique Mark and Move. It is a way to do BAT 2.0 in situations in which we can't just follow the dog, but need to be more directive to avoid the dog getting overly aroused.

Mark and Move

With the Mark and Move BAT technique, you mark the best behavior you can reasonably wait for, move away, and then reinforce. You can mix and match markers, behaviors, and reinforcers given after moving away. If you are familiar with the older version of BAT, think of this as clearer, more flexible version of the "stages."

The order matters for Mark and Move: *reinforce after moving*. This gives the dog a chance to notice she is moving away and also reinforces that behavior. I call the reinforcer that comes after the movement a **bonus reward**. Bonus rewards are consequences that your dog likes that aren't related to the particular behavior. Unlike a functional reinforcer, this is more of a bonus than a paycheck. Give bonus rewards *after* the functional reinforcer, so your dog is allowed the time to appreciate the functional reinforcer first, i.e., to learn that the replacement behavior leads to the same desired consequence as the behavior you're trying to remove.

Marking a behavior

You can mark any behavior that's appropriate in the situation, such as looking at the trigger or any of the various cut-off signals. In other words, any movement that's not about aggression or a frustrated outburst is fair game. Looking at the trigger is still worth marking if the dog hasn't barked yet, since it's still better than barking. Don't worry that you might accidentally be reinforcing staring: in a human behavior study by Smith and Churchill (2002), reinforcing precursors to aggression (i.e., behaviors that predictably came before aggression for the subjects of the study) actually reduced the frequency of aggressive behavior.

BAT: Mark and Move

Survival Skills for **Real Life** or **Smaller Spaces**

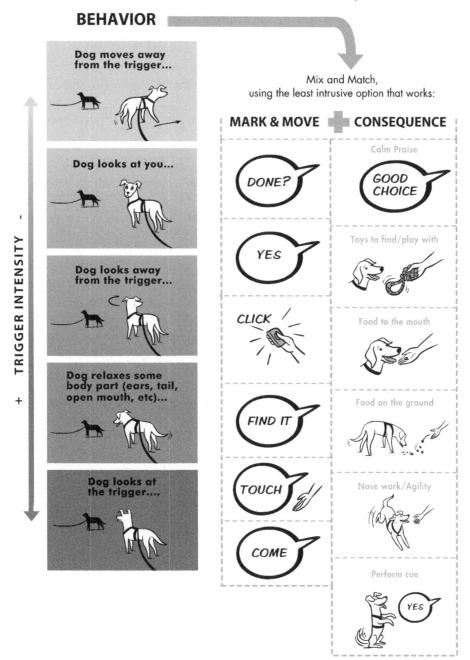

BEHAVIOR

Dog moves away from the trigger...

Dog looks at you...

Dog looks away from the trigger...

Dog relaxes some body part (ears, tail, open mouth, etc)...

Dog looks at the trigger....

TRIGGER INTENSITY

Mix and Match, using the least intrusive option that works:

MARK & MOVE + **CONSEQUENCE**

DONE?

YES

CLICK

FIND IT

TOUCH

COME

Calm Praise — GOOD CHOICE

Toys to find/play with

Food to the mouth

Food on the ground

Nose work/Agility

Perform cue — YES

Notice that in the illustration, the top of each column has the least intrusive option with more intrusive options listed as you move down the column. Always use the least intrusive option that will work in each situation. For example, when dogs are first greeting, I might click for the student dog just looking at the helper, move away, and treat with a big party. Or I might say "Yes" for sniffing the helper's rear, then move away, and give the student dog a chance to find some treats in the grass for a while. You can decide on your own, whatever motivates your dog.

Why don't we just use the biggest, most exciting marker and reinforcer? The more exciting it is, the less they actually seem to remember about the greeting. They also greet awkwardly and less skillfully. When you choose big reinforcers, dogs can become overly motivated to do the behavior we choose to reinforce, and they can miss out on the small details of the social situation.

Let's put this in human terms. Imagine you're on a TV show where you can win a million dollars if you can quickly learn some new handshake with another contestant. You probably totally miss your partner's smaller social signals, like eye contact, laughter, needing a bit of space from you, etc. You were too focused on the handshake, because that was being reinforced.

If intense experiences like that were the only interaction you have with your species, your social skills would end up being a bit awkward. You'd be great at fast handshakes but may be awful at actual communication, like making small talk or noticing body language. The same applies to dogs. In BAT, we do Mark and Move to make sure that the dogs don't rush in before they are ready. As soon as possible, however, we reduce the intensity of how we help, so that our dogs can stop playing the million-dollar handshake game and learn in a more natural way.

Let's go through an example. Let's say that I am doing a set-up with a student dog, Reactive Rudy, and the helper dog, Mellow Mia. We could start out with having Mia move away and Rudy following. We work for ten minutes, take a five minute break, and then start again and work for another five minutes. During that time, Rudy has been gradually getting closer to Mia, and this brings the working distance between the dogs to about ten feet (three meters). If a dog has done other BAT set-ups before, this is often enough introduction time for the student dog to be comfortable going in for a sniff (and the amount of time needed before a greeting shrinks as training goes on). So our example dog, Rudy, is ready to greet. We would then walk where there's a fence between Rudy and Mia, or Rudy can wear a muzzle, which he has been pre-trained to do. Then we start doing Mark and Move Move as a way to transition into working up close.

When safety has been put into place, we then allow Rudy to go a bit closer to Mia, with Mia facing away from Rudy. They are both walking in the same direction or they could be stationary. Having the student dog walking and following the helper is usually the safest. As Rudy starts to sniff his handler immediately marks (clicks), calls Rudy if he's not already coming, moves about fifteen feet (five meters) farther away from Mia, and tosses some treats on the ground. Mia's handler could also feed her a treat as hazard pay and so that she doesn't turn to follow Rudy. Clicking Rudy right away makes it so that he doesn't have a chance to start going over-threshold after smelling Mia from that close. Allow Rudy to return to Mia, but don't lead him there! Repeat that a few times and then after about five times, hold off on clicking until a little later. You can just wait for an extra second or you can start selecting good cut-off signals, if you are getting any. Each time you mark, you move away, then reinforce. After about five more treats, switch to clicking even later or selecting for even bigger cut-off signals. By fading out Mark and Move, you gradually give Rex more control over the situation and allow him to experience the naturally occurring reinforcers.

Here is a series of six photos illustrating the Mark and Move technique.

The dog stops at the choice point.

As the dog begins to disengage by looking away, mark the behavior.

The dog begins to move toward you in anticipation of a reward.

Start to back up to move away from the trigger.

Reaching for the reinforcer happens after moving away. (Ignore cute puppy Bean, who was our fake trigger).

Deliver the reinforcer.

Using treats

Depending on the student dog, you may need more treats, or you may be able to get away with fewer. When the dog is showing fear/avoidance behavior, you usually don't have to do much Mark and Move at all, because she is able to move away on her own. On the other hand, she may only want to avoid, so you could mark for looking at the trigger to build up some interest in approaching. For dogs who are rushing in to play or are otherwise frustrated, then you might need to do more Mark and Move to counteract the large force that pulls them toward the trigger. Reinforcing for movement away makes the approach-move away chain stronger, so the dogs neither avoid nor get stuck in a greeting.

But as I wrote above, if you are using a lot of trainer-provided reinforcement, the dog isn't really greeting at all, but rather performing a trick. Don't get stuck with using a lot of treats for greeting, even in the form of Mark and Move. It is just there to jumpstart the natural social behavior. As soon as possible, fade out the excitement of the clicker and treats.

So in the Rudy example, the handler would do the fifteen treats worth (that's just an estimate) and then switch to a lower intensity marker and reinforcer, like marking with "Done," shifting her body to move away, and reinforcing with praise. This gives Rudy a chance to move away but isn't artificially motivating him to do so. That way, he can pay attention to the social situation and leave when he's ready, not just to earn a treat. Fairly soon, I'll have the handler stop marking altogether, or mark just occasionally, to allow for more natural movement and flow between the dogs. Rudy's behavior continues to change due to naturally occurring reinforcement he earns by adjusting the level of social contact with Mia. After a while of walking and exploring things together, Rudy has a new friend. This goes a long way toward changing how he feels about all other dogs!

Note: With all aspects of BAT 2.0, when the student dog is aware of the trigger, we let her control her movement toward the trigger. That means you don't lead her toward the trigger. That advice becomes harder to remember during Mark and Move, because it is a more directive technique. So watch yourself on video or have a helper look at you to see if you are accidentally leading your dog toward the trigger by shifting your weight or positioning yourself between the dog and the trigger. Pat yourself on the back every time you see yourself getting out of your dog's way or resisting the desire to lead!

Out for a walk

Mark and Move is also great to use when you are out for a walk, especially when your dog sees a trigger out of the blue. Whenever you think you can't just let your dog work things out on his own, you can use Mark and Move to reinforce a better choice. If you absolutely can't move away from the trigger, just click and treat for good choices, and then figure out how you can avoid such situations in the future.

Random intrusions

If you are doing a BAT set-up with a helper where you don't need Mark and Move, but a random trigger appears, you can switch to Mark and Move with that trigger. When the trigger is gone, give your All Done hand signal to indicate that you have no more treats, and then go back to doing your set-up with the helper. You may need to secretly scatter some treats to get your dog back in the mood to explore.

Severe cases

When a dog bites with minimal warning, it's usually because the dog's requests for space were severely punished in the past. If that is the case, I use more Mark and Move than I normally would when up close. I focus on teaching avoidance of the trigger and attention to the handler. Unless all of the dog's caregivers will consistently use the muzzle when the dog is around triggers, avoidance is far safer than teaching a dog with minimal warning signs to interact with his triggers.

More on the last ten feet/greetings

I see a significant change in attitude when the student dog is able to really interact with multiple helpers. I like working to the point where the dog can engage in 'conversation' and is not concerned about approaching or being approached by the helper. At first, you'll probably need to work with the same helper for multiple sessions to build up to greeting. You can work with other helpers in between. It's important to make sure these greetings are safe, so if you're ever not sure whether you should let the dog greet the helper, the answer is probably no. There is still plenty of benefit from having friends that the dog goes on walks with but doesn't actually touch. One of the most challenging parts of working with dog reactivity is figuring out what to do when they are actually close enough (within about ten feet) to bite another dog, person, animal, or object. I've already given you some safety tips for working up close, but here are some more ideas.

First and foremost, keep things moving. Dogs who are standing still around their triggers are likely to get themselves in trouble. Use a following or parallel walking procedure, as mentioned in the last chapter. Allow only very short greetings, keep walking together in some way, or do something else that lets your dog move his body. If they have to concentrate on where to put their feet, dogs pay a little less attention to the triggers, which can help avoid reactive responses.

Greetings should be very short at first, like a quarter of a second or less. That's where Mark and Move comes in handy. Work up to longer greetings using a tangible reinforcer (treat, etc.) after moving away. Gradually fade into using just praise as the reinforcer after walking away: wait for the dog to be done with the interaction and then encourage him to walk away from the trigger. Eventually, you'll just let your dog decide when to end the interaction and move away on his own. Throughout the process, empower your dog to move away on his own; watch your body language and make sure that you aren't blocking the exit or leading the dog back to the helper (like we used to do in BAT 1.0).

Face-to-face greetings are much more challenging than face-to-rear greetings, regardless of whether the trigger is another dog or a person. I've listed a general order of difficulty for most greeting approaches below. Keep in mind that every dog is an individual, and your dog may not have read this list to figure out which kind of approach is supposed to be easy or hard. This is also not broken into these steps based on scientific research, but rather on my own observations with clients. As you read this, also be mindful of the variable dimensions I listed in Chapter 6, like vocalizations or other objects in the picture.

Note that when I write "stationary," that means the helper playing the role of the trigger is basically in one place. This could be in a fixed position, like a sit, or could be sniffing the ground in one general area.

1. Your dog approaching trigger, who is walking away (student following trigger)

2. Your dog approaching stationary trigger from the side. As your dog begins moving, trigger walks away to the left or right (angles can vary)

3. Trigger approaching your dog, who is walking away (trigger following student)

4. Your dog approaching trigger, who is stationary, but turned fully away

5. Your dog approaching trigger, who is stationary, but turned sideways

6. Your dog approaching trigger, who is stationary and facing student

7. Trigger approaching your dog, who is stationary, but fully turned away (and possibly being fed)

8. Trigger approaching your dog, who is stationary, but turned sideways

9. Trigger and your dog approaching each other head on (slowly, possibly offset first)

10. Trigger and your dog approaching each other head on (rapidly).

Remember, this is not true for all dogs. For example, sometimes #6 is more challenging than #9, because the dog is stationary as the trigger approaches in #6. In #9, you can observe body language more carefully as the dog chooses to go forward or avoids doing so. Experiment with your dog. You can add more steps in by considering different ways in which your dog and the trigger might approach each other—a straight approach is usually more likely to cause a bad reaction than an arced approach. The tightness of the leash has an effect, too.

Most of the time, you should be trying to set this up so that you aren't leading your dog into these situations. As people, we tend to be greedy for progress, and that actually ends up slowing things down. Try to let these encounters happen more naturally, when the your dog is ready. Certain types of engagement are, by definition, initiated by the trigger. If getting closer to the trigger was not the dog's idea, move away after disengagement to give the dog the option of returning to the situation. If he doesn't want to, you may have pushed too quickly.

I like to work through all of the variations at a distance before doing them up close. For number #10 (dogs moving rapidly toward each other), I recommend stopping at a choice point that's at least twelve feet away before trying it within striking range. When you start working close enough that the dog could physically reach the trigger, go back to the easiest ways for the dog to interact, and then work up to the challenging ways systematically. This isn't as necessary when you are working at a distance. For example, let's say that I'm the helper and a client has her dog fifty feet away from me. I might begin with full (but brief) eye contact with a dog and talking to the handler about what to do. If that is too much for the dog, my first adjustment is to increase the distance between the dog and the trigger. I'll mix it up so there are times without eye contact and times with eye contact—just make sure the handler is aware of what's happening.

When I am close to the dog, I physically arrange the situation to make sure it goes well, because: 1) it's a safety issue; and 2) our training may have missed some aspect of the trigger. To avoid trigger stacking, I take it down to what I think is the easiest for the dog when working within ten feet. So if I'm the helper, I don't make eye contact; I'm turned away, walking away, or sitting down; hands are in my pockets, etc.

Working up close is dangerous unless you put some safety devices in place (and honestly, even then). Until you are very sure that your dog will respond without teeth, always have at least two barriers between those teeth and anybody's skin. The leash counts as one and in many cases, working far away is another 'barrier'—assuming the dog is not intent to run across a field to start a fight or there's a location close by for the helper to escape to if that leash gets dropped. When working up close or with a dog with a history of injuring other dogs or people, a second layer of defense is to work with a fence between your dog and the trigger or to have your dog muzzled.

As I mentioned before, take the time to get your dog acclimated to wearing a muzzle before he actually uses it, so the muzzle itself is not a stressful event. Otherwise, you run the risk of your dog associating the stress of the muzzle with the trigger, and instead of learning that the trigger is safe to be around, you've made things worse.

If you're using a muzzle instead of a fence, have your dog on a leash for the initial up-close sessions. To avoid tangling, stay alert and keep moving, following the instructions in the illustrations on the next page. Unless you are very, very comfortable using a long line, I recommend using a shorter line for close-up work.

Have a good grip on a loose leash. Hold the leash close to your body and your center of gravity, so that if your dog suddenly lunges, you can control him. Be ready to step back to get the dog out of the situation. Dogs are much faster than humans, but if you're ready, you can do a fairly good job at helping them avoid a bite. That's because dogs usually give multiple warnings, so you have a bit of time to get them out of there. If you don't see the warning signals, hire a trainer to help you.

Tips:

- Have a good grip on the leash for greetings.

- Make sure it's short enough to avoid tangling and has a few inches of slack so that it feels loose to the dog.

- Be ready to prompt the dog away if you see any stiffening, staring, holding breath, or other signs of trouble.

The illustration on the next page shows proper leash handling during greetings. When your dog is on leash, it's critical to keep the leash from tangling or wrapping around someone. To do this, position your body so there are no obstacles between you and your dog, especially not the trigger! In particular, your dog's head is directly between you and the trigger and your leash is almost perpendicular to your dog's body. Your hand, your leash, your dog's head, and the closest point of the trigger should all be on a straight line.

If your dog or the trigger moves, walk around to maintain the right position relative to your dog and the trigger. If the trigger is also a dog, then his head, leash and handler should be in the same line as you and your dog. The reason for this arrangement is that you are now able to get the dog(s) out of there as quickly as possible, because the force of the leash can pull the dog directly away from the trigger. While I don't use the leash for punishments, I do use it for safety. Since I'm not a giant person, and I have slow human reflexes, I want every ounce of force that I put on the leash to help move the dog quickly away from the trigger. Of course, use the least amount of force that you can, to avoid injuring or scaring your dog. Mime Pulling can come in very handy for prompting a dog to come away, but of course you'd first want to try your happy, trained recall cue to just call your dog.

How to Hold the Leash
For Greetings

Handlers stay on opposite sides, with dogs in between.
Have a good grip on the leash, but do not attach it to your wrist. Keep the leash loose, if possible, but not so loose that the dogs step over it.

When the dogs change relative positions, handlers should move too. Handlers need to stay opposite each other, with no obstacles between them and their dogs. If one person calls their dog and moves away, the other person should too.

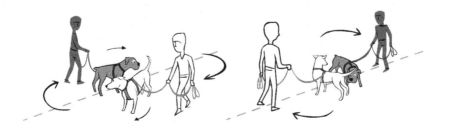

Don't let the leashes tangle. If the leashes tangle, breathe and stay calm. Immediately untangle them, call your dog back and give a treat.

Some dogs will react with a huge snarly display or even bite the other dog when there is any pressure on the leash. As soon as the leash tightens, the emotional tension is likely to go up, which is why we practice relaxing the leash after a Slow Stop. This goes for all dogs, not just those that need rehabilitation. Don't just tighten the leash unless you are specifically working on that as part of the context (usually I do that practice at a distance). Either keep the leash loose or use it in an emergency to steadily pull the dog away from a scuffle. We always avoid leash pops, especially in this situation, because they tend to add to the stress and cause redirected biting (dog biting you). You can teach your dog a better response by using the "Silky Leash" technique for leash walking from my *Ahimsa Dog Training Manual* (see Resources). You can also do some training practice with Mime Pulling. Keep that fun by tossing a treat or toy for your dog when he moves with you

When dogs are greeting, don't pull the dog out with the leash just because you want to leave, or as your first prompt if there's trouble. As they teach kids in pre-school, "use your words." If you want to interrupt a tense moment, call your dog, yawn, sigh, start to walk away (without tightening the leash), Slide, tap the leash, make a kissy noise, or any number of things that I discussed before under the topic of graduated prompting. If you're rock climbing outside, you have a safety rope and a belayer (support person), but the rope is not your first line of defense against hitting the ground—you use your brain and do your best to avoid putting yourself in a position to fall. It's a big deal to use your safety line, because something could still go wrong. Equipment may fail, the belayer may be distracted, or you might hit an outcrop of stone. The same goes for pulling the dog out of a conflict with the leash: it's good to have a safety line as a backup, but it's better to avoid being in the position to need it.

When do you get rid of the leash? You only need to work off leash if interacting that way is part of your goals. In most cases, you will start BAT on leash and then naturally work up to having the dog off leash. After you have gone through all of the various ways to have your dog interact with the trigger on leash, and have built up a solid recall, you can start working off leash with a fence in between and then with no fence but a muzzle (if needed). If your dog has a fabulous recall and the helper is far enough from the fence that the student dog is comfortable, you can actually start off leash, without doing the on-leash part first. This is in a contained area, of course, so that you aren't breaking any leash laws or endangering passersby.

If you see tension during a BAT session, help lower the dog's stress level quickly, by moving the trigger away from him, calling him away from the trigger, or otherwise diffusing the situation. Before doing off-leash work, it's important to work on your dog's recall cue (see Coming When Called in Appendix 1). Your dog should be able to come away from big distractions before working off leash. Another way to make this work is to have a helper who is able to calmly move away from the student dog and a barrier to keep the student dog from following. However you do it, if a dog gives a cut-off signal, there must be a way to reduce the stress or excitement.

When the dog is close enough to cause harm, it's especially important to know what you're doing. If you are at all unsure how to keep your dog safe at this point, hire a professional trainer and film your sessions!

> Tip for Pros: If you are just getting started working with aggression cases, I suggest hiring a CBATI or other experienced trainer or behaviorist as a consultant. This can be done in person, on the phone, by video chat, or in an online school like my Animal Building Blocks Academy.

Mark and Move for frustrated greetings

I use Mark and Move more for frustration cases than with fear. Otherwise, the dog is not as likely to move away on his own and tension builds up. It also builds up a reinforcement history for moving away. The most effective replacement behaviors for frustration-driven reactivity are similar to the ones you want to see with other kinds of reactivity, but not exactly the same. When working up close with dogs experiencing frustration, I mark for short micro-greetings at first, then shift to reinforcing any sign of self-control, and finally return back to the "follow your dog" way to do BAT 2.0. I also will sometimes use Mark and Move for the behaviors below when the dog first enters the training area. Here are some self-control behaviors that you could reinforce:

- Looking away from other dog
- Turning head away
- Turning body away
- Backing away
- Sniffing the ground
- Sitting
- Lying down
- Looking at you
- Slowly stretching

Mark and Move for Greetings

After you've done set-ups further away and your dog is no longer reactive toward a particular Helper at a distance, you can work on greetings. For safety, use a muzzle or have a FENCE between your dog and the helper. Keep things moving using following or parallel walking.

MARK ENGAGEMENT

1.Click!   2. Move Away   3. Treat

MARK DISENGAGEMENT

cut-off signal: Looking away

1. Wait or Call   2. Mark   3. Move Away   4. Treat

FADE OUT FOOD

cut-off signal: Nose lick

1. Wait   2. Mark   3. Move Away

As soon as possible, shift back into regular BAT 2.0, where you can just follow the dog.

Some of these may actually be problematic in certain dogs, so choose wisely! For example, a Border Collie may lie down just before pouncing on the other dog, so that's actually something to avoid, not a good choice for a replacement behavior. But in an English Mastiff, lying down might indicate a relaxed state, because getting up from a Down is not worth the effort.

When a dog really wants to greet the helper, moving away after marking may increase frustration, even when you offer a bonus reward. When working with Bean, I found that sometimes I was frustrated myself! After a few BAT set-ups, I knew that if he could just calmly get to the other dog, he would warm up quickly with careful management of the greeting (less careful management would lead to snapping). One time he got so worked up that I just kept having to move farther and farther away. Then I tried doing a zigzag version of Mark and Move. When he started focusing on another dog, I would walk perpendicular to the line between Bean and the other dog, to suggest turning to his left or right. As usual, I'd Slow Stop his direct approaches toward the other dog. I clicked for disengagement and then tossed a treat about 10-15 feet ahead, so he would move in the direction I was walking. This repeated, bringing us toward the other dog in a zigzag pattern: when Bean walked toward the other dog, I'd start walking back the other way, still perpendicular to the line between Bean and the other dog, and do a Slow Stop. One important key of zigzag Mark and Move is to still avoid leading the dog toward the trigger.

If you are doing Mark and Move and the dog is still suddenly drawn toward the trigger, you may have just gotten too close to the trigger, too soon. If you get straight-on approaches or other signs of increasing arousal, like breathing faster, aligning the spine toward the trigger, ears up, etc., then do a slow stop or walk in a curve away from the trigger. On the way to the helper, if you do a Slow Stop and your dog disengages but moves right back toward the helper again, call your dog. This is different from the older version of BAT for frustration, where they would disengage and then we'd walk directly forward. The more curvature there is in the approach, the better the greeting usually goes, so you can introduce zigzags, loops, etc. Enrich the environment a bit more and go back to a distance where you can do regular BAT 2.0 (the one where you follow your dog). Or do following/parallel exercises so the dogs are not as fixated on each other, where you may not need to use Mark and Move. That said, even from far away, you may need to switch to using Mark and Move with great treats for a bit, if the 'magnetic' pull of the other dog is just too great. If your dog seems more frustrated by meandering in slowly, the structure of Mark and Move could help.

Many dogs with frustration act crazy from a distance but can actually greet just fine once they actually reach another dog. For dogs who can greet well, all you need to work on is a calm approach and the problem is solved. Just practice several polite approaches with different dogs and let the dogs greet whenever they are close enough to do so.

Other dogs tend to show the "Tarzan" behavior that Jean Donaldson mentions in her book *Fight!* (see Resources). These dogs eagerly go to greet other dogs, but lack the subtle negotiation skills dogs use to avoid conflict. They seem to want to interact, but they just aren't good at it. For example, instead of approaching in an arc and sniffing the rear first, Tarzan behavior would be to try to start a play session with a new dog by running straight at the new dog and tackling him, which can then start a scuffle or a real fight. I like the techniques that Donaldson mentions in her book, including interacting with a group of well-socialized dogs to set boundaries and facilitate learning. Finding enough dogs who can tell a Tarzan to back off without actually hurting him or starting a fight is a challenge, but if you can do it, it is really useful. If you have a dog with a lot of frustration and poor social skills, that's a great book to add to your library. I especially like Jean's use of warnings followed by time outs for rude behavior. That way, your helper dogs don't have to set all of the boundaries. It's not fair to them.

When the reactivity comes from frustration and the student dog is just very motivated to go greet the other dog, I tend to use Mark and Move for longer. I do that to counterbalance the motivation to go running in. But be careful not to rely on it forever—they still need to learn good social skills based on feedback from the other dog, not your treats. That said, using Mark and Move during the first part of greetings comes in very handy for these dogs, because you can mark appropriate greeting behavior, move away, reinforce, and then let your dog try again. Even though they have good intentions, dogs who come on strong can irritate even patient helper dogs, so be careful to keep things short and appropriate. Teaching dogs to greet in short bits with Mark and Move reinforces the behavior of moving away as well as the polite greetings, so it's win-win.

Because dogs with frustration and poor social skills don't necessarily know how to reduce the excitement level of greetings, you'll need to keep the interactions very short, just as you would with dogs who panic or escalate into aggression. Call your dog after a short greeting (about a quarter of a second), walk away, reinforce, and return to the other dog. If you don't have a great recall, work on it! During Mark and Move, the clicker usually gets your dog's attention (and marks desired behavior), but you also want a good recall cue.

Use the information on clicker training in Appendix 1 and the *Ahimsa Dog Training Manual* (see Resources) to learn how to get started with coming when called. You can also use clicker training to teach a bow as a default behavior. A side-effect of rewarding a lot of bowing in your dog's interactions with you is that it becomes a part of his repertoire, and he's more likely to offer it to other dogs, too. When he does that, he signals his peaceful intent, which most dogs will respond well to, and the interaction will go more smoothly.

Greeting with a tight leash and an improperly fitted harness can lead to reactivity. Keep greetings brief by calling away or using Mark and Move.

Part of your dog's frustration is that she may not know when you will allow her to interact with other dogs and when you won't. One way to make that really clear is to never allow your dog to greet another dog when you are out for a walk. I have to admit that I don't have the heart for that, but I trust the trainers who say that it works, like Pia Silvani (see Resources). I prefer to have a cue that signals that the dogs will be allowed to greet, like Go Say Hi and a cue that signals you are not going to allow greetings, like Leave It or Let's Go. Any time we can be really clear with dogs, they have a better chance of success.

Tight spaces: Parallel play

In therapy or school for children, **parallel play** means that the children are doing their own tasks in the presence of other children. It's an independent form of socializing. The exploration that the student and helper dogs do during a BAT set-up is an example of parallel play. When you don't have a lot of space for free exploration and wandering, dogs can do parallel play activities that are a bit more distracting. The downside of parallel play activities is that the dogs are more distracted and there are more contextual clues for you to fade later. But the upside is that the activities boost the dog's mood and reduce the threshold distance so that you can do BAT indoors. This is helpful in the winter, in urban locations, or in smaller areas than the dog could otherwise be able to handle.

Here is a list of some parallel play activities:

- Sprinkles (see Resources)

- Balance/**proprioception** activities (pilates disks, etc.)

- TTouch ground work (see Resources)

- Scent games (treats in boxes, hidden odors, toy, keys, helper's item)
- Food puzzle (may cause guarding)
- Massage
- Relax on mat
- Dog sports
- Physical play with you
- Clicker training a new skill

Any task that your dog enjoys is a potential parallel play activity. With parallel play, your dog is engaged in what she's doing, but she should also be aware that the trigger is there, as well. Watch body language and allow for safe, sub-threshold interactions, as you would with a typical BAT set-up. I prefer low arousal activities for parallel play because that's a more ideal state of mind to have when interacting with other dogs. Most dogs are less likely to go into a barking frenzy during a relaxing massage than during an intense flyball match. I wouldn't usually do a BAT/flyball combination unless a client specifically wanted to work on reactivity in the flyball setting. Even then, I might encourage a different sport that isn't quite so frenetic (or send the client to some of the few specific trainers that manage to keep flyball safe and quiet).

The illustration on the next page shows two dogs simultaneously doing BAT and other activities, with a fence for safety. Let your dog move around the space as much as possible. For example, if your dog is doing agility and stops for a moment to look at the other dog, let her take in that information. Don't immediately prompt your dog to look at you again; you'll actually get better focus and more rehabilitation if she has a chance to sniff and look. Just wait, relax, breathe, and then when your dog moves on, follow her. If she looks at you, shift your weight away from the trigger to ask her if she wants to move away, like you'd do in a normal BAT set-up. When your dog looks like she's gathered all of the information she needs for now, and is interested in working again, go back to the parallel play activity, such as scent work.

BAT Set-Up: PARALLEL PLAY

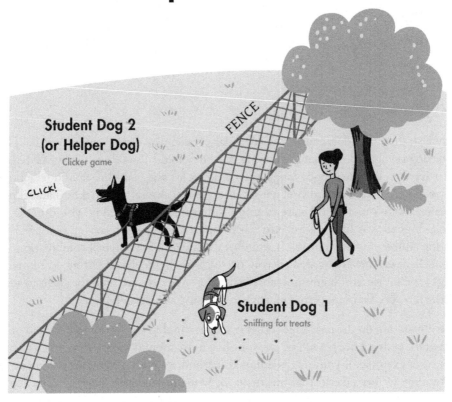

As always, if you see arousal going up and think your dog will explode if you don't call her away, then do so. But that tells you that she is too close to the trigger, so change something about the situation. You shouldn't need to call her away in order to prevent explosions.

Tips for small spaces

When there isn't room to just let the dog wander around, as in a 'real' BAT set-up, I tend to do more Mark and Move. Well, actually, when I realize that the space is too small for a particular dog, I just tend to work harder to try to find another location that will be large enough for the dog.

Sometimes there is no other option, so I'll do parallel play, add in a lot of barriers, and/or do Mark and Move. In a small space, many dogs will charge in like a bullet toward another dog to fight. If you were far enough away, they would be happy just to leave—when they are done gathering information. In a smaller location where the dog is overly drawn toward the trigger, you can click for small behaviors, like blinking, sighing, or softening the jaw—on their own, the dog may not want to leave until he is done checking the trigger out, but if you click, he is likely to disengage and move away with you. I'm saying "click" here, but you can use any marker as mentioned above.

Click to mark the good behavior, walk or jog away (call dog if necessary), and give a treat or toy. Walking away also becomes more likely because it leads to a treat. Once a dog gets into the habit of walking away, the dog gets less stuck around the trigger. Make sure to do the full retreat first, so the dog notices that their behavior has effectively reduced the stress of the situation (functional reinforcer), and then you can give the bonus reward of food, toy, play, etc.

Another way to use Mark and Move in a small space is to start by pre-training Go to Your Bed. During the BAT set-up, have a visual barrier with the dog's bed behind it, so that the dog can retreat behind the barrier—by choice or on cue. The barrier can be a full visual block or just a partial block so that your dog can see the whole room, but still feels a bit safer. The barriers should be low enough for you to see over. That way, you won't accidentally let her walk right into another dog.

If possible and safe, leave a door or gate open so that your dog has the option of leaving the area without passing by the trigger. You should *always give your dog a way to opt out of being near the trigger.* I have seen classes where the dogs were eating treats but clearly not happy to be there. Even if you are giving hundreds of treats, if your dog is over-threshold, you need to find a better way. Having an exit door available is one way for your dog to opt out. Can you think of any others?

Before your session, put lots of interesting items down for the dog to sniff and explore. This can be something as interesting as a towel that's been used to dry a cat's fur or as normal as an empty cereal box. If the dog couldn't just sniff around without going over-threshold, use Mark and Move:

1. Mark appropriate behavior

2. Move away

3. Reinforce

For example, you might set up the room with her bed behind a barrier and some interesting things scattered throughout the room. Let your dog explore the area, being sure to keep her from accidentally getting too close to the trigger. When she does notice it, that's time for Mark and Move. For example:

1. Dog looks up and sees the helper (who is probably facing away to make it easier)

2. Click

3. Happily encourage her to go to the bed

4. Treat

5. Release cue—add a little calm massage if she is interested

Then follow her again as she explores. Watch your posture and where you go, to make sure you aren't accidentally leading her back toward the trigger. It's so tempting!

Here's a slight variation you could do with a dog who is already trained to go to bed on cue. Instead of clicking in Step 2, you could mark with the Go to Your Bed cue. That would look like:

1. Dog looks up and sees the helper (who is probably facing away to make it easier)

2. Go to Your Bed cue (dog runs to bed and lies down)

3. Treat

4. Release cue—add a little calm massage if she is interested

There really is no limit to the creative ways that you can use Mark and Move and enrich the training space. Just remember this is a jump-start to be able to do BAT, not the whole technique. Don't get stuck thinking that you've really tried BAT if you've only ever done Mark and Move, and only with treats. In my experience, the intervention of cueing, marking, feeding, etc. tends to slow down progress if you aren't also doing proper BAT 2.0 set-ups with the dog fully in control. The goal of BAT is to empower the dog to make good choices on his own, in a natural way. Let that be your compass as you choose what to do.

CHAPTER 8

Troubleshooting BAT Set-Ups

As I mentioned before, progress is never really linear. In the early phases, there will be times when you are amazed at your dog's social abilities, followed by other times when he freaks out just like he used to. In general, however, you should be seeing progress in terms of intensity and frequency of reactivity. Here are some tips that will help you when the overall training is taking longer than you think it should, you've hit a plateau, or you are having a setback in a particular session.

More stress means more help

The deeper your dog is in the water (the more stress he's experiencing), the more you will need to help out. Like the lifeguard, you will rescue your dog in the smallest way that will work with his current state of mind. Using the right level of intrusion avoids micro-management and helps your dog practice decision-making and active coping strategies.

Your dog is stuck in working mode

If your overall progress is slow or your dog only does well if you are paying attention to him, it might be because your dog isn't really doing BAT, rather he's working for reinforcers from you. Here's what that looks like: your dog looks at the trigger, disengages quickly, and then just stares at you without going anywhere. He might even offer some other behavior, like a trick.

A dog in working mode is not taking in as much information about the trigger. This is handy for escaping a situation, but not useful during your BAT set-up.

Your dog needs more direction

The dog may need more direction and allowing him to wander freely around the set-up area may make him feel unusual or uncomfortable.

- Walk near interesting smells, so he can take his focus off of you. You can also casually drop treats behind you so that your dog can discover them later.

- Do some wandering walks with no triggers around, using the same trick of casually scattering treats mentioned above.

- The dog may not know he has a choice. Use your body language to ask him where he wants to go. Take a slow step in a couple of different directions and see which one your dog most readily goes in. Gradually teach him that he has the choice of where to walk in the training area.

- The dog may be stressed and looking to you for help. In that case, regroup and start again away from the trigger/helper.

Your dog is over-threshold

If any of the following situations happen, you are probably waiting too long to stop your dog; he's walked right past the shoreline and into the water. Whenever you have to prompt the dog away from the trigger, go far enough away that he doesn't glance back right away. If you use a recall cue, move your dog away from the helper and then *always reinforce,* say by tossing some treats on the ground. I know some people prefer not to feed the dog on the ground, but it takes more time to eat that way and it encourages exploration. In my experience using a heart monitor during training, searching for treats reduced arousal.

Signs that your dog is over-threshold include:

1. **It's difficult to Slow Stop your dog in the first place.** He's already in over his head, so call your dog away. I like Treat Party as a recall cue (See Appendix 1).

2. **He walks directly toward the helper after disengaging.** Call him away, unless you are really sure that he is relaxed enough to handle it. Most of the time when this happens, the dog is too focused on the trigger and at least a few steps into the water.

3. **It takes your dog more than two seconds to disengage.** His toes are in the water. Don't take control right away, but be ready to suggest where to go next.

   - Relax and wait for him to disengage on his own, and then suggest that he move away, using the smallest level of intrusion (control/ prompting) that works:

      ◦ If your dog was air-scenting (gathering info) and pretty re-laxed, prompt in a small way by shifting your weight away from the helper.

      ◦ If turning away was a little challenging, use a more obvious prompt: ask aloud if he's "Done?" and shift your weight away from the helper.

   - If he's getting more excited while you wait (face muscles tight, taller, up on toes, breathing faster, heart rate going up, mouth closing, lean-ing toward the helper, spine pointing directly at the helper, chest puffing out, ears forward, tail up, forehead wrinkled), *call your dog away!* He's moving deeper into the water at this point, so you can't give him time to check things out.

Dog is drawn to the helper

Most dogs seem to be drawn to the helper in some way. Learning about something that is scary usually makes it less frightening, so there is a good reason to get close enough to gather information. Ideally, your dog will gradually want to go closer and closer to the trigger, but it's a slow process, especially the first several times. Some dogs want to run in right away and your job is to keep that from happening. It's all about the pace. You might even start out at one distance and then you or your dog will real-ize you actually have to be farther away. In the beginning, you'll experiment to find the right working distance, and then keep assessing if things are still okay. That's critical: working at the right distance is the most reliable way to help your dog overcome these issues.

Dog, what dog?

If your dog completely ignores the helper, you are too close or too far away, or he just hasn't noticed the helper yet. Take a look at whether or not his motion pattern seems to be influenced by the helper. Here are some options:

- Walk him further away and see if he starts to look up at the helper.

- If you are sure that your dog just doesn't know the trigger is there, you can get him to notice in a couple of ways.

  ○ Jingle tags for helper dogs or have helper humans say something to make sure he knows the helper is there.

  ○ Sneakily put down some treats so that as he searches for the food, he works his way closer to the helper. Make sure he doesn't sniff his way up so close that he is shocked and starts barking when he notices the helper for real.

  ○ Zigzag your way back and forth across the training area, gradually getting closer. As soon as the dog becomes aware of the trigger, stop leading. If the dog is aware of the trigger, don't lead him toward it.

Dog is very distracted by prey

Sometimes there are very exciting odors in the area you choose for a BAT set-up. I've had squirrels run through and the dog becomes so focused on that, it's like my helper has disappeared. There are at least a couple of options on what to do after that.

- Think of the squirrel obsession as a parallel play activity, and work as described above. You could just do the regular 'follow your dog' or you might need work closer to the helper. Be ready to use Mark and Move. Watch for signs that the dog is paying attention to the trigger again or getting too close. You could even do some following or parallel walking where the dogs 'hunt' together. Cooperative squirrel hunting can be a bonding experience.

- Train the dog to pay more attention to you around squirrels, using that training as a parallel play activity. For example, you're heeling and clicking the dog for being near you, or you are clicking and treating for every look away from the squirrel. So you're watching for the need to keep your dog at the right distance from the helper, but also reinforcing good choices relative to the squirrel. Your dog will be drawn to either you or the squirrel (both, really) and may not notice the helper until they are too close, so keep a watch on that.

- Stop the session and move to a location with fewer exciting distractions. This may be the better choice if your dog is getting really worked up, the squirrel is freaked out, or your dog is paying absolutely no attention to the trigger.

- Thank the helper and just work with the squirrel as the trigger, doing something like Mark and Move. Use an equivalent functional reinforcer, like a tug toy.

Dog runs all over the place, really fast

Some dogs zoom around, and it is hard to keep up. BAT should be a fairly relaxing activity, like walking meditation. Dogs do walk at different paces, so it's okay if they don't look like a 12-year-old Golden Retriever, padding along, sniffing quietly. But if your dog is zigzagging quickly all over the place and scanning, then his arousal level is so high that you probably won't be making a good association with the helper.

- Work farther from the trigger. It may just be that you are too close.

- Stop the set-up. Do separate exploration/leash skills sessions without a helper, to get your dog used to exploring at a slower pace. Work in a smaller place so it's easier to catch up with your dog. Implement a stress-reduction plan for daily life, using food puzzles, massage, diet changes, supplements, routine changes, environmental management, etc. Be sure to read Chapter 3 on management.

- Use your long line as an actual long line. Some people have a death grip on their leashes. Even though the line is 15 feet (5 meters), they still keep all of the loops in their handle hand and don't release them as needed. That said, be sure to not give away all of your braking distance; when the leash is fully let out, you should still be able to relax your arms in Basic Position. Any time your dog stops to sniff, casually move toward her and shorten up the line, so you get back into Basic Position. That's very important.

Whenever your dog stops, go to her and shorten leash to Basic Position.

- Look at the enrichment in the space. For most dogs, a lot of interesting smells is a good thing, but sometimes that can be overwhelming. Are there any items in the space that might trigger an emotional or excited response, like training cones or urine from a female in heat?

- Relax yourself. Breathe and walk at a slow pace. If you find that your dog is walking much faster than you, just do a Slow Stop and catch up.

- Look at the value of your treats. If you have scattered your dog's very favorite food on the ground it might be way too exciting. If you crumble in a treat that he likes but doesn't go crazy over, you might get milder behavior.

- Exercise before the session. If your dog is amped up from being in the house all day, he will likely zoom around a bit too wildly. For example, go on a walk, have your dog use a treadmill, or have her search for kibble or a toy in the backyard. Fetching tends to cause more excitement to build-up, so I usually do a search with toys instead of throwing them.

When I filmed the BAT set-ups DVD, I was working with a pit bull mix who was way too excited to work. His issue was barking in frustration and an intense greeting that would lead to fighting. Before starting our BAT set-up, we did several recalls up and down the hill to help him settle down. Then we did Sprinkles—a helper scattered some treats and we explored the area with no trigger. That got him settled down more after the excitement of the treats and the recalls. By taking ten minutes to get him into the right state of mind, we set up him up for success and could move forward with doing a proper BAT set-up with the trigger.

Dog just pulls toward odors

Odors can distract dogs in the set-up area. Some dogs react by walking the same pace all the time, sometimes they want to go more quickly. If you walk through the woods with your dog off leash, you'll notice a pattern of trotting, then walking, over and over. If you want to let your dog sniff during a set-up, you can facilitate that by being ready to let out more leash or you can make the area interesting enough that your dog doesn't need to run off to explore something else. Just make sure not to let your dog run at the trigger.

Your dog should be able to sniff a lot as you walk along. If your dog walks faster than you can, let out some more leash so he can get to the odor. But if your dog can't reach the smell without pulling on the leash, don't let him just pull you there. Do a Slow Stop, catch up, relax the leash, and move on. If that's just looking like stop, go, stop, go over and over again, then change direction after you stop the dog each time. Try to go toward an area of more intense odor, like a fence line or areas with bushes. That way he doesn't have to go far to get to the next great smell, and you can easily keep up.

Dog sees the trigger and leaves the area

This is because either the dog is avoiding the trigger or drawn to something outside of the area. You could potentially be leading the dog away from the trigger with your own body language, so watch for that on the video if you film. There could also be an odor, sound, or visual stimulus that's drawing your dog in toward it and away from the helper. One option for testing this theory is to take the trigger fully out of the picture and see if your dog still behaves the same way. Better yet, follow my tips above and have a session in the training space in advance. That way, you can see how your dog normally acts when you are wandering around using BAT leash skills in that context. Testing the spot in advance may tell you that you need to make the area more interesting in order to keep her willing to walk around the space.

If your dog avoids the trigger and leaves the area, you're too close. I know I'm repeating myself here, but it's important. Most of us humans are very goal-oriented and we want the dog to make progress from where we started the session. Maybe last week, the dog got closer, so you try to start out at that distance, not taking into account that she just went to the vet for shots, time has passed, and this is a new helper.

When and where to start the session

Even though we try to take a lot of factors into account, the start point for training sessions (with any technique) is pretty arbitrary. We can only take the dog's internal state into account inasmuch as we can observe it on the outside or with monitors. We can do our best to look at the direction of the wind, the odors in the air, the sensation of the surface on the dog's paws, medical issues, body language, and more, but in the end, we can't really predict how the dog will feel when she first notices the trigger.

What we *can* do is relax, be adaptable, and observe the dog's motion. *Let your dog vote with her body on where to go.* Stop the session or have a snack break (for the dog) and brainstorm on how you can make it easier. At all moments throughout your session and in life with your dog, think, "Is there anything I can change to help my dog feel safer?" I have had very good success with just making my training area larger. This can be done by moving farther away, if there is room to still see, or by switching to a totally different spot. Once they are at the right distance, the 'magnet' kicks back in and the dog will gradually want to go a bit closer.

Having the helper walking away when the student dog encounters him is usually the easiest, so you can do a following version of BAT, as described above. Bringing along a dog friend who is more brave and curious may also help, but again, keep an eye on whether that accidentally pulls the dog closer to the trigger than she can handle.

If you go to a truly gigantic space and the dog still wants to move farther away, that's some big information on your dog's threshold distance and quality of life. It's very rare that I work with a dog for whom we can't find a big enough space, even in urban environments. Look into anti-anxiety treatment, using nutrition, exercise, TTouch and possibly medication or herbal anti-anxiety supplements. Check out Anders Hallgren's excellent book, *Stress, Anxiety, and Aggression in Dogs.* BAT set-ups in this situation look basically like I described in Chapter 7, when your training space is too small for the dog's needs. You also might need to do Mark and Move, clicking for any approach behavior, then moving away and tossing a treat. If you do parallel play activities, like Find It, training, or sports, still notice when your dog wants to move farther away from the trigger, and help honor that request.

If you are having any other trouble with your set-ups, please reread the section on how to do BAT. Many of the mistakes that people make come from just not fully digesting the material before they start training. Also learn as much as you can about dog body language, and film your own dog in many situations. Play the videos back in slow motion so that you can see behavior that tells you how she's feeling or where she wants to go next. Consider hiring a CBATI or other professional trainer or behaviorist who is familiar with BAT 2.0. Film your sessions and participate in the BAT Chats on my site. Join a local discussion group for BAT so that you can meet up with other people in your area. A lot of times, another set of eyes will help you see what is going on.

CHAPTER 9

Surprise:
Sudden Environmental Contrast

When it comes to surprises, a lot of dogs bark first and ask questions later. Dogs respond more strongly to stimuli that appear suddenly, compared to those that the dog is aware of from a distance. Given how common it is, your dog probably has an issue with Sudden Environmental Contrast or Sudden Environmental Change (SEC) too. SEC is a change in the surroundings that happens quickly, like a child popping out from around a corner, a dog suddenly appearing out of a car, or a guest standing up to leave the house. For some dogs, the appearance of a trash bin in a different place than on yesterday's walk can stress them out. "That is NOT supposed to be there." Dogs are not particularly great at generalizing information that something is safe to a new context, so the concept of SEC needs specific work (see Appendix 3 for some technical information on generalization).

Most of the time with BAT, the helper is in view throughout the session, except during the frequent breaks. The chance to gather information is the primary way BAT teaches dogs to be comfortable with their triggers. It takes some planning to create situations that teach dogs when triggers suddenly appear, or suddenly move, that they are no more dangerous than before. So first get your dog comfortable in the presence of the trigger, and then begin to work on SEC. This can be at the end of a session with a helper, woven in during the session when your dog is comfortable at a particular distance from the trigger, or in a separate session. Also practice SEC with helpers your dog hasn't worked with before.

Having enough distance between your dog and the helper is the key for all of BAT, including Sudden Environmental Change work. When you change any aspect of the trigger, you may need to stay at a greater distance from the helper, and that's especially true for SEC. Let's say that your dog, Lola, is comfortable with the helper approaching to five feet away, but has trouble with the helper suddenly appearing around a corner. Start with Lola walking and suddenly encountering the helper, say around a corner, at fifty feet away (that's ten times farther). Note that the helper is not moving toward your dog at that point, just standing there. Practice this concept at gradually shrinking distances, in various locations, so you don't end up with a dog who thinks that the hedge at the corner of 5th Avenue and Main Street is okay, but surprises everywhere else are scary.

After doing set-ups to get Lola comfortable with moving into a space that has a Scary Monster, you could have her stationary or moving and have the trigger pop into view at fifty feet during SEC training (notice that I bumped the distance back up again because the trigger is now coming into Lola's space, not the other way around). For SEC training with your dog, you can remove the trigger after your dog disengages or you can do one SEC appearance and then just keep the trigger in the area and let your dog explore, as in a normal BAT set-up. The latter is a nice way to work SEC training into your regular BAT set-ups. Just make sure it's not stressing your dog. If you learn nothing else from this book, learn this: *there is always an emotional take-home message for your dog.*

With Peanut, the initial BAT training made him become comfortable with walking down the sidewalk and encountering a trigger at a distance and while moving up close, but if he was standing still and the trigger suddenly appeared, it was a different story. So, we worked SEC on scenarios where humans would suddenly appear from behind a hedge, get out of a car, walk around a corner, or otherwise suddenly appear. You can do SEC sessions just like your regular BAT 2.0 set-ups or you can use Mark and Move for the SEC part. Because this was several years ago, before BAT 2.0, I used only Mark and Move with Peanut. I now would do a combination, starting with Mark and Move for SEC triggers and later doing regular BAT wandering for the reappearance of the same triggers.

We began by having helpers surprise Peanut from one hundred feet away, which was interesting, but not enough to startle or elicit a bark. That was a great starting distance. He turned away, sniffed the ground, looked at me, or offered another replacement behavior and was rewarded with a verbal "Yes," walking away, and praise (that's Mark and Move done in one of the least intrusive ways). The helpers then ducked out of sight and we turned around and headed toward them again. We used cell phones with hands-free sets to coordinate the training. That way, we didn't accidentally surprise him at only twenty feet away and end up with a barking episode.

Some SEC variations:

- Your dog suddenly encounters trigger while walking

- Trigger suddenly appears (around a corner, through a doorway, etc.)

- Trigger suddenly moves (turn to go, face away and pivot toward your dog, stand up, lift hand to pet, clap hands, jump, trip over something, etc.)

- Trigger suddenly makes noise or pays attention to your dog

- Moving trigger suddenly stops
- In a group of people or dogs, one does something different from the rest—steps out of the group, stands while they move, etc. This is especially important for herding and livestock guarding breeds who pay careful attention to such things (think "sheep, sheep, sheep, wolf!").

If you do accidentally put your dog over-threshold in an SEC trial, use graduated prompting to get your dog back to a thinking state. I usually keep the trigger stationary instead of removing it, because having the trigger disappear could reinforce the bark, but I also balance it out with whether I might be causing more stress. If moving the student dog away is not immediately calming, I will have the trigger move farther away or disappear. After you've moved your dog away and he's not over-aroused, let him take a look at the trigger. Mark that very first look, move farther away, and put some treats on the ground so he can self-soothe by sniffing. If you think he can stay below threshold, go back to the wandering version of BAT with the trigger still in view. If you think your dog needs more help, do some more Mark and Move instead of just following the dog. Since you've already taught your dog to be comfortable with a stationary trigger, your dog should quickly acclimate to the situation. Remember, it's not just about behavior; it's about teaching the dog that the world is not so scary or angry-making after all.

Varying the exposure step of BAT allows your dog to encounter the trigger in more natural ways. Depending on the situation, you may also need to reinterpret "move away" for Mark and Move. For example, I worked with a Great Dane in a small apartment where my standing up triggered his aggression. We had already worked with me just sitting there, and the dog was comfortable with approaching me as I sat, even to the point of soliciting my attention and petting (while muzzled). I tried standing up with him ten feet, fifteen feet, and twenty feet away, but that was too much, and it resulted in this 150-pound dog with a damaging bite history lunging at the end of his leash toward me.

For his safety, and mine, we moved to create the maximum amount of distance between us and I changed how I moved. From the other side of the apartment, he was now easily able to look at me and then look away if I rose only halfway. At that point, however, there was nowhere for him or me to go so we were unable to use walking away to reinforce his cut-off signal. This would mean that his behavior had no effect, which would be bad. But he was comfortable with me sitting, so my returning to the sitting position reduced his anxiety. My return to sitting was his functional reinforcer.

So I'd start to get up, he'd look at me for a little bit, and then turn away. His owners verbally marked his choice and I then sat back down and relaxed as his owners told him that he was fabulously brave. He relaxed, too. If I were to do it over again, I'd probably also have had the owners give him a food treat. After a few repetitions, we were able to move him about five feet away from the wall, closer to me, with me half-rising as the trigger. Then, I'd return to sitting and he could walk a few feet away within the apartment (a bigger functional reinforcer than before, now that there was room). We gradually moved the choice point closer to my chair, and then we increased the distance and began working on having me stand all the way up. To make it easier, we had him move to the far end of the unit when I stood all the way up as the trigger, and sat back down as his reward. He made great strides in that session.

Another way we could have varied this was to have me sitting in a chair in the hallway, outside. Better yet, we could have started in my training center, so that he could become comfortable with the trigger at a proper distance away, without the extra stress of me being inside his home. We didn't do the hallway because we were afraid random neighbors would arrive and put him over-threshold. But we could have done the training center. Why would that be better? He'd have less stress and also more behavioral control. He could have moved more, and we could have done a set-up more like BAT 2.0 (except that this was many years ago and I hadn't developed it yet). I'll talk more about how to do set-ups for territorial issues in Chapter 11.

CHAPTER 10

BAT on Everyday Walks

BAT set-ups can work quickly to rehabilitate dogs (think ten to twenty set-ups for dogs with straightforward issues), but if dogs are rehearsing aggression, panic, or frustrated freak-outs during their everyday walks they will lose the new skills they have learned in the set-ups. The good news is that Mark and Move works well in unstructured encounters with a trigger as might be experienced on a walk. You can also gradually start to use 'real' BAT 2.0 where you just follow the dog. You may be meeting triggers frequently on walks, so you and your dog can practice the skills learned in your BAT set-ups in a variety of locations. Just be sure that you really are doing the set-ups as well.

I mean that—please don't just skim through this chapter and practice BAT on your walks. It's not going to be enough. Your dog needs a chance to make friends, not just acquaintances.

Mark and Move revisited

In the chapter where I introduced Mark and Move, we talked about bonus rewards. Tangible bonus rewards like treats are used primarily on walks rather than in set-ups. Formal BAT set-ups don't usually use trainer-delivered reinforcers, because dogs seem to learn more about the trigger without them. There is no competing motivation to earn a reinforcer from you, so they can attend to the naturally occurring reinforcers in the environment. In particular, that means your dog has more attention to focus on the social situation at hand. Dog (and human) brains file away information that they focus on. Background information may or may not be retained. Dogs seem to miss subtle information in social settings when distracted by the temptation of food or the threat of punishment from their human.

I am more likely to use Mark and Move when I do BAT set-ups with inanimate objects (slippery surfaces, scary rooms, getting into cars). They don't require nuanced interactions. Those situations also don't have the natural magnetism of social situations, so we first try to enrich the environment to make it more interesting. If that doesn't work, dogs may need bonus rewards to stay engaged with the trigger.

Even though bonus rewards can get in the way during set-ups, they are extremely helpful during walks. The three main effects of bonus rewards are to: 1) help your dog make good choices when close to the trigger; 2) make the training more fun for your dog; and 3) decrease stress.

On a walk, for example, your dog might randomly encounter triggers at ten feet, thirty feet, and then at fifteen feet. This is in contrast to set-ups, when you control the exposure and can make sure your dog is likely to stay relaxed. On a walk, however, you may need a little extra help on your side to encourage your dog to avoid aggression or panic. Even though the bonus reward comes *after* you walk your dog away, knowing that his human is carrying freeze-dried liver can take some of his attention off of the triggers and puts it on to you. As I mentioned in Chapter 7, this is especially useful for dogs who are really frustrated and want to go say hi. Those dogs are basically just chanting, "Go, go, go," so it's useful to have something tangible with which you can reinforce self-control. Regardless of the emotional reason for the reactivity, the presence of treats or toys makes your dog more likely to hold herself together around a trigger in real life.

Sniffing is a lovely self-soothing behavior, and looking for treats puts your dog in a seeking state of mind which helps relieve any stress that's building up. A simple version of using scent work as a bonus reward while on a walk is to toss a treat into the grass behind you while your dog looks at a trigger. When he disengages, you can mark with "Find It." If your dog doesn't already know a search cue, you'll need to toss the treat after she disengages, so she sees you doing it.

I'll take this chance to remind you that even though having food or toys on you to use Mark and Move will make a dog less likely to react in the moment, it's not an ideal long-term solution. Actual BAT 2.0 set-ups will make it so you don't need to be ready with those treats and scanning for triggers all the time. But Mark and Move on a walk helps dogs keep things together, and that's good for you both. To summarize: use calm praise, petting, or other non-distracting bonus rewards with impunity, any time you want to. Use food, toys, scent work and other tangible bonus rewards when the distraction works in your favor.

Let's take a look at the main way that Mark and Move can be used on walks and other uncontrolled environments. It should give you a better idea of how and when to use tangible bonus rewards.

Example: Look, move, treat

This is the simplest version of Mark and Move. It is one of the most distracting ways too, so it is useful for handling big surprises in real life. Use this whenever the dog is likely to bark and lunge or panic if you were to let him check things out on his own. For example, if a child pops out from behind a fence, just click (or call your dog) and go.

Behavior: Looking at trigger

Marker: Click

Bonus: Treat—the type and how it's delivered will change the value

The behavior you are reinforcing here is simply noticing the trigger. As soon as your dog perceives the trigger, click, guide your dog away as you praise, and then give your dog a tangible bonus reward. The order matters! If the dog is afraid or showing aggression, the treat is a bonus, not the main reinforcer, which is the relief of escaping from the trigger. If the dog is frustrated, then moving away is a difficult behavior that needs to be reinforced. Either way, treating after you move is ideal. Mark, walk, or jog away, and then surprise your dog with the delicious or fun bonus reward. As I mentioned before, if the issue is frustration, you might move away by zigzagging side to side, rather than going directly away from the trigger.

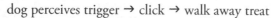

dog perceives trigger → click → walk away treat

Mark: click when your dog sees the trigger.

Move: walk or jog away from the trigger.

Bonus: After your dog walks away, feed a treat or play with a toy.

Notice that this means there will be a few seconds of delay between your click and the treat, as you reward your dog first by going away from the trigger. If you're in a tight spot, you can click and then do something else to reduce your dog's stress: go as far away as the space allows and block your dog's view, then treat like mad.

When you are really trying to get your dog's attention and mark good behavior at the same time, I recommend using a clicker, rather than a verbal marker. The clicker serves two purposes here. It marks the behavior, but it also cues the dog to turn toward you for the bonus reward—away from the trigger—which helps your dog avoid an outburst. If a clicker just makes you feel clumsy or your dog is afraid of the clicker, stick with your regular verbal marker or use your dog's name, recall cue, targeting, etc.

> Tip for Pros: Don't worry about weakening the power of the clicker. A few second's delay, especially when the treat is predictably given in the "click → walk/run away → treat" pattern, is not harmful to the click/treat association. Furthermore, in most cases, the dog is still getting a reinforcer immediately after the click—the functional reinforcer. If you're still worried, jog or run so that the delay between click and treat is shorter, and praise after the click to bridge the time between your click and the treat.

This use of Mark and Move is very similar to what Leslie McDevitt calls "Look at That" in her excellent book, *Control Unleashed* (see Resources). The basic version of Look at That is to train it as a cued behavior by clicking and treating dogs for looking at a neutral stimulus first, and then reward them for looking at (or listening to) a low-level version triggering stimulus, like another dog or a person. Leslie does use release of social pressure (walking away from the trigger) as part of Look at That in some cases. A lot of the *Control Unleashed* exercises complement BAT very nicely, and her work is worth looking into.

Example: Choose, move, treat

This example of Mark and Move adds more responsibility for your dog, but you are still using a tangible bonus reward, usually food. The only difference between this example and the last one is the behavior you are marking. In this case, you would wait for a good choice. So you would wait for the dog to disengage first instead of just clicking when the dog perceives the trigger as you would do above. This is less intrusive than the previous example, giving the dog a chance to learn more on his own. It's still more intrusive and distracting than a regular BAT set-up, where the dog has a lot more freedom. I would use this on a walk when a student dog sees something across the street and it's challenging, but not impossible, to disengage on his own.

In this example, your dog notices the trigger, then you wait for him to look away or do some other cut-off signal, and that's when you click. Here's what that looks like:

dog perceives trigger → wait for good choice → click → walk away → treat

Wait for and mark disengagement whenever you would bet money that your dog would be able to do it. If you can't make that bet, mark earlier, when your dog first looks at the trigger, as we discussed above. If your dog sees a trigger in a particular situation where you think your dog could do the replacement behaviors even without the bonus rewards, go for it. You don't need to treat all the time. The appropriate social responses by the trigger are probably naturally reinforcing, and staying out of your dog's way helps him notice them.

Note: If you use Mark and Move every single time your dog sees a trigger, you may get a false sense of how close the dog can be to the trigger. The distraction helps your dog handle the situation but robs him of the opportunity to gather information. Be patient when you think your dog can disengage and move on without your help. Use tangible reinforcers when you need them, but the more 'proper' BAT you do, with following your dog and using naturally occurring reinforcers, the less you have to fade out to create a realistic context.

More BAT tips and examples for walks

Doing BAT on a walk provides a great opportunity to generalize what the dog is learning from BAT set-ups. Unfortunately, if the dog is put over-threshold, walks can also reverse some of the gains made in those set-ups. If you follow the safety tips from the Chapter 3, you should be able to keep your dog below threshold most of the time. That doesn't mean avoiding triggers altogether; that is almost impossible on walks. On the contrary, you may find that you actually start walking your dog more often and start stalking your dog's trigger—following other dogs from a distance or doing "undercover BAT" in other ways (this has also been called "Stealth BAT" and "Ninja BAT"). Look for triggers who are relatively stationary or walking in a predictable way:

- Dogs behind fences
- Gardeners
- People and/or dogs at coffee shops
- Kids at playgrounds
- Dogs tied up at a football game (from a distance only!)
- People or dogs on walking paths
- Dogs in training class or at pet stores

Example: Encountering children on walks

How exactly would you do BAT on a walk? Let's say your dog is reactive to children. If a child is walking directly at you on a sidewalk, you have a lot of choices, so I have created a checklist of examples of what you might do in this situation on the next two pages. As you're reading these examples, some of them will seem impossible or unsafe for your dog and some will sound reasonable. Do the reasonable ones and keep the other choices in mind for later, as your dog progresses. Remember, the stages are situational—just pick a behavior that you think your dog is capable of doing and reinforce it, if you think he needs that help from you.

Always do the least intrusive, least distracting version of Mark and Move. Use management (muzzles, etc.) to keep everyone safe. This list goes from most to least intrusive. It is not meant to be a recipe, because there would be steps in between. It is just an example of what your dog might be ready for in real life at any given time.

As you read through each of these examples, visualize doing them with your dog. Make a mental check as to whether you think each one would work yet or not in cases where your dog encounters children. If you have a print edition of this book, you can even write in here, if you don't mind marking it up, and then come back in a few months to see if anything has changed.

	Distraction (management, not BAT). You are just stuck until they go by, so you shorten the leash (without tightening it, if possible), stand between your dog and the child, and drop treats on the ground, away from the child.
	Distraction. You see the child first and know that if your dog sees the child, he will start barking right away. You do an emergency U-turn to get out of there, and feed your dog a treat for coming with you.
	Distraction. You have to keep going, for some reason, so you feed your dog a non-stop series of treats as you pass by.
	Your dog looks up and notices the child as you are walking. Click as soon as he sees the child, then say "Let's go," jog in the opposite direction, and feed a treat.
	Your dog looks up and notices the child as you are approaching. Click as soon as he sees the child, then walk away and tell him to "Find it" with several treats tossed on the ground.
	You want to avoid getting too close. Do a Slow Stop and wait for your dog to notice the child. Click as soon as he sees the child, jog away into a driveway, and then stop to play tug as the child passes by. (This is a tough one because the child is still moving.)
	As soon as your dog sees the child, you click, walk into a driveway, and treat. The child passes by you. You wait a bit and then you and your dog follow the child down the sidewalk, from a safe distance. As you're walking, he looks at the child, then looks away. You click for the lookaway, then pivot and walk him away from the child, and then give your dog a treat. Successful repetition is the key to progress, so if you can get a few trials in with the triggers you encounter in public, do it!
	Do a Slow Stop and wait for your dog to notice the child and then look at you. Click as soon as he looks at you, jog away into a driveway, and then stop to play tug. (Again, this is tough because the child is still moving. This may be better to do when the child is walking perpendicular to you instead of right at you.)
	Your dog has calm body language on the approach, and stops, so you stop to say hi. Your dog looks at the child and then looks away, so you click, walk away, and give your dog a treat, praising her massive bravery.

	Walk your dog a little off the sidewalk and wait for the child to pass by. Your dog looks at the child, then sniffs the ground. Wait until she's done sniffing and then Mark that choice by clicking, praise as you jog away from the child, and then give your dog a treat.
	Walk your dog a little off the sidewalk and wait for the child to pass by. Your dog looks at the child, then sniffs the ground. Wait until she's done sniffing and then Mark that choice by saying "Yes." Praise as you jog away from the child.
	Keep walking toward the child along the sidewalk. As you're walking, the dog looks at the child, and then looks away. Mark that choice by saying, "Yes" and take a step off to the side so that you're arcing around the child (slight increase in distance/decrease in stress as the functional reinforcer).
	Follow your dog to the child and allow your dog to greet the child. After a little petting, your dog looks away from the child. You say "Yes, let's go" and continue on your walk, telling your dog he's fabulously brave.
	Follow your dog to the child and allow your dog to greet the child. After a little petting, you ask the child to pause and step back to see if the dog wants more. Your dog looks away from the child and walks away. You follow your dog.
	Follow your dog to the child and allow your dog to greet the child. After a little petting, you ask the child to pause and step back to see if the dog wants more. Your dog nuzzles her hand for more and the petting resumes. The child stops again and this time your dog walks away. You follow your dog. Cool, huh?

Note: If there is any risk of a bite, of course, you won't do all of these, especially with a stranger. Use distance and consider having your dog wear a muzzle for unforeseeable surprises.

That brings me to the sad fact that walks are unpredictable. They just are. By doing BAT 2.0 set-ups, your dog should get better and better at handling triggers without your help. In the meantime, your dog may bark and lunge when you misjudge the situation or life happens and suddenly she's too close to the trigger. Sometimes, even distraction may not work. Don't yell at your dog for freaking out when she ends up too close to her trigger; just get out of there as soon as you can using whatever means possible, including the survival skills I gave in Chapter 3. See what you can do about avoiding such a situation in the future. If avoiding triggers is really hard, there may be a location that's easier for your dog to walk in without going over-threshold. Your dog might benefit from indoor exercise before heading out, stress relief of some kind (medical and/or training), or may need more BAT set-ups before the real world is not overwhelming.

If your dog's worst nightmare suddenly appears, use an emergency U-Turn or Mark and Move.

BAT can almost always be done on walks, in one form or another. Try to do the regular "follow your dog" version whenever you can. Any time your dog is exposed to the trigger, you should be aware of his body language so that you or the environment can reinforce good choices. Be aware of your location, so that you know the best direction to head for a retreat. When you walk away, you can turn around entirely and head in the opposite direction or turn at a right angle and cross the street or walk into a driveway. Remember that you, not your dog, have opened the door to your home to take your dog for a walk, so it's your job to help him out of trouble. Doing BAT on walks can help your dog learn that he has the power to reduce the stress of living in a world orchestrated by humans. And that means less work for you, too.

CHAPTER 11

Love Thy Neighbor:
Fence Fighting

Dogs are great at alerting their families that an intruder has entered their territory. That's part of why people have dogs. Knowing that my dogs will sound the alarm if someone were to break into my home comforts me. Several years ago, a man opened our door at 2 a.m. and two hundred pounds of barking dogs kept him outside. Even 'friendly' dogs take this job very seriously. Unfortunately, *a lot* of dogs also consider it imperative to keep all other dogs and people away from their fence line, especially the 'intruders' that live in the house next door.

To work on fence fighting issues, I always recommend starting with management, because environmental changes can quickly reduce stress. Environmental changes combine well with passive training, active training, or both. Let's look at each of these three approaches in turn.

Change the environment

If a dog is fence fighting, he is probably getting a fair amount of reinforcement for the behavior, especially if he is reacting to dogs who are on the sidewalk, on the other side of the fence. Look at it from your dog's perspective. A stranger appears, he charges out to bark and growl, and the other dog or person leaves in defeat. It doesn't matter that they were leaving anyway. He still may feel that he has successfully guarded his territory. To make solid progress, this naturally occuring reinforcement for barking needs to be removed. A lot of this can be handled by the management techniques discussed below.

If your dog fence fights with neighboring dogs, one simple technique is to work out a schedule where the dogs are out at different times. You should also do all of the steps I mentioned in the "out of sight, out of mind" section of Chapter 3.

Even if you have a fenced-in yard, you may need to walk your dog on a leash in the backyard for a while so he can avoid getting sucked into a conflict at the fence. You can also tether your dog with a long leash that doesn't allow him to reach the fence—the further away he is from the fence, the less likely he is to bark. Always supervise a tethered dog—go outside with him. The safest way that I've found to tether a dog is to have a bungee attachment at the end that secures the leash to the stake, house, or other solid object. Use a long lead that is not likely to get tangled, like climbing rope. Clip that lead to the back of a harness on your dog. That way, if your dog does decide to charge out and hits the end of the leash, there's a bungee to absorb the shock and the harness distributes the remaining force instead of choking your dog on a collar.

Bungee shock absorbers make long lines safer when the dog is tethered.
Use a back-attachment harness, rather than the collar pictured here.

If possible, landscape the yard so that your dog can't get right up to the fence. Plant something thick and/or prickly next to the fence. In addition to reducing visibility, plants can absorb more of the noise that the 'intruders' make, which keeps your dog calmer. If you are on good terms with your neighbor, suggest that they consider some landscaping that might keep their dog away from the fence, too. It can be easy to start getting mad at each other because your dogs don't get along, so try to consider this a problem you can work on together. If it's possible, plant something like arbor vitae between your fence and the sidewalk as well. It will keep passersby further away from your fence. If you need some more ideas, Cheryl Smith has a book on creating gardens and landscaping that are both beautiful and dog-friendly (see Resources). If you are not on good terms with your neighbor, read the section on social psychology, especially the Fundamental Attribution Error in Appendix 3.

Use your creative human brain to look at the situation and see if there are any other changes that can be made to reduce the chance of barking in the backyard. Environmental changes (management) can be quicker and easier than training, so think long and hard about what you can do. Question your assumptions, too. Does your dog need the whole yard? Are you giving your dog front yard access when the backyard will do? Is your dog's life really improved by having your dog door open all day, or is that just causing more stress? If you have an older dog who really needs to go outside to pee during the day, but your young dog is fence-fighting, could you get a dog door with a sensor so that only the senior dog can go out? Changing the external factors in the environment can help everybody relax.

Passive training: Lazy Bones BAT

Lazy Bones BAT is a way to arrange the situation so that your dog can succeed and be reinforced by the environment, much like our regular BAT 2.0 set-ups, but even easier because you are not even following your dog around. Lazy Bones BAT is a form of passive training. It gives your dog an entertaining focal point, which can help to minimize exposure levels of various real life triggers. One example of a simple way to do this is to stuff an easy, but long-lasting food puzzle and give it to your dog out in the yard. This, combined with attaching a harness and long leash to keep your dog away from the fence, should help keep your dog calmer (remember to still supervise).

In a situation like this, the stuffed food puzzle acts as a magnet for your dog's attention. If it's set up well, as other dogs pass by, you'll see your dog look up, think about barking, and then go back to work. Yay! He ignores the other dog and the other dog leaves (they were going to, anyway), so your dog gets his functional reinforcer for behavior you like. Magic! If you're still getting barking, then do Lazy Bones BAT with your dog and the food puzzle closer to the house or even inside with the door open (as in a formal set-up, you are increasing the distance to the trigger). You can also train your dog to "Get your toy" and if you think he's about to bark, cue him to get the food puzzle that he was just eating. That worked well for Peanut.

We are all busy, and if preparing a food puzzle takes too much time out of people's day, they won't do it. Here's how I made the preparation process efficient and quick at my house. Get some kind of food that comes out as a paste, without chunks, so that you can easily get it into the food puzzles. If you're really into food prep, you can grind your own meat. For Peanut, I mix cooked oatmeal and some other ingredients with canned dog food or dehydrated raw dog food to which I add hot water to rehydrate. You can buy a pastry tube or scoop the wet dog food into a baggie, close it, and cut off one of the bottom corners of the baggie, so you have a hole about half an inch wide. Now you have a homemade version of a pastry tube, so you can squeeze just the right amount in each toy. The toys can then go into baggies or a reusable container in the freezer. As your dog empties the toys, just put them back into a big container in the freezer. You can stuff a bunch all at once, which saves you time. Putting the used puzzle toys back into the freezer ensures that any leftover food doesn't mold. I have a portion of my freezer dedicated to the dogs, so we have about a dozen stuffed Kongs and other food puzzles. Consider getting a bottle brush and dishwasher safe toys to save time.

If your dog is busy with his food toy, he's not doing this.

For fastest learning, feed your dog all his meals this way while working on his fence fighting issues. If you do need to feed the rest in a bowl, for some reason, do the food puzzle outside first, and the bowl inside afterwards (so he's more interested in the puzzle). Make sure to take into account how many calories your dog gets from the food puzzle each day. Remember that treats are often more calorie-dense than dog food. The last thing you want to do is make your dog chunky. Overweight dogs have more health problems and shorter lives, so don't overstuff your dog! Overfed dogs are also generally less food motivated, so Lazy Bones BAT doesn't work as well for them. How can you tell if your dog is the right weight? About sixty percent of dogs in the U.S. are overweight, and I've seen overweight dogs pretty much everywhere. So you may not be able to just compare to other dogs that you see. You can ask your vet at your annual checkup, and you can also test it yourself right now. You should be able to feel your dog's ribs without having to really press in your hands to search for them, and if you look at your wet dog from above, you should see that he has a waist.

Back to Lazy Bones BAT. As your dog completes the food puzzle, she is more likely to react to triggers again, so stay out there with her so that you can see when she's done with the food puzzle. You don't have to just concentrate on the dog while you're outside. You can read a book, do yard work, talk on the phone, etc. as your dog plays with the toy. Be ready to either bring her in or give her another food puzzle (or set multiple puzzles out from the beginning). While you do Lazy Bones BAT, allow her to be out in the yard only for potty time or when she has a food puzzle. It may take several months for her to learn to ignore the background noise—less time if she's new to fence fighting. Once she's doing well, you can start to remove the long leash and harness. You can even gradually shorten the long leash and have her drag it around so that there's not such a big contrast between being tethered and being free in the yard. Again, make sure an adult is supervising when your dog is on a leash.

Continue doing the food puzzles for every non-potty trip outside until your dog is not reacting badly to any of the passersby or the neighbor's dog. Once that's gone well for a month or two, then start having more gaps in between the food puzzles, so that your dog has more time out in the yard without distractions. Gradually have the puzzle less and less full. You might still want to leave some kind of toys out in the yard, so your dog can self-soothe as people or dogs pass by. Here's a puppy tip. Use the food puzzle to reinforce eliminating outside. Then you can do Lazy Bones BAT at the same time. Prevention is quicker than rehabilitation.

Active training

If you're willing to take a more active role, there are some other exercises that you can do to reduce or eliminate fence fighting using BAT. The first active training that you can do to work on fence fighting with a neighbor is to do a regular BAT set-up with both of the dogs involved, so they can become friends or at least friendly acquaintances. When dogs actually know and like each other, they don't usually fence fight. If there are multiple dogs in each yard, start with the pair that fights most intensely, and work your way down.

I tend to do a lot more Mark and Move with fence fighting, still using the least intrusive/distracting version that I can get away with. Doing BAT with the dogs 'on location' in their own yards may pose some difficulties: 1) there may not be enough room to maneuver (although opening the door to retreat inside the house can help); 2) it's an emotionally charged area; 3) the fence between the dogs may be part of the trigger and 4) you may need to add extra enrichment to encourage exploration.

Most of the time, I have neighbors do set-ups on the sidewalk first, with the dogs on-leash, far away, and no fence between them—or a 'neutral' fence if that's needed for safety. Get them to the point where they can go on walks and ignore each other or interact well. If they can play safely off leash in a neutral area, like a park or someone else's yard, that can help. Try to find a neutral fence to have in between them for your first set-ups, i.e., not their shared fenceline.

> Tip for Pros: If you are certain that their fence fighting is based on frustration relating on not being able to play together, you can use the Premack Principle (see Appendix 2) and let them play as reinforcement for appropriate behavior. Before you try that, have them play in a neutral location, to be sure the play really is appropriate.

The farther your dog is from your house, the less reactive he is likely to be.

After they have gotten used to each other on the sidewalk, you can do a BAT set-up with each dog in their own yard with the fence in between, on leash. Remember to do this with just the pair you have been working with, without adding in extra dogs. It's a big enough criteria leap to go to the backyard, without adding in the stress of a third dog. Once you have success with the most challenging pair, set up sessions to train all of the pairs of dogs and then work all of the triplets, quadruplets, and so on until you have worked with all of your dogs and all of the neighbors' dogs. The people on the other side of the fence may not be willing to work their dogs, but may allow you and a friend or trainer to do so.

If your neighbor is unwilling or unable to help you, then the task is a lot harder, because you won't be able to take the dogs out of the high-stress area or keep your neighbor's dog away from the fence. You may still be able to do BAT with the off-leash neighbor dog in the yard as the unwilling decoy. If you have multiple dogs, work with each of your own dogs individually, then in pairs, and so on, using the neighbor's dog(s) as the trigger each time. This will be most successful if you first do some land-scaping and make the neighbors less visible/audible/sniffable by putting up a solid privacy fence and some strong-smelling bushes in front of it. One of my dogs really hated the smell of ladybugs. I could have planted marigolds and other plants that attract ladybugs near the fence to discourage her from sniffing in that direction. Get creative!

What if it's not the neighbor's dog? If your dog doesn't just have the one 'nemesis' barks at all people or dogs walking by, recruit helpers and decoy dogs for several BAT set-ups, including some work on Sudden Environmental Contrast (see Chapter 9 for more info on SEC).

If there is no place within the yard that your dog can see the helper without barking, then you'll need to do more distracting Mark and Move with quick clicking or do set-ups outside on the street, so that she gets used to people, generally near her house first. This kind of barking is usually part SEC and part territoriality, so you will probably need to do basic BAT set-ups as well as SEC set-ups. If the problem is just SEC, or the territoriality is mild, you can just go right to having helpers walk up to and away from the fence. When the student dog is off leash, expect that she will be standing at the fence for most of the session. If there is some distance from the fence at which the helper can walk without your dog barking, then your dog can be off leash. If not, start with your dog on leash and away from the fence.

The helper should walk all of the various routes by the house that pedestrians normally take. The only difference is that the helper should walk up, stop or move slowly, and then time his exits so that they serve as functional reinforcers for your dog's behavior. You can watch your dog and mark with "Yes" for an acceptable replacement behavior and signal the helper to walk away as a functional reinforcer. So the helper walks or wheels parallel to the fence, stops at some approach point, waits for you to say "Yes," and then goes back the way he came or leaves in some other way. Don't forget that there are all sorts of passersby—so try this out with kids, bikes, people with walkers or wheel chairs, people in cars stopping by to say hi, and pedestrians with and without dogs. Try to get some of each at some point in your training. A person jingling his keys or playing a recording of dog tags can make your dog think that the person is walking a dog, so you may be able to get away with using fewer helper dogs using that trick. You can even train alone by playing own sounds on a Bluetooth speaker outside the fence that's controlled by your phone.

You can also do Mark and Move with treats from inside the yard. A good option is to use remote control treat dispensers like the the PetTutor or Manners Minder. The Manners Minder remote works from about one hundred feet away, even with walls in between the remote and the dispenser. When you press the remote, the machine beeps and then dispenses food, so your dog knows that they've earned a treat. A remote control treat dispenser allows you to watch good behavior in the backyard and click the remote to signal your dog to run away from the fence to the dispenser for her treat. Because she's got to run away from the trigger to get her treat, she's getting a functional reinforcer of distance as well as a bonus reward. You can train while your dog is outside and you are inside the house, or you could also be handling the neighbor's dog, remote in hand, while you reward your own dog for good behavior. The PetTutor also has an automatic bark detection system and a timer, so it can feed your dog for silence. The PetTutor may develop mobile apps to control the dispenser. This could be combined with a remote camera to train while you are away from home. The Petzi Treat Cam, iPooch, and PetChatz Video Phone already have online treat dispensing technology, but I haven't tested them. Whichever device you use, place the feeder so that your dog runs away from the trigger for her treat.

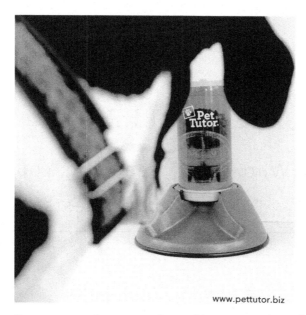

www.pettutor.biz

*Treats from a remote dispenser make good bonus rewards, as the dog
must run to the machine for the reward.*

Teaching dogs to react well around their triggers, even while off leash and inside their
own fences, can be a challenge, but the peace and quiet that you get at the end is worth
it! Whether you are doing active or passive training, be patient with the process and
make changes to the yard in order to keep outbursts to a minimum. Now let's talk
about what to do if you actually want to bring guests inside your home.

CHAPTER 12

"Who Is It?" Teaching Your
Dog to Enjoy Guests

What do you want your dog to do when you have company? I personally like it when my dogs welcome guests when the door is opened, no matter who is on the other side. If I freak out, of course, I would appreciate my dogs helping me out by barking. But you probably don't have to train for that part; most dogs automatically know when there is really a threat. The hard part learning to welcome a stranger into their territory. We can help dogs enjoy visitors by using BAT to help them know that they have choices and by creating a pleasant association with people coming into the house.

With punishment-based training, **flooding** is a pretty standard procedure: just bring a visitor into the home and give leash corrections or shock the dog whenever she communicates discomfort. When the dog stops reacting badly, you've 'trained' her. Dogs are not humans, but they have a lot of similarities in their mammalian brains. Can you imagine if you were nervous about clowns, for example, and someone just brought a bunch of them into your house and then choked you when you screamed or tried to defend yourself? It's like a horror movie. You may end up looking compliant, but that doesn't mean it made you comfortable with the situation. There are a lot of similarities between the symptoms of PTSD and the 'calm submissive' dogs seen on television.

In modern training, by contrast, we set the dog up for success. Many great trainers that I know would start off by having the owner feed the dog any time a stranger comes in (or better yet, start outside and work their way in). That is a good start, and it often works, but I prefer empowerment: giving dogs control of their safety as the primary vehicle for change and use treats as needed to build a good association

Don't get me wrong: as I described in the management chapter, I do use treats, toys, and whatever else I can to help dogs stay more relaxed when they haven't yet been taught to handle the situation. Put management and other safety measures in place whenever you can't avoid bringing a person into your home before your dog is ready.

For training, I recommend using BAT outside with a helper and then, over time, working on bringing the helper inside. Your BAT set-up outside will probably have a leash or a fence for distance. If there is a history of biting or a risk that it may happen, use other safety measures like a muzzle, exercise pen, or baby gates. Work all the way through to friendly interactions in a few locations before you have the helper come over to the house as a guest. That is, the first several times you bring a 'stranger' into the house, it shouldn't really be a stranger, but rather a guest that your dog knows and likes outside the home.

Many dogs are great with people outside, but have trouble as soon as they step inside.

Ideally, the very first person you do a set-up with should be a family member or friend who your dog already welcomes into the home, so that you can get some baseline information about how your dog may behave in the set-up situation. Using Mark and Move and having a leash and other safety devices may signal to your dog that something is different, so you should test that out and see how she behaves. Doing Mark and Move in 'normal' situations also keeps your dog from making an association that this kind of behavior from you means there's danger.

Let's take a look at how you would work with a stranger. Your dog may take more time on this with your first helper, but then the process of turning a stranger into an accepted friend will go faster and faster. Eventually you will skip the pre-work and go right to letting the people into the house. But laying down this foundation makes things run more smoothly for your dog. I have very specific steps laid out in the example below. It might still be going too quickly for your dog. Be ready to add in more gradual changes to set your dog up for success.

Say you start by doing BAT with your dog, Denali, and your human helper, Max, outside the home. In this example, I'm assuming you have a house and a yard. If you have neither of those things, don't worry. Everyone's setting is different. It does take some extra brainstorming and creativity to figure out how to arrange a low-stress environment when you live in a high-rise apartment, but it's possible. In any case, I recommend hiring a professional trainer to help you through these steps, because the details are so important, and they are different for every dog and every family.

Let's get back to our example. Let's say Denali has a bite history and she is has been taught to wear a muzzle. For the first session, you meet Max in a totally neutral location, like a park. Denali quickly warms up to Max in that location and you go on a walk together. Even though Denali seems very comfortable, you have her wearing her muzzle so that everybody is safe. By the end, Denali has greeted Max nicely. If Denali solicits petting, Max uses the 5-second rule for petting (see Chapter 13). In the second session, you take Denali on a walk around your neighborhood in her muzzle and you encounter Max, who is walking away from you. You do a following version of BAT and sometimes Max moves farther ahead and then walks back toward you in an arc.

You take a 10-minute break near your house where Denali does Sprinkles or works on a frozen food puzzle or muzzle-cicle that you have prepared in advance. Max stays out of sight for the break but has some way to stay in contact with you, like a cellphone. When the food puzzle is finished, you message Max, put the muzzle back on and do a bit of Sprinkles. After a minute or so, Max returns. The activity is so that Denali isn't standing around stressed out. You could also just be walking and having Denali sniff real things in the area. When Max returns you do BAT some more, being aware that Max coming back into view is a Sudden Environmental Contrast.

Now that you've done your prep work, Max will actually go into the house on the next visit. Start like the second session above, where Denali is out for a walk and encounters Max. Do a bit of BAT so that you know Denali remembers Max and is comfortable. Walk back toward the house together, with Max in front. Have Max move to various places around the outside of the house, while you follow Denali around using BAT 2.0 and a long leash.

The main thing we are doing outside is to recreate the triggers your dog will experience inside. This lets us work at lower intensity, because your dog can move around more freely outside and the context is different. For example, have some lawn chairs out so that Max can sit in them and occasionally get up and move to another chair. At first, only have Max stand up when Denali is at a safe distance away, because that's usually a trigger for dogs. Max standing up is a Sudden Environmental Contrast, so use the same tips mentioned above for SEC, like starting out with Mark and Move. Other variations for your helper: getting up and disappearing around a corner for a bit, then coming back (as guests do when using your restroom—build up duration from a very brief exit, as dogs behave as if they have forgotten the guest was there), sitting next to a family member, hugging or interacting with a family member, etc.

Mark and Move is good to use when beginning with SEC work, but another reason to use Mark and Move is that you're working close to the house, which is a less interesting spot for Denali to just sniff on her own. Boredom can build up cortisol and make an outburst more likely. Doing Sprinkles is another option to relieve boredom. Max can even be the one to scatter the Parmesan cheese or treats. If you use treats, make sure that Denali can actually eat them with her muzzle on. If Max gives Denali any treats, they should be tossed in such a way that Denali moves farther away in order to get them. That gives Denali the option of stopping the interaction or choosing to return. Do be careful, though. Some dogs may misinterpret the hand motion and react.

When Max opens the door, Denali may become alarmed, so you would want to do that only when Denali is a safe distance away (and she is outside). Try to keep things casual and light. Next have Max go inside and sit somewhere, followed by Denali. Use the tips on parallel play when working inside. Why? Chances are, even with all of that prep work, there will be a trigger you didn't plan for, and the small space may make Denali less likely to use her new skills. You might need to have a shorter leash (still loose) or an ex-pen around Max for safety. Denali could have a muzzle-cicle or muzzle-friendly food puzzle to work on so that there's something to do besides for just obsessing about Max. If you are not worried about biting or you have a physical barrier, then you can go without the muzzle and have a regular food puzzle.

Do this for a bit and then have everybody head outside to reduce the arousal. Be sure to have Denali away from Max (maybe even go outside first) when Max stands up, because this could be a trigger. Go for another short walk together. In the next round, have Max sit somewhere else. That is probably already plenty for one visit. You might stop at the lawn furniture or the door-opening scene, for example, or after a few minutes of sitting in the first chair inside. Watch your dog's arousal level. It should be low throughout the process. In the next visit, you do an abbreviated version of the outside work and then have Max come in and sit in a new chair. Pay attention to the relative position of Max's chair and where Denali normally rests, as that may be more of a challenge than a chair farther away.

For the next visit, you do the things you practiced outside but now you are inside the house. Over time, you'll take less and less time to introduce Denali to your guests. You'll also provide fewer distractions inside, but I would recommend having a food puzzle for Denali when you have guests for a good long while. Try to have the food puzzle appear as a result of the guest arriving, not the other way around. If you're at the point where you are going without the muzzle, you can even put a pre-stuffed food puzzle outside the door and have your guest bring it in. At first they would just hand the puzzle to the dog, but as she's gets more and more comfortable with company, have Denali sit, then they give her the puzzle. That helps build and maintain a positive association.

When it's time to go off leash, use pretty much the same techniques, paying extra attention to whether you need to interrupt a build-up of excitement. Make sure you have a solid recall cue trained with positive reinforcement. Stationing, such as a positively trained Go to Your Bed cue, is another great way to move the dog around because you can tell her to go somewhere else, not just back to you. If you are trying to separate two dogs with issues, having them both come back to you is not the safest option. Your dog's station (where he goes on cue) can be a bed, chair, crate, or other target. Watch body language to be sure that your dog is not stressed at her station. You can use stationing to get movement when doing Mark and Move. For example, say you are sitting next to Max on the couch and you see Denali give a cut-off signal like turning her head away from Max, you can say "Yes, Go to Your Bed." Denali then runs away from Max, over to her bed. Then you can get up and feed her on her bed, use a remote treat dispenser like the PetTutor, or cue her to get a toy and bring it to you.

Even when your dog is pretty comfortable with guests, it can
help to have a chew toy as an outlet for extra stress.

As I mentioned, you may need to take things more slowly or you may be able to progress faster than what I described here. Keep an eye on what happens when Denali first meets a stranger outside. If you have been pushing things, and going too fast, she may start to make a negative association with meeting people outside. She might start barking or scanning the moment she realizes that this is a set-up. If that happens, take a look at your training plan and change something. You may need to work with more distance, do shorter sessions, etc. You can also do pseudo-set-ups where you act as if it's a set-up to bring in a guest, but really you're just going for a walk.

For a dog who is afraid of and/or aggressive toward people, having guests in your home is really big deal. It's like winning a gold medal at the Olympics. Training for such a difficult task takes time and careful practice. As they say, it's not "practice makes perfect," but rather "perfect practice makes perfect." To build a solid foundation for years to come, take your time to set your dog up for success. This may be in the form of rehabilitation, as we have talked about so far in this book, or early socialization, which we will discuss next.

CHAPTER 13

BAT for Puppy Socialization

Don't skip this chapter. You may not have a puppy now, but chances are you will have a puppy or an older dog who is new to you some day. You can use what you have learned so far about Behavior Adjustment Training to help that puppy or dog during the socialization process. Getting things right the first time is a whole lot easier than rehabilitation! If you are a trainer teaching puppy classes or working with rescue dogs, please pay special attention to this chapter. If you have a puppy, you can use this information to help your puppy avoid reactivity problems. You can also use it as a litmus test when choosing whether a group class is the right choice for your puppy, and if so, which one.

Raising a puppy is like launching a space shuttle—you have a tight schedule to prepare for the mission (of life), and repairing things afterwards is a whole lot harder than the initial assembly. Unlike launching a space shuttle, everybody thinks they already know how to raise a puppy. But things change over time, as new information comes out, and all dogs have different needs and personality quirks, so we can't stick with the way we have always done things.

I wish I could do Peanut's puppyhood over. I would have tried to get him before he landed in the shelter, or urged his family to wait just two more weeks until his fear period was over before they gave him up. Most importantly, I would have integrated BAT into his everyday life, which means that I would have watched his responses more closely and honored his requests for distance from triggers so that he could have become brave. I would have stopped shoveling so much food in his face so that he could notice the naturally occurring reinforcers he could get from interacting with strangers. I am doing my best to do all of those things with my new puppy, Bean.

You can weave BAT into a puppy's socialization process by watching her behavior. When she goes to check something out on a walk, use your BAT leash skills to let her investigate without leash pressure. Follow her if she is still curious and wants to approach or learn more. Slow Stop or call her back if it looks like she's going to get herself into trouble or is scaring a person or another puppy. When she decides that she has investigated enough and is ready to move on, say your Let's Go cue and walk her away. Feel free to praise and/or treat her for coming with you.

That doesn't mean to forego heel altogether, but heel for only a short period and then let your puppy go back to learning about his world. The time your puppy spends focused on you is time that he is not expanding his map of what's 'normal' in his environment. Even though you have been a million places with your puppy, if he never stopped working with you in those locations, you still risk under-socialization, one of the key causes of reactivity.

Training with treats is important, but if puppies are always in working mode, they miss out on learning about the world.

Socialization with people

People love petting dogs. I do, and I have to admit that's a huge reason why I have dogs and why I love working with dogs full time. Unfortunately, most people disrespect a dog's need for space. They walk straight up and shove their 'paws' in the dog's face. Or worse, they excitedly put their 'paws' up on a dog's head and shoulders and pat. Vertical play is something we usually try to avoid in puppy play time (lots of jumping up on each other's shoulders), but ironically, that's what people do to dogs all the time. Then we wonder why they get so excited and try to jump up!

Children hug and kiss dogs and do all sorts of things that primates find soothing, but which are rude from the dog's perspective. People cause dogs pain sometimes—kids pull at their tails/ears/fur, vets poke them with needles, groomers clip their nails. (I think nail clipping probably feels like a bite to a dog.) Given all of those things, it's actually kind of impressive that many dogs don't bite more often.

Dogs do need body contact from loved ones, but much of what kids do to dogs is risky for bites.

One key element of socialization is for a puppy to enjoy meeting and greeting people, despite their unintentional rudeness. You can use some of what you have learned about BAT to make this process a success. As children or adults come up to your puppy, you can tell her to "Go say hi," and then allow an interaction to occur based on the puppy's behavior. This is an optional cue, based on what she wants at the time, not something you are paying her heavily to do. If the puppy walks up to say hello, then let the person greet your puppy.

When your puppy turns away from the person, shift your weight back or step back to create some space, that way the puppy has the option of moving farther away from the person. If you think the puppy wants to move but is stuck, happily call the puppy back so that she is out of reach of whoever she just met. Praise the puppy for coming back to you, and then go back to the 'follow your dog' aspect of BAT. If she wants to go say "hi" again, let her. It's also fine if she doesn't want to go back to the person. Just keep things upbeat and walk away with her. Better yet, if the person has time and your puppy is not trying to get away, you can also just stay with the person and let your dog explore around. Move away if that's what the puppy wants. Chat until the puppy decides to go check the person out again, and repeat the above process. If she's jumping up to greet, just kneel down and slip your finger through the chest strap of her harness so she can move around but can't jump up. Ask the person to kneel down too, so they are less scary and/or your puppy is less likely to jump.

Don't let people scare your puppy during a greeting. This puppy can't escape.

Help the children in your life learn to respect your puppy's requests for space. There's a great mobile app illustrated by Lili Chin called Dog Decoder. It shows body language in an easy-to-use format. Socializing your puppy with children is a great chance to educate them on dog body language and the **5-Second Rule**. Actually, adults could use that rule, too. Let the puppy start the greeting, no more than 5 seconds, then pause to wait for the puppy to start the process again.

Here's an excerpt about the 5-Second Rule from the *Ahimsa Dog Training Manual:*

> *After at most 5 seconds of petting, pull your hands away and see what your dog does. If she nuzzles your hand or looks at you, she probably enjoyed the petting. If she holds in one place or turns/moves away, you were pestering her.*

The cut-off signals that can be reinforced for reactivity—like lookaways, head turns, body turns, ground sniffing, shaking off—can and should be reinforced in puppies. Ideally that would be a naturally occurring reinforcement, but you may need to step in to reinforce the behavior with space. Very young puppies learn cut-off signals during play fights in the litter and with other dogs. We can help continue their normal development by reinforcing those behaviors in their new homes. Kids should learn to calmly step back and/or turn to the side in response to puppies who do cut-off signals. This is for the child's own safety and helps empower the puppy.

Puppies have short attention spans and when they give a cut-off signal to 'ask' for distance, they don't mean that they want to be alone forever. They just need a little relief from the social pressure. When a child steps back after seeing a cut-off signal, the puppy will pause only briefly before following the child, and the game will be on again. Doing this kind of exercise can help make children aware of what a dog's body language says about the dog's emotional state and willingness to engage in petting or play. Children can use their own cut-off signals to calm down boisterous puppies.

When a puppy's requests for distance are being consistently reinforced, she becomes more resilient and can learn to be more patient with humans and persistent with her polite requests for distance. In the first BAT book, I wrote that we can wean off the reinforcement of responding to the puppy's need for space. I now know that not to be true. For one thing, in real life, we automatically have to ignore some requests for space. There's no need to add that in deliberately. So if your puppy needs space and you can make that happen, go for it.

As you work with a puppy, she should gradually be getting braver. At some point, there may be a period where things are suddenly more scary—there is a sensitive period at about eight to ten weeks of age and then later in adolescence for a few weeks when they're about six to twelve months old. If you see your puppy suddenly get stressed about something that's minor, she's probably in a sensitive period. In that case, just be patient and tone down your puppy's experiences so that she doesn't accidentally become sensitized. *Always help your puppy stay below threshold, respond to requests for space whenever possible, and be aware that the threshold changes as the puppy develops.*

For a puppy who shows a lot of fear, make sure people don't accidentally punish her tentative explorations by trying to pet her (if she's afraid of people, she may perceive their petting as punishment, something to avoid). As the puppy goes up to the person, have them toss a treat and then back away. This can happen repeatedly, and it builds up confidence and interest very quickly. What I just described is one way to do "Treat and Retreat" by Suzanne Clothier. This isn't just for puppies; I also like using Treat and Retreat for adult dogs who are afraid of people. BAT also applies here: if you can't ask the stranger to back away, just use Mark and Move—call your puppy away before the stranger can pet her. Give her a treat and let her go investigate again. Just be sure to fade the food!

Socialization with dogs and other non-human animals

Dog-dog interaction is another important element of the socialization process. Puppies need to become friends with dogs of all breeds and sizes and also meet the various other animals that they might encounter in their lives. I discussed socialization with people separately because dogs definitely view humans as being in a different category—some dogs are only reactive to people, some only to dogs, and some to both. So puppies need to be socialized to people and dogs, as well as other species of animals. With animals (including humans), help your dog make several real, beloved friends—not just acquaintances—of each species; this builds a positive connection and practice communicating on a deeper, more advanced level.

Tip for Pros: The BAT leash skills are really useful for puppies, but long leashes are hard to use in a puppy class. Group walks are an excellent service to offer to your puppy clients (or even all of your clients). Just be sure to take vaccination status into account. You can work on socialization, leash handling skills, leash training for the dog, proofing, and everything else that might be encountered during the walk. For marketing, share videos on social media and/or have a specific route that stops at a locally-owned pet store or other pet services. Check in at the shop on Facebook with a photo of your students.

Nowadays, many puppies get their first major exposure to other puppies outside of their family in puppy kindergarten classes. Puppy classes are not appropriate for all dogs. Please consider your own puppy's socialization as well as the experience of the other puppies in class. Most dogs already do a form of BAT naturally—if another dog turns away, sits facing away or shakes off, for example, then most dogs will pause for a bit or play bow or do something else to decrease the stress of the situation. That's really all BAT is: facilitating the natural socialization process. While some puppies learn these body language skills from their mother and littermates, some are not adept at reading other breeds of dogs, or are clumsy because of growth, so people often need to step in during puppy play. If a puppy is bullying or scared in class, or if you are experienced and can spend time setting up sufficient opportunities, it may be better to do initial socialization in very small groups instead of classes.

If you have a puppy, it's important to recognize when your own puppy is giving cut-off signals to request distance from another dog. Let's say that your puppy is in a playtime and you see him turn his back on a female puppy and start to slowly walk away from her. The other puppy follows, pouncing. Help honor your puppy's request for safety by going in to distract the other puppy: pet her calmly or call her away to give your puppy a chance to escape. Let her caregivers know what you are trying to do, and why. If the other puppy is persistently going after your puppy, you or her caregivers can pick her up and set her down somewhere else in the room. Do not yell, shake the puppy, or add anything else scary or painful.

If a puppy is consistently bullying the other puppies (ignoring cut-off signals), it's the trainer's responsibility to find a way to provide socialization experiences for that puppy which are safe for the other puppies. Here are some options for trainers: separate play groups so that dogs are in with appropriate play partners; a toy for the puppy to carry might keep her teeth busy (or could cause resource guarding, so watch out); consistent time outs; or a well-socialized/clean/vaccinated adult dog to play with instead of the other puppies. If you can't bring an adult dog to the class, the puppy who is bullying can play with the owner or do self-control exercises during puppy play. Then schedule some individual play sessions with well-socialized adult dogs—supervising yourself for a fee or by sharing a resource like a list of other dogs looking for playmates. I created a database for Ahimsa Dog Training clients and it has been quite useful for that. Keeping play sessions short and encouraging the caregivers of the puppy who is bullying to exercise in advance can also help. If they're willing to do private lessons, some BAT set-ups would do the puppy a lot of good! Use the advice in this book to teach replacement behavior for frustration.

> Tip for Pros: If there is an aggression issue, puppyhood is the time to work on it, and part of our responsibility as trainers is to help people see the red flags. Encourage the caregivers to do private lessons or point out other resources for reactivity. They may still be able to attend class in a limited way, but if it is not in their best interest (over-threshold) or the interest of the other puppies, then find another solution.

Your puppy is not the only one doing cut-off signals, so it's important to notice when your puppy doesn't respect those signals from another dogs. Puppies are still learning, after all. Watch the other dogs and puppies that your puppy greets. If you recognize the other dog giving cut-off signals, wait for your dog to respond to them appropriately. But, if she doesn't, call your puppy to redirect her or go pick her up and give your puppy a time out (fifteen to thirty seconds of boring time in your arms). You can also use Mark and Move, as described in Chapter 7.

Give your puppy a chance to meet cats and other flight-prone animals in a way that won't make the other animals run away. For example, have the cat up on a surface, like a couch or cat tree, with the puppy on leash and in a harness. This gives the cat a safer position and makes her likely to stay put. When your puppy investigates this new animal and then turns away, calmly praise the puppy and step back to see if he wants to move away. If your dog was a little too focused, you may need to step up your training a notch: motivate the moving away more by doing some Mark and Move, with a food puzzle as a reinforcer. This lets your puppy settle down more between repetitions, lets the cat relax, and also creates an association: See Cat → Go Get Kong. Switch back to the 'follow your dog' version of BAT 2.0 as soon as you can. If that's not working, then stick with and generalize the concept of See Cat → Go Get Kong. It's not BAT, but it's useful!

It's ideal to have your dog meet other species when he is very young.

If you know that your cat will be afraid of your puppy, do BAT with the cat as the 'student.' Start with the puppy in a pen with a food puzzle to keep her busy. Let the cat approach at her own pace and calmly retreat. You might also see if your friends have cats that are comfortable with dogs and will not run away. Meeting those cats first gives your puppy a chance to meet cats as companions, versus chase toys. You can reinforce social behavior or self-control using clicker training (see Appendix 1) or Mark and Move. I used to go to a pet supply store that had three cats who were very dog savvy and held their ground. They made excellent puppy socializers.

Exposure to surfaces, crates, noises, and other experiences
In addition to socialization with humans, dogs, and other species, puppies need positive exposure to inanimate objects, noises and all sorts of things. They need to learn how their bodies work, and how to control them on a variety of different surfaces. As with rehabilitation for reactivity, I tend to use more treats with puppies in situations that don't require them to be aware of social cues. When socializing with dogs and people, I want the puppy to pay a lot of attention to the dogs and people so I use treats carefully. When I'm just trying to get her to walk on a slippery floor or get into a crate, I use Mark and Move with treats much more freely, but I still try to stop using food soon, so that they can get a sense of what their bodies are doing and how best to move. Proprioception is an important part of learning how to exist in the world, and if we are always distracting them with food, they miss out.

Like a child learning to ride a bike without training wheels, when socializing a puppy treats should be used with care and faded quickly so the dog can get his own balance.

In my first BAT book, I gave an example of a puppy named Lulu who was afraid of slippery floors. I would have trained slightly differently if I knew then what I know now. To illustrate the updates in the BAT technique, I have shared an edited version of my original example.

Lulu loved the clicker, so I used it to mark her good behavior of approaching the tile floor of the kitchen. I worked with her off leash, starting in the carpeted hallway. I tossed a treat at the edge of the kitchen tile to make it more interesting, and then walked with her in the hallway toward the kitchen. When she sniffed toward the treat, I clicked and walked her away from the kitchen down the hall a few feet and fed her a treat. I turned around and we approached the kitchen again. (With BAT 2.0 you would stay out of the way and wait for her to turn around in that direction, not lead her there.)

This time she snatched up the treat, I clicked, called her away from the kitchen, and gave her another treat. I tossed another treat into the kitchen, this time about six inches into the tile floor. As she headed in for the treat, I clicked, walked back away from the kitchen, and fed her. She was free to go get that treat or come with me, but my leaving gave her the option to leave the kitchen, which she did. Then I tossed a treat into the center of the kitchen and clicked/retreated/treated about ten more times, each time trying to click while she was still moving into the kitchen, but further and further into the room. On our next approach, I clicked as her nose headed toward the floor, as she snatched up the treat from the middle of the room. We retreated and I treated again. After that, I repeated without food on the floor for a few more trials, still clicking for the same behavior of kitchen-ward motion.

After about a total of fifteen treats worth of Mark and Move, I started just clicking for having four paws on the tile floor, treating in the kitchen, and then walking away as the reinforcer, for another thirteen treats. Note that's not quite Mark and Move any more, but I was building up the value of the location. The relief of leaving the kitchen was weakening, and the joy of getting treats in the kitchen was getting stronger. Remember that she was off leash, and after those thirteen additional treats in the kitchen, she didn't want to leave the kitchen any more. I came back and gave her a jackpot: a handful of treats all over the kitchen floor.

This kind of training can apply to any spot that the dog doesn't want to be in, whether it's a crate, a car, a surface the dog doesn't feel comfortable being on, or a location with a scary noise. The key is that the dog can leave whenever she wants, but you actually call her away before she's uncomfortable and gradually increase the value of being in the scary place or on the scary surface. You can do the same sort of thing with socialization with humans, too, if the dog is very avoidant.

With sounds, like thunder, fireworks, or babies crying, you can get a recording to help your puppy get used to the sound. Terry Ryan has a CD series called *Sound Socialization* designed to acclimate dogs to such types of sounds, the Company of Animals has a CD called *CLIX Noises & Sounds,* and Victoria Stilwell has the *Canine Noise Phobia Series,* which has calming background music (see Resources). You can also get sounds for free from YouTube. For example, Epic Fireworks in the UK has a YouTube channel to which they upload a new short video each day. I subscribed to their channel so that YouTube would send me a reminder to play firework sounds every day for Bean.

Take the time to get your dog comfortable with the sound of fireworks,
but don't go to the show!

Help your dog desensitize to a variety of firework sounds. On YouTube, you can play multiple videos in a row or you can focus on one type of firework. The volume may be higher on some and lower on others, so watch out for that. The squealing fireworks tend to be scariest for the dogs I have had, but your dog may be different. When playing sounds, always test the volume with your puppy out of the room, so you don't accidentally play it too loudly. I start with the volume down to the lowest notch on my computer and also reduce the sound within the YouTube player. If you have a Bluetooth speaker, you can help your dog generalize by playing the sounds in many locations, not just right next to you or in one particular room, or even only inside. Using a phone, you play the sounds from a Bluetooth speaker all around town.

I like desensitizing a dog's response to noises by using those sounds as markers for behavior. This is an empowering way to do counter-conditioning, because the dog controls the onset of the noises. In other words, you can play a recording of the sound just as if you were clicking a clicker with a behavior your dog already offers easily, like a sit. You only cue the behavior a few times, to jumpstart it, but mostly the dog should be offering the behavior, then you mark (play the sound) and reinforce. The behavior becomes what I call a **More Please Signal**, a way for the dog to say "please play that sound, because I know it leads to treats." I talk about this concept in the Cooperative Care member videos in the Animal Building Blocks Academy. More Please Signals are great for teaching a dog actively cooperate in grooming, vet care, etc. The dog can use them to indicate readiness for counter-conditioning procedures. For example, a chin target is a good More Please Signal for a jugular blood draw. The dog holds that position and then you touch his neck with a finger and feed a treat. Building up slowly over time, you can do an actual blood draw with little to no restraint.

You don't necessarily need to use the More Please Signal for sounds, but it is more empowering than standard counter-conditioning. The standard way is, however, a bit easier: all you do is play the sound at a low volume, give your dog something great (like his breakfast in a food puzzle), and turn off the sound just before he finishes the food.

A third way is to teach your puppy about the sound in a relaxing way that gives time to process the information. Choose a time when your puppy is resting, but not asleep. Play it at low volume, just enough that you think the puppy can hear it. What you are looking for is no response or a very tiny one, like the ears turning toward the sound or a slight shift of body position. When the puppy is done listening, the ears will shift back to neutral. 'Overtrain' by playing the sound for another several minutes. Note: don't confuse lack of interest with fear—if your puppy is moving away from the sound in avoidance, the ears are pinned back, the breath rate goes up, or you see any other signs of stress, it's too loud.

Replay the same sounds again but this time, turn it up tiny bit higher than before. Over many sessions, you can eventually have it pretty loud. *The point is not to see how loud you can get it, but to try to turn the volume up gradually enough that the puppy barely notices the difference.* That's how you measure success. If you do this with an older dog, expect to go even more slowly. If the puppy gets up or shows signs of distress, turn down the sound halfway and do something fun for your puppy, like tossing a handful of treats to find, feeding a food puzzle, or doing a little easy clicker training, then turn the sound off. Wait for a while and next time, increase the volume more gradually.

The point of socialization is not just to teach the puppy about specific stimuli that he might encounter as an adult, but also to give him experience coping with novelty. BAT allows for a puppy to learn this kind of skill, rather than just what my dog Peanut initially learned via our classical counter-conditioning phase, which is that "people give me food, other dogs make mom give me food, and skateboards make mom give me food." That was helpful in getting him over a lot of his fears, but I felt like he didn't really take the time to check things out without my interference. Looking back, it was like I was trying to make up his mind for him by treating him whenever something potentially scary came along. He didn't really learn to trust the world on its own merit or to accurately determine the safety of a situation, but he made many positive associations. This didn't serve him well as an adult when something different came along. By contrast, a puppy socialized with BAT learns to gather information about his environment, trust what he learns, and to diffuse tension when he needs to. He knows how to cope with the world as it is, because his handler gave him time to check things out.

CHAPTER 14

For Trainers and Behaviorist Consultants: Using BAT with Clients

Note: I have chosen to use citations in parts of this chapter and in Appendix 3 where appropriate as trainers and behaviorists may wish to read additional material on the subjects covered. Sources cited are listed in the Resources section at the end of the book.

Before you start coaching your clients how to do BAT, please watch some of my videos on how to do it! It's one thing to get the description from a book. It's different to actually make decisions, moment to moment, that set the dog up for success with BAT. I love that you are reading this book because it gives you the theoretical underpinnings and a way to apply that knowledge. But there's something about actually watching it happen. I have a lot of videos out there, including free videos on my YouTube channel and GrishaStewart.com and the full-length DVD series that is also available in streaming format. If you find a BAT video on YouTube, make sure what you are watching is the most current version of BAT. And if it's not me, make sure it's actually done in a way that I would recommend. There are a lot of BAT videos online that have some room for improvement. If you aren't sure about the accuracy of a video, you can always post to the Grisha Stewart Facebook page to ask. If you really want to make sure you are doing BAT well, share videos for assessment in the BAT Chats on my site, take an online course or attend an advanced BAT seminar with hands-on practice. If there is a CBATI near you, they can provide 1-on-1 mentoring to improve your coaching skills. I also mentor trainers via video chat.

Clients want to know how to help their dogs become safer and less reactive immediately, if not sooner. Trainers need to assess their canine clients' reactivity and then guide the caregivers through a behavior modification plan. In this chapter, I'll discuss some of what I do to teach clients how to use BAT in private lessons with dogs who are reactive to people, dogs or both. I will also talk about BAT in group classes for dogs who are reactive to other dogs. You can also use BAT in puppy classes and private lessons to provide socialization experiences, as I covered in Chapter 13.

Keeping your clients and their dogs safe

The big picture is that you should let the dog have maximal control within a safe zone that you create and maintain. Make sure the handler understands the leash skills before doing a set-up with a trigger. My favorite way to do this is to use TAGteach, which is used to teach skills when time and precision matter. The free *BAT Leash Skills* handout on GrishaStewart.com breaks leash handling into several distinct behaviors for your clients to rehearse. Start with role-playing—the client is the dog, you are the handler, then switch—rather than trying to teach two species at once. Have the client tag you (with the clicker) for doing each of the leash skills correctly, then swap roles and tag them. Next, have them practice the leash skills with their dog. Do this in a spot with interesting smells and no triggers in view. You may even want to subtly scatter some treats in the area, so that the dog will move around.

Think of the shoreline on a beach as the threshold between curiosity and fear/aggression/frustration. The handler should follow the dog as long as the dog is below threshold. If the dog approaches the threshold, the handler should slowly stop the dog, wait for disengagement, praise, and then follow the dog's next move.

If you didn't immediately see the stressed body and tight leash, don't coach BAT to clients yet.

If the dog goes over-threshold during your set-up or if you have no way to create a set-up in which the dog is fully below threshold, use the least intrusive prompt to help the dog disengage from the helper. In a very small space, like an apartment, that might involve something like clicking or calling the dog as soon as the dog sees the trigger, then moving away to regroup and eat the treats off of the floor. Whenever you need to intrude on the process beyond slowly stopping the dog at his threshold, take another look at your antecedent arrangements and change something to set the dog up for success next time. For example, if you have to immediately call or click when the dog sees the trigger in his home, is it possible to work outside where you might not need to prompt at all, and then gradually get closer to the door and eventually move inside? (See Chapter 12 for details.)

The illustration of the beach with the Support Scale in Chapter 4 has suggestions for what you might do from the least to most intrusive option. As a professional, you may have your own favorite ways to intervene or your own ways to prompt disengagement (for example, by laughing, sighing, or singing if the dog appears stuck) or to reinforce movement away (say, with agility jumps or scent games after he moves away). Just remember that we still want to avoid working mode; we want the dog's attention to be focused on taking in information as a dog, not on working for you.

Distractions and food

A lack of distraction allows the dog to practice more natural social skills with the trigger. The research on attention in desensitization is mostly on humans and the results are somewhat mixed, but except for situations in which something is physically happening to the body (like a blood draw), distracting the person seems to reduce desensitization effects (Telch, et al., 2004; Mohlman and Zinbarg, 2001; Haw and Dickerson, 1998).

Avoid always having food in your set-ups. Food is a giant context cue, and as we know from what I discussed above, fear is likely to return when the context is different from the training context (Thomas, Cutler, and Novak, 2012; Capaldi, Viveiros, and Campbell, 1983). That means that treats or toys can become like Dumbo the Elephant's magic feather: the fear comes right back if your client doesn't have them. Fortunately, treats are not required for BAT set-ups, so we can easily avoid having the treats become a context for the good

Only use food when you need focus. Working mode is not ideal for BAT.

experiences that dogs have during BAT. Additionally, your prompts and cues also provide context, they distract the dog, and they are intrusions to the dog's control over what is happening. Prompts and cues should be used only when needed.

How BAT has changed for trainers

The new version of BAT has the handler more in the background, with fewer prompts. If you are familiar with the older version of BAT, I would like you to notice that this new version is more fluid and has the dogs working at a distance where they are truly below threshold. If you are one of the many people who have been successfully using BAT with clients, you will be happy to hear that the old Stages can still fit within this model as ways to prompt behavior if the dog accidentally goes over-threshold. Prompting after the cut-off signal in the old Stage 3 can be used as a way to encourage the dog to walk away at times when he is up to his ankles in water on the stress chart—for example, when the dog takes more than two seconds to disengage. Stage 2 can be used for times when the dog is up to his neck in the water (say, your training space is too small for him to cope otherwise). Stage 1 can be used whenever the dog is in over his head.

In this section, I'm mentioning the old BAT stages to help you integrate BAT 1.0 with the new 2.0 info. I don't actually recommend teaching these variations of Mark and Move as numbered stages. Simplify it for your clients. You can just teach a solid recall cue or use a clicker for Mark and Move. The clicker in the old Stages 1 and 2 marked behavior you like, but it also basically serves as a recall cue in those cases. Yes, I did just write that the clicker works as a recall cue here. It does, of course, also mark acceptable behavior. In this use of the clicker, however, you are in survival mode and its most useful feature is that the dog returns back to the handler for the treat or other reinforcer. That is, it is operating as a recall cue.

The prompt or verbal marker in the old Stage 3 also moves the dog away, and is useful if the dog is a bit stuck on what to do next. Even though they are useful get-away tools, it is better to set up situations in which we do not need the old Stages. That said, when you are close to the trigger or have to work in tight spaces, you will probably need to use more Mark and Move because the dog is more likely to quickly go over-threshold. It is always good to be on the safe side, because when we mess up, it is the dogs who suffer the consequences.

I have always emphasized that the Stages were not meant to be done in numerical order, but rather to be used whenever necessary, using the highest Stage the dog can do at that time. I've done away with the concept of Stages for the current version of BAT for a couple of reasons. For one thing, people used Stage 1 and 2 too frequently during set-ups. This resulted in the training getting stuck in management mode, versus 'real' BAT. More importantly, Stage 3 was often done over-threshold—even by me—in the early years. I am hoping this new conceptualization of BAT will encourage people to truly set things up so that the dog is consistently below threshold and in control of the direction this process takes.

The Stages in the older version of BAT were useful for teaching handlers to notice the various bits of body language that they need to know. You can certainly do a separate exercise to practice body language skills before the first BAT set-up with a trigger. For example, you can place a treat pouch at a distance and have the handler click for signs of disengagement. Click and treat for behavior that you want the handler to notice, and then have handlers do the same.

What's the dog's problem? Get a good history

I recommend getting most of your client's history in advance, so that you know what to expect and save time. You can always ask follow-up questions to get information that you still need to choose a behavioral intervention. The easiest way to do this is to provide an online form for your clients in private lessons and Growly Dog classes. A written history gives clients a chance to efficiently share their dog's history, target behaviors to eliminate or change, and goals. My form includes the dog's major medical history, how and why the dog was acquired, the dog's daily lifestyle, training history, and more. I can quickly read through this form and then ask other questions in person during the session. Keep in mind that people are not always honest or detailed enough in a written form, so you may need to pry a bit to get all of the details of a dog's situation.

Even with a history of allergies, pay attention to itchiness. Stress makes itchiness worse.

Questions should always be directly related to helping the situation, not just satisfying your curiosity. Only ask questions that affect what you do with the client or what you do with the dog. In terms of the client, your questions should be directed at things like building relationship, determining their motivations/reinforcers for working with you, seeing the amount of homework they can handle, and what style of explanations would most benefit the person. For the dog, you are collecting information that will help you choose the intervention (BAT or something else, or a combo), reinforcers that will work for this animal, thresholds in various situations, and what management needs to be put into place for safety and stress reduction.

Here are some of the topics that I ask about on my form and in the interview for an accurate functional assessment to create an individualized plan:

- Contact information

- Names and ages of humans in home

- Names, ages, species, weight, and breeds of non-human animals in home, including the student dog

- How and why dog was acquired

- Primary trainer in the home

- Whether someone has given up on the dog and do they have authority to euthanize/rehome

- Detailed description of behaviors the client wants to change—antecedents, behaviors, consequences (dig into this further in the interview)

- Ranking of behavior the client wants to change (what is their priority?)

- Goals for what they want the dog to do (this is almost always not a measurable goal, so you can help the client rework these)

- Other professional trainers or behaviorists with whom they have worked. Are they still with them? If not, why not? (If you know the other trainers in your area this may give you a lot of information. Always take what the client says about previous trainers with a grain of salt, as it may just have been miscommunication.)

- What they have done to work on the problem in the past / how that worked

- Books, TV shows, etc. about dogs that they like

- What type of training they have done—clicker / choke chain / treats / shock

- Medications / last vet check / have they done a thorough vet check / vaccinations (A lot of behavioral issues have a medical basis, so they need a check-up, especially if the behavior chance was sudden)

- Bite history including puppy play biting

- Does the dog have any dog friends (more is better)

- Response to various stimuli and situations—men, women, children, being picked up, having food taken away, grooming, animals, etc.

- Behaviors that the dog knows, including tricks. How well does the dog know those behaviors? (gives indication of client's interest in training)

- Is the dog accustomed to a muzzle? If so, why and how? If not, why not?

- What type of building does the dog live in?

- Is there a fence? Real or invisible? How tall? Fully secure?

Knowing the dog's full history will help give you an idea of what needs to be done. BAT is a part of most of the training plans I come up with for reactivity, but it's rarely the only thing. There is always some management and some behavior modification for the dog's other issues that may not involve BAT. I might change antecedent arrangements or apply tools from *Control Unleashed* (see Resources), classical counter-conditioning, or clicker training, for example. To do BAT or any of these other methods well, you also need to tailor it to the individual dog in terms of where to start, how and when to change criteria, etc. Most importantly, though, watch the dog as you train. Regardless of what you know from the history, be ready to respond to what the dog is bringing to the table that day.

Private lessons

The show must go on! No matter what else is happening, we must keep dogs and their families safe in their daily lives. My first advice to new clients in private lessons is almost always along the lines of management—finding environmental changes that can be made to make the situation safer and improve everyone's quality of life. That's why this book focuses on Safety and Management Essentials (Chapter 3) before really digging into BAT. Look at the whole picture of the daily life of the dog and the family and see what can be done do in terms of distant or proximal antecedent arrangements. In other words, address the contributing factors in the environment, such as diet, exercise, use of barriers, etc. to set the dog up for success. Step one is to prevent dangerous situations. Step two is to reduce the dog's overall stress, so that the training you develop has a chance to kick in. That includes teaching some of the management tips from Chapter 3, but not so many that it overwhelms the client.

My private consultations are ninety minutes. Some cases are straightforward and I can quickly run through the history and management pieces and talk about training for most of the first session. In others, I find out that there is something dangerous happening and see that the family needs a lot of help with management. I need every last detail of what's going on, so that the clients and I can create a 24-hour management plan for the dog. In cases like that, we spend most of the first session going over things like muzzle training and ways to guarantee that doors and gates will be kept shut. This is usually the case when there are children in the family who are in danger from the dog or who might let the dog into an unauthorized area. It's also the case when dogs within the home are fighting. Careful planning and consistent execution of the plan are essential.

Safety and management are also important within the session itself. Most of my canine clients have issues with humans, including me, so I meet them online, at my office, or another neutral location to reduce their stress and ensure my safety. To set the dog up for success, the initial consult can be done completely without the dog, with the client bringing in a video. This is not always possible, but it's a good policy.

When clients do bring their dog to the first session, I have them leave the dog in the car for a moment (if it's safe) to talk about the plan for entering the training area. When they bring in the dog, I am already seated, so the dog is less likely to react badly to me. For the sake of the dog, my chair is placed a bit away from the family's chairs and is turned slightly sideways. The training area is enriched in advance with smells and various things for the dog to do, rather than just focus on me. I may have treats and give them to the dog if he comes up to me. I read the dog's history in advance, so that if I feel it's necessary, I can take other safety measures like putting an exercise pen around my chair, requiring the clients to use the wall tethers for their dog, or doing the first session completely without the dog. Most of my clients' dogs are not already used to the muzzle, so I use the fence and leashes and do not muzzle until later sessions, when the dog is ready.

Avoid making the client feel guilty or defensive when you suggest a safer muzzle and a harness.

If they have their dog on a prong collar, choke chain, or similar device, I discuss why I prefer harnesses. Empathy is important; people are just trying to do the best that they can. They have these kinds of collars as a way to try to fix the problem and want what's best for their dog and their families. Don't shame them if they have a tool that you wouldn't use. Instead of spending a lot of time on what they should not do, focus on what they do already know and link that to the benefits of your training advice. Don't say, "I'm not judging you," because that means that you are, indeed, judging them. Like dogs, people are not very receptive to new information when they're defensive.

If they forget their harness or want to try one out, I loan them one with a front- and rear-attachment. They have to put the harness on the dog themselves, making sure that the dog is not off leash at any point. I may supervise as they fit it, but I don't put it on their dog myself. Because the dog is usually reactive to people for my private cases, I can't move without stressing their dog. Even when the client reports that the dog has no people issues, I have the client fit the harness for the dog. For one thing, the client can be wrong about her dog's comfort level and for another, dogs don't really like having a stranger interact in that way. Why add extra stress?

Before I go to the home of a dog with reactivity to humans, we have already had training sessions outside of the home on the basics, like leash skills, a BAT overview, body language, and management. Whether or not their dog liked me outside of the home, I assume that these dogs won't love me coming over for a visit. Even if they will 'only' bark at me, with no history of biting, I try to limit any stress that I can. Besides, trigger stacking may create trouble during our session, so I usually start in-home sessions with a short walk. I message when I arrive and the clients meet me outside with their dog, in a carefully orchestrated introduction, basically the same way that I mentioned in Chapter 12, on teaching dogs to be comfortable with guests. I wait at least twenty feet away from their door, and start walking away when they come out. When the dog sees me, his first impression is of a person with treats, dropping food and walking away. That's not a huge threat. We just keep walking and they gradually catch up to me, using Suzanne Clothier's Treat and Retreat (see Appendix 2). If it's a safe enough situation, I eventually allow the dog to eat the treats from my hand.

If the dog has a history of biting, I have them condition a muzzle before I go to their house, have a physical barrier between us, or have the client keep the dog out of reach throughout the session. It's really important to me that the dog does not feel forced to bite me. I haven't been bitten by my reactivity clients, but a Golden Retriever puppy in kindergarten class really nailed me one time and I was bitten on my forehead and scalp as a child. Although I do have first-hand knowledge that dog bites hurt, my biggest concern is for the dog—I can heal, but the real damage is that the dog now has a more substantial bite history. In my opinion, a trainer should never risk causing a dog to bite him or her. Whatever you do, set up your session to be safe. For me, this includes escorting clients with reactivity to dogs to their car at the end to be sure there aren't loose dogs on the way.

Here's how I explain BAT to clients in private lessons. I start with a discussion of what they think is motivating the dog to bark, lunge, flee, or offer other reactive behaviors. Then we explore the concept of needs, primarily safety, and talk about distance as a functional reinforcer (without necessarily using that term). I describe how to do BAT set-ups and animate the BAT set-up illustration drawn by Lili Chin as I talk, to explain how we will basically be walking all over the place (see Chapter 6).

After a short overview of BAT, I explain the purpose of the leash skills and we begin practicing them. The leash skills are a practical way to get started, because they tend to immediately strengthen the client-dog relationship and reduce pulling. Besides, you can't really do a BAT set-up well without proper leash skills, so we begin there. I like to devote an entire session to leash skills, often without the dog. First I demonstrate and explain, and then have the client practice with me, an assistant, a stuffed dog, or even an office chair on wheels. If the student dog is comfortable being there, then we finish up by practicing with the dog. I know several CBATIs who bring their own dogs to these sessions and have clients handle the leash. When you practice with a real dog, I recommend setting up Sprinkles or other enrichments in advance, so the client can practice the concept of following the dog.

Some skills may be very easy for the client to do, so you can just demonstrate and they can immediately copy you. Other skills may take some specific focus, using TAG-teach, for example. Break it down into a simple behavior, and then start by tagging yourself (with the clicker) as you do the skill, then they tag you, then you tag them.

Your client must feel comfortable with the long line before you do a BAT set-up.

Knowing when to do a Slow Stop (and how to do it) is probably the most critical part of helping the dog stay below threshold. We spend a fair amount of time practicing the Slow Stop and learning about when to use it. Even after they know how to do a Slow Stop, the client will still need coaching on which behaviors indicate they should stop the dog. To get a fast response from the client during a set-up, I've found that it really helps to practice having the handler respond to specific cues from you to stop or call their dog. Otherwise, in the heat of the moment, they end up taking way too long to stop the dog and he goes over-threshold. Use consistent phrasing so they don't have to think about it, they can just react with what you taught them to do.

We are essentially doing a cue transfer. The cue that people learn most quickly is a vocal cue from the trainer, like "Slow Stop." The cues they are still working on come from the dog. Whenever you transfer a cue, you give the less familiar one, followed by the one that the learner knows well. In this case, your learners are the clients. They watch their dogs and if you see a need for a Slow Stop, say "Slow Stop," which translates the dog's body language into a previously learned verbal cue.

New Cue → Old Cue → Behavior

Cue from dog (moves directly at trigger) → Cue from trainer (Slow Stop) → client stops dog

I show my clients a video of BAT in action to demonstrate what a good set-up should look like. While they are learning the leash skills, it is hard also pay attention to the dog's small signals. I will certainly point out body language as we go, but video is really useful here. When we review a video from their own leash work, they can learn more about the specific body language that their dog does and how best to best respond. As we get into doing BAT and talking about Mark and Move, going over Lili's Good Choices illustration from Chapter 4 helps people notice those behaviors.

Before they begin working with the dog, be sure to discuss what to do if their dog starts to go over-threshold: call the dog back and take a break. They shouldn't have to wait for you to do prompt them during a session, but of course you will, if need be. Teach your clients to recognize the precursors to reactivity, i.e., behaviors that dogs typically do before they bark, growl, panic, etc. Depending on the client, I may also explain why it's counterproductive to give a leash correction or yell at the dog for overreacting. I usually sum it up by saying that *suppression just shuts down the warning system and we may end up with a silent biter*. I don't know about you, but that's the scariest kind of dog for me—one that looks ok, but then bites. This is an important point to get across if the client has previously done that type of training.

To help clients fully understand the concepts, I either print out or email links to the BAT handouts. You can find them at GrishaStewart.com and you are welcome to print them out for your clients or share the link to them on your website. Just please don't upload them to your own site, because I want to be able to have only the most up-to-date version of them online. Thanks to many kind translators around the world, the BAT handouts are available in several languages—if you don't see yours in there, but can translate, please let me know. Clients can share the BAT Basics handout with people doing set-ups with them, so that the helpers have a general idea of the process before they start (see Resources). Of course, this book is also a good resource. ☺

Before we start BATting with a trigger, the clients should be proficient at doing the leash skills and have a solid understanding of what to expect. Our first set-up is usually with a fake dog as the helper (for dogs who are only reactive to other dogs) or with me as the helper (unless the dog already loves me because of using Treat and Retreat). The client needs to know his role in the set-up before anything gets going. The client's tasks are to: 1) follow the dog; 2) listen for me to say "Slow Stop" and then do so; and 3) listen for me to say, "Call your dog," and then do so.

That's it. The client has already rehearsed doing 1, 2, and 3 without the trigger present. So he now just has to put it together with the dog potentially being more reactive. If he can also Slow Stop his dog if he sees his dog walking in a straight line toward the trigger, even better. That makes things more efficient. You can also practice this before the real set-up by having a super-fake trigger, like a treat bag or backpack, on the ground during the leash skills practice with Sprinkles.

With Mark and Move, I point out that the first and most important consequence is to move away. In the beginning, I do the marking and the client just needs to move away from the trigger and praise the dog as the bonus reward. You don't need to explain the many possibilities for Mark and Move the first time you teach it. Just tell them which behavior(s) you are marking and that you'll be using a verbal marker, like Yes. When you mark, that's your client's signal to walk away with the dog and praise. This is a useful activity to do when you are trying to coach the client, but the dog is reactive to you. Because you are a trigger who is also talking and watching the dog, it can be easier to start with Mark and Move than with the standard 'follow your dog' version of BAT 2.0. When they use a standard 6-foot leash, the leash skills don't technically have to be fabulous for Mark and Move. You can teach some Mark and Move first and do the leash skills later, if that makes more sense for a given client. One risk is that they get stuck on Mark and Move, rather than the full BAT 2.0.

As the client practices doing Mark and Move with you marking, have him start to mark too, and eventually it's just him marking. Give your client specific feedback but don't chat too much, because it's distracting. For example, you can point out success keeping his hands relaxed, the timing of the marker, Slow Stopping at the right time, or a useful choice to stay out of the dog's way. I mention that if I mark and the dog is relaxed but not ready to walk away, then the handler should wait—staying to gather information is more valuable to the dog than moving away. I tell them to exhale, take a breath, and wait until the dog's next disengagement. Next time, have them do the Slow Stop farther from the trigger. Remember: this may indicate the dog might be a bit too close. Watch for precursors to reactivity that indicate the need to do a recall.

Another variation of Mark and Move is to use a clicker and treats. If the client isn't already clicker-savvy, I coach some easy, useful clicker training first, like hand targeting. We've already marked using a verbal marker, and I initially do the clicking myself, so now the only real change for the client is that he feeds treats instead of just praising after walking away. Most of my clients are couples, so I usually do the clicker myself first, then have one of the clients do it as the other one continues to do the dog handling and treating. Then they switch who is clicking and who is handling the dog. Finally, each of the clients practices clicking and treating on their own.

Some clients have trouble with feeding too soon, so that instead of Mark→Move→ Treat, it's Mark→"Move & Treat." In that case, I have the treats placed at the retreat point, on a table or chair, or held by the dog's other caregiver. So the dog walks up toward me, I click, and they run back to the food to get a treat. This helps them get the concept of giving the bonus reward *after* moving away. If the click is too distracting, coming from me, we immediately change it up and have the client or other caregiver do the clicking.

I teach Mark and Move to clients this way because it's easier to build up handling skills by adding in one new thing at a time. Besides, humans tend to default back to whatever they learned first. I want them to do BAT in the least intrusive way that they can, just using the leash skills and following their dog.

As time goes on, I gradually put the students more in charge of running the set-up, because it's a lot more cost effective for them to learn to do BAT sessions on their own, instead of having a trainer present at every set-up. As the trainer, I'm basically the 'director' of the first few set-ups: I'm in charge of the flow and the client follows my instructions. The first set-up is with a fake dog or me as the decoy, and the client's role is mostly just to handle his own dog. Next, I often coordinate a BAT set-up with a real dog or myself as the helper near their house. In the next session or the one after that, the client is the director and I'm there as an advisor to observe, give feedback, watch for external triggers, and coach the client when they need help with training or safety. I teach the client that an important part of the director's job is to coordinate with the helper. You should always be watching the helper's stress level or assign that role to someone else. I usually work with clients for about five sessions, but I'm always available for follow-ups in person or through my online school if they need troubleshooting. Over the course of your work with the client, try to include all people who might be handling the dog in 'real life' at some point, including the dog walker or pet-sitter.

Clients seem to understand the idea of BAT and really like using this natural way to empower the dog and reinforce better choices. They appreciate that it's not about intimidation, nor is it all about treats. I feel I'm getting less resistance than I did with open-bar counter-conditioning, but it does take a little more time to explain. The key in presenting BAT to clients is to keep them from feeling like they have to do too many new things at once, and to point out progress as you go.

Group classes

For group classes, I find that it is safer and more productive to include only dogs who have issues with other dogs, but not with people. If I had more space or a smaller pool of dogs to work with, I might choose to do it differently, but so far we've had a lot of candidates. The way I structure the classes involves everyone being able to watch the dog work, so if the dog is uncomfortable with people, that doesn't set the dog up to be successful. Group classes for human reactivity can work, but in the models I've seen, the trainer basically ends up doing private lessons, because the other students have to be far away. It's also a liability issue, which is my main reason to stick with private lessons for reactivity to people. Students tend to bring their dogs too close to the other people in the class, ignore other dog's need for space from them, or otherwise put the dog at risk. When the dogs are not reactive to people, students can also coach each other, which is a very valuable part of the group format. That said, BAT walks with advanced students work well even when people are the triggers.

The students who don't bring dogs learn by being paired with a working team to watch for warning signs.

I have done a couple of different models for group classes, and with BAT 2.0, we found that it was very helpful to do an introductory workshop without dogs for body language, survival skills, and the BAT leash skills. Without the distraction of dogs, this information can be efficiently taught to a fairly large number of students in a two-hour session. Registering for the intro session is the prerequisite to the four-week class with dogs, but it can also be used as a cost-effective way for private clients to get a good set of foundation skills. At the intro session, students learn what BAT set-ups look like (using video), learn about the various cut-off signals and stress signs, get tips on management, and do role-playing to learn the leash skills.

The actual class with dogs is for BAT set-ups, and the dogs work as each other's help-ers. These set-ups are almost always outside for new clients. The class has four canine students and weekly one-hour sessions for four weeks. Students fill out a comprehen-sive questionnaire online after they register. A copy of the BAT book is included with the course. Before the class, the trainer does a short call with each student, to make sure they are in the right class and pair them with an appropriate set-up partner. In the first week, there is one set-up with two of the dogs. The other half of the class attends without their dogs so they can assist and learn from the first set-up. In the second week, they swap who brings their dogs and who assists. In weeks three and four, all students bring their dogs. There are two simultaneous BAT set-ups, close by but in view of each other. With the introductory part in a separate workshop, students are then able to repeat the four week session for further practice without being bored or feeling like they paid for something they already knew.

An ongoing course is another option, because this training doesn't just take four weeks. That said, you still want to have a way to keep people motivated. The four-week ses-sions give you a chance to check in and demonstrate progress.

Motivating clients

For any long-term program, like BAT, counter-conditioning, or even basic training, it's important to keep people motivated. As with dogs, functional reinforcers are bet-ter than bonus rewards for our human learners. The main functional reinforcer for participating in the training is to improve their dog's behavior. That means the key is to make sure they are really noticing the progress their dog makes. There are other reinforcers that you can facilitate or provide, like positive social interaction with other students, attention from you, certificates, discount coupons earned by perfect atten-dance, etc.

There are a lot of different ways to point out the success students are having. Many students prefer a personal comment on their progress, while others may prefer to have success noted in front of the group. If you have a group class with a monthly check-in, you could have open-ended questions like, "What's one thing that you or your dog can do now that you couldn't have done before BAT?" or "What's one thing you no-tice about your dog that you didn't see before?" This doesn't just apply to group classes. You can have a scheduled check-in time every month or two for your private clients, too—in person, by video chat, or by phone.

Take notes during your sessions so you can refer back to some specific bits of progress they have made in the previous month. If you have assistants, have them jot down notes too. If there hasn't been any progress, figure out why! Use the check-in call as a chance to dig in deeper and share a plan for how things can go better the next month. A lot of times, students don't realize that trainers actually have more tricks up their sleeve. So if clients aren't seeing progress, they leave, rather than asking you for troubleshooting or changes to make to what they are doing.

Students in group classes still need some individual contact. You could have a phone or video chat scheduled at the end of the session (or monthly for ongoing classes) where you take 10-15 minutes to talk about their case. Be sure to make the time allotted clear to your clients when you schedule the call. Calling each client takes extra time, however, so I recommend that you adjust the cost of the class accordingly. Trainers tend to undercharge, because a lot of people do this for a hobby; that isn't good for the industry. Just keep in mind that a phone call like this is a chance to get your clients enrolled in another class, so you might not need to increase the cost of the course very much to make this worthwhile. It is also a feature that sets you apart from other training classes, so mention it in your marketing material.

A quick video chat helps clients stay motivated.

Another way to demonstrate progress is to have clients use some version of the data sheet from Chapter 6, and then go over it with them from time to time. You can fill it out or you can have them do it. In your debriefing sessions, make sure that you are not shaming anyone for not having progress. Definitely don't put too much emphasis on distance to the trigger as your measure of how much progress they have made. You get what you reinforce, so if they are working to close the distance, then they are going to be encouraging their dog forward, which is the opposite of what we want. For example, progress can be measured by the number of times the dog was in the Yellow Zone or higher during the sessions in a particular setting (that number should go down or stay low). They could also get a "Leash Skills Certificate" by demonstrating their ability with the various leash skills. This could be done all at once or just as the class goes on. Being able to check their skills off the list, one by one, shows their progress.

Filming is another way to collect data to demonstrate progress. If you have your clients film their set-ups, one option is to give an assignment to them to find their "best BAT moment" or something else that you want to reinforce or build confidence in. This can be done either once a month (better for group classes, because you kind of need a projector) or after each session (can work well for private lessons). Not all students will be able to do this, technologically, but it does help. You can also do it yourself, but editing video takes a ton of time, so I'm not sure it's a good idea. Dogs may also show more fear with a fake dog unless you move it realistically.

Finding helpers: dogs and people

Getting helpers is one of the hard parts of any rehabilitation program that relies on the dogs being sub-threshold. The good thing about BAT is that it can be done on walks and in real life, not just in set-ups. That said, dogs definitely make the fastest progress when they encounter triggers in a systematic way that lets them fully make their own choices, i.e., set-ups.

I recommend creating a way for your clients to set sessions up with each other, like an online group or a bulletin board at your school. BAT sessions can be done with both dogs working at the same time, so they are approaching and retreating from one another. You just have to make sure that both dogs are comfortably below threshold. In my experience, people with dogs who have issues with humans are quite willing to swap roles as helper for each other's dogs. This is also good for motivating your clients to continue doing set-ups, because there's a social component.

It is easier to get helper dogs if you have something to trade. This table shows who in the family can serve as a helper for another dog. The first column assumes the other dog is reactive to dogs and the second column assumes the other dog is only reactive to people.

	Can be a helper for dog reactivity	Can be a helper for human reactivity
Your dog with reactivity issues	X	
Another dog in your household	X	
Humans in household		X
Friends		X

I don't often use my own dogs as helpers, unless I'm also doing BAT work for their own benefit. Life-sized plush fake dogs also make great helpers for distance work. Once they get up close, the dog usually figures out that it's not real within a few minutes, but it works well from farther away. It's great practice for starting out, because the handler is more relaxed. I used to also use fake dogs for assessment, but I rarely do that any more, both for safety and because it's not necessary. Every moment of doing BAT is like a mini-assessment. Most of the time a fake dog will get some kind of realistic response, but sometimes, dogs will ignore the fake dog because they have experience with a fake dog or a big stuffed toy somewhere else.

While it can make it easier for the student dog to have a stationary helper, that can be hard for the student dog. I often have the helper dog handlers follow their dog around the training area as well, as long as they aren't approaching the student dog in a way that's stressful. Another option is to do Mark and Move with 'veteran' helpers. By 'veteran,' I mean that the helper dog's handler already knows how to do Mark and Move and can do that and still pay attention to the other dog. Meanwhile the student dog is working on the more standard 'follow your dog' version of BAT 2.0.

Being a stationary helper from time to time is fine, but it's the sort of thing that can burn a dog out, and honoring the helper dog's own needs by doing BAT is helpful. Make sure clients understand that. If they're loaning out their other 'good' dog as a helper dog over and over, they should basically be doing BAT and following their dog during the set-ups (within reason), so that their 'good' dog continues to have effective cut-off signals. This is also useful for dogs who are helpers for other techniques, like open-bar counter-conditioning.

Caregivers of helper dogs should also make sure their dogs encounter dogs without issues on leash during their daily lives, to help them unwind. That doesn't mean they need to play on leash, just that you don't want the dog thinking, "How come I never see friendly dogs on leash any more?! Everybody seems to have a problem." This advice goes for dogs used as helpers for other techniques, too. For example, in the open-bar/closed-bar version of counter-conditioning, you can time the helper dog's appearances and disappearances based on the helper dog's behavior.

Hopefully this chapter has given you some ways to successfully integrate BAT into your training toolbox. BAT is not meant to replace solid techniques that already work well for you, but rather to add another tool to help make your training more efficient. With some explanation and practice, caregivers can fully grasp BAT 2.0 and make significant progress with their dogs (see Appendix 4 for some examples). Trainers and behaviorists around the world have reported similar successes, so it's definitely worth trying out. Your turn!

CONCLUSION

Thanks for taking the time to learn about BAT 2.0. As I mentioned in the first version of this book, BAT is always going to be a work in progress, based on practice and the best information we have available. I urge you to look at everything you do with animals and see if there is a way to make things better—not just faster or easier for you, but also more empowering for the animals themselves.

Here are a few final take-home messages about BAT:

- Create safe situations that allow your dog to learn with naturally occurring reinforcers.
- Once the dog knows the trigger is there, don't lead him closer to the trigger.
- When your dog needs help, do so in the least intrusive way.
- Practice leash skills for safety and freedom.

If you haven't tried BAT with a dog yet, now is the time! Find a friend to help you, film a session of just wandering around using leash skills, and then go over the video, paying close attention to the stress level of the dog(s). When you do set-ups with a helper, film that too, and assess it carefully. If you are a trainer, I recommend working pro bono on some cases, or doing BAT first with your own dog. The Animal Building Blocks Academy is a great way to continue your education and get feedback on your videos. Be sure to check out some of the BAT videos on GrishaStewart.com or purchase one or more of the DVDs or streaming videos on BAT.

Above all, it's important to just give BAT a try, starting with the leash skills. The proof is in the pudding, as they say. As long as you set things up to keep your dog below threshold, you can't really mess things up. Of course, getting the details of BAT right will speed up your progress, so don't hesitate to seek some additional help from an expert. It's also a great idea to work through this with a friend and/or a video camera, so that you can get another perspective on the training sessions. Good luck!

APPENDIX 1

Clicker Training Foundations

If you haven't seen a clicker or tried clicker training yet, now is the perfect time to learn! Clicker training, also known as marker training, uses a marker signal, like "yes," a whistle, or an actual box clicker, to pinpoint the behavior that earns a reinforcer. Clicker training is not a gimmicky fad—it's a straightforward application of the scientific laws of learning. It is effective with all sorts of animals, from South African tuberculosis- and mine-detecting rats to service dogs, housecats, and killer whales. Clear communication is important in training, and the marker signal tells the animal exactly which behavior has earned a reinforcer. The most common marker signals in dog training are clickers and verbal markers. A clicker is a tiny handheld box that makes a clicking noise. A verbal marker is a word that serves the same purpose as the clicker; it's a sound from our mouths, like "Yes" or "Yip." If your dog is deaf, you can still use anything that your dog can feel, see, taste, or smell as a training cue. Similarly, you can use a tactile or visual marker to clicker train a deaf dog.

The keys to a good marker:

1. The dog can clearly detect the marker (visually, audibly etc.).

2. The marker reliably predicts the appearance of a reinforcer.

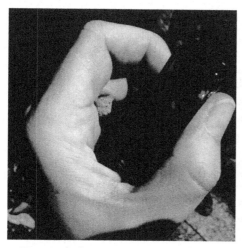 

You can hide some treats in your clicker hand for easy access.

Training clicker with a wrist coil. Push on the metal and release to make a click-click sound.

The following are some behaviors that are great for the dog to learn before or between BAT sessions. I don't require my clients to finish these exercises first, because they are chomping at the bit to work on their dog's aggression. I also don't require a specific time of pre-training, because just practicing BAT helps the dog learn these skills. But having these foundation skills in their toolbox makes our BAT work even more successful.

Attention

Attention does not mean that the dog is constantly staring at their human. In fact that gets in the way of doing BAT. By attention, I just mean that you can easily get your dog's full attention, and that your dog always has some connection with you during a walk. I like to train automatic check-ins as well as teaching the dog to respond quickly to their name.

The Lassie Protocol

Naming activities for my students is a trick I picked up from the fabulous Terry Ryan many years ago. I named this attention protocol after the famous canine television character with a strong connection to her family. The Lassie Protocol jump-starts dog training in seven days and is a simple way to train a dog to automatically check in.

> Tip for Pros: The Lassie Protocol is a great first assignment in training classes and private lessons. You can even send it to your clients in advance of your first session, so the clicker is charged up and the dogs are more attentive.

I recommend doing the Lassie Protocol with any dog who needs a little more focus. Try it on your dog after reading the rest of this section, especially if you've never tried clicker training before. Because every dog learns at a different pace, the days listed are just a suggestion. If you have an attentive Border Collie, you can fast-forward through the process in a few quick sessions. If you have a new rescue dog who doesn't even know who you are, you might need to stretch the training out to a few weeks.

Days 1-2: Mark and reward every time the dog pays attention to you on his own.
Use the clicker or a verbal marker to pinpoint any glances your way, and give a great reinforcer. Try to mark the exact instant your dog starts to turn his head toward you, so that you are rewarding the choice of turning his head.

1. If you're not going to train for a while, give an All Done signal. When you're ready to train again, say his name and click/treat the turn toward you. I recommend not doing this while you're eating your own dinner. When you sit down to eat, that's a perfect time to say "All Done," meaning there is no chance for rewards until further notice.

2. In quiet places, like in the living room, you can reinforce with your dog's food. Offer better rewards when your dog looks at you around distractions. Dogs deserve 'hazard pay.'

3. When you are using a clicker as the marker, attach a keychain wrist coil to it so that the clicker is always at hand. You can swap back and forth between the clicker and the verbal marker, so use whichever one is available first. The clicker is more memorable to the dog, so use that when you can. Don't forget to praise your dog after you mark her glance!

4. For this and all of your training, vary the type of reinforcer and where it comes from. Mark and then pull a hidden toy out of a tree or off a shelf. Mark and pick up a stick to toss. Mark and play a game of chase (dog chasing human). Mark and run to the kitchen together and grab a treat for the dog from your refrigerator. It helps to match the type of distraction the dog was looking away from, so that looking away from food gets them food, looking away from a toy gets them a toy, etc.

Days 3-4: Mark and reinforce the best look out of every two.
We are now weaning off the treats a little. That doesn't mean you aren't reinforcing attention. Continue to praise or at least acknowledge your dog for checking in.

1. Every time you mark, you still reinforce; you just won't be marking as much.

2. Get a little picky—click for the faster head turns, longer glances, or whatever is somehow 'above average.'

Clicker Training Foundations

1. THE LASSIE PROTOCOL

* Train your dog to automatically check in
* Encourage more focus & attention
* Mark & Reward every time your dog pays attention to you on his own.

2. THE NAME GAME

* Teach your dog that his name = Pay attention, the next thing I say is for you.
* Use this cue wisely. Never just ignore a dog after saying his name.
* Mark & Reward eye contact or whiplash head turn.

3. EMERGENCY U-TURN

* Train your dog to turn around and walk away
* Make your walk safer because you can quickly get your dog out of a stressful situation
* Back away from your dog. Mark as your dog turns and have her catch up to get the treat.

4. LOOSE LEASH WALKING

* Golden rule: Never let your dog move forward if the leash is tight
* Different methods to train this: Click in position, Be A Tree, Silky Leash etc.
* Mark and Reward when the leash is loosened, or when dog is in correct position

5. EMERGENCY RECALL

* Useful in emergency situations when a reliable recall is needed
* This is a special cue always followed by loads of fabulous treats.

6. BOW

* A fun alternative way for a dog to get attention (vs jumping or barking or sitting)
* A very obviously friendly signal to teach dogs who lack social skills

Days 5-7: Wean off of the treats.

Mark and reinforce on a random schedule, for about one-third of the responses. Try to mark the best responses. Reinforce by just paying attention and/or praising the rest of the time. Gradually shift to a one in four schedule, then one in five. Change the reinforcement schedule slowly, so that your dog won't suspect the odds are getting longer.

The Lassie Protocol is great to do during the first week of training, along with using Mark and Move on walks. Do it again whenever the dog needs a refresher, like when you have a baby, get another dog, or move to a new home.

The Name Game

The Name Game teaches a dog to direct her focus to you when you say her name, so that she catches the next bit of information from the human.

Let's say your dog's name is Riley. If you have said his name a lot in an angry voice, use a nickname, instead—either a brand new one or one already in use. Use a name that you don't mind saying in public. Start off with the dog in a quiet setting. It helps to do the Lassie Protocol first.

1. Say his name one time, and then give him a treat. He doesn't have to look at you at this point, but he probably will look if you're in a quiet setting. Do several pairings of "Riley" → treat. Start to say it when he's not looking, then follow up with a treat.

2. Repeat step one in several locations, inside and out.

3. Start to require that Riley actually make eye contact for his treat. Start with a 5-second 'limited hold,' meaning that if he looks within 5 seconds of you saying his name once, he can have the treat. You can click to mark the moment or mark with your word, "Yes!"

   If he doesn't look in time, just quickly walk away and take your treats with you (unless he's having fun without you, in which case you may need to make the fun stop). If he follows you, say his name without turning back around to face him. He should try to come around front to see you. Reinforce that. Another option is to walk away and then just wait for about 20 seconds and do the Name Game again. Either way, if he fails the 5-Second Rule several times in a row, you're pushing too quickly. Go back to step one or work in a less distracting environment.

4. Move on to the 3-Second Rule, then 2, then 1, then the Whiplash Rule—only instant looks get treats.

I learned of this game from Leslie Nelson from her *Really Reliable Recall* (see Resources), although I have my own spin on it. Leslie gives three reasons why the Name Game might fail:

1. **Icky treats.** So use great treats!! The dog gets to decide what that means.

2. **Not enough practice.** Do fifteen name-food pairings each day. Surprise your dog.

3. **Repeating the name.** Say the name only once, and then apply whatever rule you were using. Eat the treat, make a smoochy noise if you really must, but don't repeat the name.

I think it's fair to repeat the name after ten to twenty seconds if the environment has changed, the dog looks ready to pay attention, or you know some other reason that it's going to work if you try again. And remember, your dog is always learning from you, whether you think you're training or not. Every time you say the dog's name, he's learning what it means.

Speaking of meaning, make sure that *you* really know what the name means. To me, the name means, "pay attention, the next thing I say is for you." The dog's name should be followed by a cue for what to do next, either a release cue or some other cue. Saying "Freddie," followed by praise for looking, is fine. Saying "Freddie," followed by "Sit," and then a release cue is also fine. Saying "Freddie," followed by nothing at all or worse, something icky like patting on the head, is not fine, unless you want the name to mean "leave me alone." Pairing a cue with no behavioral response from me is exactly how I teach the All Done cue that I mentioned above, which tells the dog that their request has been denied and to stop begging at the table, bringing me toys, or offering cute tricks. I just say, "All done" at the end of a training session and then ignore the dog! Use your dog's name cue wisely, and never just ignore a dog after saying her name.

"Let's go" / Emergency U-turn

I mentioned the U-turn before as a way to get away from a sudden surprise. Two of my favorite verbal cues for emergency U-turns are "Oh Sh%@" (easy to remember in case of emergency) and "Call your dog" (double-meaning). If you have trained "Call your dog" as a cue to turn around, then shouting "call your dog" signals the emergency U-turn to your dog and communicates to the other owner at the same time.

That one signal: 1) tells the other owner to call their dog; 2) cues your dog to turn around, away from trouble; and 3) slows down the oncoming dog because of the tone. It's also easy to remember, but not quite as gratifying as shouting profanity when faced with yet another off-leash Golden Retriever. ☺ Most clients choose to teach two cues for the same behavior: "Let's go" and "Call your dog."

I first heard of the emergency U-turn in Patricia McConnell's great book, *Feisty Fido* (see Resources). Here's how I teach it now. Start inside, with your dog off leash.

1. Lure or cue the dog to get beside you, facing the same direction as you.

2. Give the cue "Call your dog," then back up (causing your dog to U-turn to face you), and toss the treat or a toy so that your dog runs past you. Repeat fifty times in different locations.

3. Repeat the above and click at the instant your dog turns when hearing "Call your dog," then toss the reinforcement, as before. Repeat exercise in various locations until dog is able to turn instantly in every room of your home (including the garage, basement, or outbuildings), with the TV on, and around distractions on sidewalks, at the park, etc. Work off leash in a safe place, on leash in public.

4. Over the course of multiple sessions, escalate the volume and tone until it sounds like what you'd really say on walks.

5. Rehearse simultaneously giving the traffic cop signal and saying (or shouting), "Call your dog."

Note that you can start right away with using the cue in the training session that I just described, because you're working in a quiet location and you are using a prompt that will already work to encourage the behavior—backing away from the dog. I love using a toy as the reinforcer, because it builds up a really strong drive to run in the direction you've prompted. Dogs who don't fetch toys still usually love the chance to chase treats, and you can feed your dog's meals this way. Whenever possible, training should be part of your daily routine. U-turns should be repeatedly rehearsed on regular walks, so that you and your dog have it fresh in your minds.

If your dog already has another positively trained cue for the U-turn, such as "Let's go," you can use a cue transfer instead of starting from scratch. To transfer the meaning of a cue, start with the second step, above, and have the old cue follow the new cue, over and over, as in "Call your dog" → one second pause → "Let's go!" followed by backing up a few steps, clicking, and tossing the treat so that the dog runs past you. Even though backing up may get in the way of the verbal cue acquisition, it's important because it's good for you to rehearse your own role for real situations.

Just to make sure that the cue transfer concept is clear, let's reverse it. If you teach "Call your dog" as the first cue and want to add "Let's go" as a cue, then the order would be opposite of what we had above. That means you'd practice this way: "Let's go" (new cue) → one second pause → "Call your dog" (old cue as a translation) followed by backing up a few steps, clicking, and tossing the treat so that the dog runs past you.

The emergency U-turn makes walks safer because you can quickly get the dog out of stressful situations. Learning to walk politely on leash the rest of the time is also helpful.

> *I love rehearsing the emergency U-turn with squirrels as the distraction and a tug or a tossed toy as the reward. Many reactive dogs also love to chase prey, and eliminating this opportunity to pull on leash makes walks more pleasant.*

Leash walking

I think I can count on one hand the number of reactive dogs I've seen that walked perfectly on a leash. Even though a client may come to me for her dog's aggression or fear issues, one of the presentations of that reactivity is that the dog pulls and lunges toward the trigger or panics and pulls home. A tight leash can cause reactive dogs to get into fights, so I like to teach both the client and the dog to keep the leash loose. I also like specifically teaching the dog that any leash pressure is just a cue for where to walk, not a signal to freak out.

The BAT leash skills in this book teach *you* how to stop pulling on the leash. There are lots of different techniques for teaching the dog to keep the leash loose, too. I like using a combination of several techniques. The Lassie Protocol from above is a great start. Here are some of the other methods that you can use, which I cover in my *Ahimsa Dog Training Manual* (see Resources). I will go over Focused Walking here below.

- Click for Attention
- Turn and Click
- Focused Walking
- Being a Tree or Backing Up
- Speed Training
- Penalty Yards
- Silky Leash

Focused walking (touch and you're heeled!)

Sometimes the trigger is so close or so intense that if your dog even notices it, he will explode. In those cases, Mark and Move isn't useful, because that first glance is already too much stimulation. You can just feed a ton to distract, but Focused Walking is a more elegant solution to get past big distractions when you think that Mark and Move won't be enough. This technique will help you teach your dog to focus on you instead of distractions. In particular, she'll be looking at your finger as you walk along (also known as "finger targeting" or "hand targeting"). Once your dog knows this behavior well, you can use it to walk past things that might otherwise ruin your lovely walk.

The idea is for this to be a fun, fantastic game for your dog, something you occasionally play on walks. I build up excitement first by asking, "Reaaaady?" to tell my dog we're about to play this or other fun games.

The behavior here is that your dog touches her nose to a human's hand, but you can also apply this to a target of some sort. I'll use "Touch" as the cue in this example. You can use it to move the dog around in space. You can also teach them to Heel nicely beside you.

Let's say you're right-handed. Start out with a treat and the clicker in your right hand. You can have your target hand a flat hand or whatever you want, but I like to do it the following way. Make a fist with your left hand. Present that hand to your dog. Your dog will then probably go toward your hand, expecting a treat. Ignore any pawing.

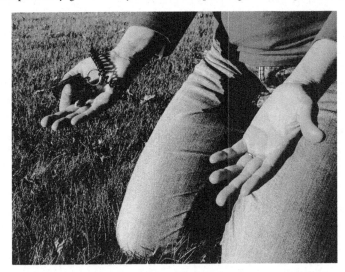

Start with a treat in your clicker hand.

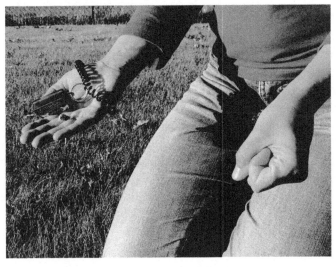

Make a fist with your (usually empty) target hand.

When she touches the target hand with her nose, click and place the treat in the target hand to feed her. While she's eating, put your target hand behind your back and then present it again when you're ready to click and treat again. For some reason, having the hand move away makes it 'brand-new' and interesting again.

Do this several times before beginning to teach a cue. Once she's got the hang of it, and you're relatively sure she will touch your hand, do the same activity, but start saying "Touch" right before you put your target hand out.

Click when your dog touches the target.

Pass a treat to your target hand.

Your dog eats the treats from your target hand.

If your dog stares at you and doesn't touch the hand, then either wait her out or put your hand behind your back and bring it back out again. Don't lean into her or stare (that's a bit scary). Your hand may also look like a hand signal you've already been giving her. If that's the case, change this to a new signal—hand flat, one or two fingers out, or other signal of your choice. If she is biting your hand rather than gently touching with her nose, make sure you aren't clicking for the bite. Click sooner to reward her before her mouth opens, or click later, waiting for her mouth to close before clicking. Changing where you put your hand may help.

Next, begin to move the target a bit, so the dog has to walk a step or two to touch your hand. Test to see if your dog will touch the target hand even if it's right beside you, instead of being in front of him. After this step, you're ready to use it for Heeling.

Next, be a moving target. After you have practiced "Touch" for a while and your dog is readily touching your hand, next you will present your hand and when your dog moves to touch it, back up so your dog has to follow you a few steps in order to touch the target. Click and treat when the dog touches the target. You can also move in a semi-circle while offering the target. The key is to get your dog following the target to touch it.

Now we'll start getting your dog to follow the target hand when it's beside you. Now it's going to start looking like Heel. If you want your dog to walk on your left, your target hand is your left hand, and vice versa if they're on the right. You might work both sides, but work only one during a particular session.

Start practicing this off leash in your house. Say "Touch" and present the target hand with your arm straight down, against your leg, and walk a few steps away from your dog. Wait for your dog to catch up to your hand and touch it. Click and deliver the treat slightly behind with your hand straight down beside your leg (never ahead of you). This ensures your dog doesn't surge past you and out of Heel position.

After your dog gets a treat, say "Touch" again and continue to walk forward. As the dog catches up to you and touches your hand again, click and treat. You're Heeling!

After the dog is doing well at this, you can begin to say "Heel" instead of "Touch," or say, "Heel," and then "Touch," if the dog gets confused.

Next, it's time to start random treating. Put Heel on a variable reward schedule by gradually spacing out the amount of time or number of steps between clicks and treats. Increase every other interval. The numbers below can be seconds or number of steps.

Ex. 3, 5, 3, 7, 4, 9, 4, 11, 5, 13, 5, 15, 6, 17, 6, 19…

(easy, hard, easy, harder, not quite so easy, harder still…)

Heel for a short time after each long stretch, so the dog doesn't notice the long pauses between treats are getting longer. You want to keep the dog thinking, "Maybe it's only two more steps before the next treat!" Note that even the short pauses are getting longer. Random treating works for extending duration in Stay, too!

If you encounter a bigger distraction, go back to rewarding more frequently or reinforcing continuously.

Once it's working at home, try it for a few blocks at a time out on your walks, when there aren't big distractions around. When there are big distractions like one of your dog's triggers, you can use the same technique, but put some extra-tasty food in your target hand, and make it easy for your dog by putting it to her nose and then moving the treat toward you.

Coming when called

Coming when called, directly and without hesitation, can save a dog's life. When a dog is likely to get into fights with other dogs or bite people, it's also an important way to keep others safe. If all of the physical safeguards fail—the leash, the fence, or whatever else—then the recall is there to get the dog back. Many dogs have no dangerous bite history and the goal is to get them to play well with others, off leash. To be around other dogs off leash, they definitely need a reliable recall. There are bound to be times when your dog gets in over his head, and the only way to get him out, from a distance, is to call him.

I've actually already covered a sneaky way of getting a dog to come when called. The "Touch" cue is great because in order to touch their nose to your hand, the dog has to come over to you. She's also close enough to grab her harness, if needed (make sure to treat after that!) My *Ahimsa Dog Training Manual* has several more ways to create a solid recall for everyday use (see Resources), but the "Touch" cue can be enough if you practice in lots of different places.

I like to teach a separate cue for an emergency recall. This cue is not eroded by everyday use, but remains strong because you practice it with amazing rewards, in several situations. I teach the dog to come to a special cue using an adapted version of Leslie Nelson's Really Reliable Recall (see Resources). My students usually use the cue, "Treat party." At my house, the cue is a high-pitched, "Boop," because that's not something the dogs ever hear, except when they are about to get a load of fabulous treats. This is straightforward **respondent learning** (also known as classical conditioning), which pairs two stimuli or events together. Here's how it works.

1. (Optional) Say your regular recall cue. Starting with this adds the joy of the treat party to your regular cue, so you get twice the training power.

2. Say the cue, "Treat party."

3. One after the other, hand out about twenty small, extraordinarily fabulous treats; bits of meat or leftover macaroni and cheese work great for this. Set them on the ground near the dog so he scarfs them up. Just before you hand out each treat, say, "Treat Party!" That way, within about twenty seconds, you've conditioned the phrase, "Treat Party" twenty times, plus you have the cumulative effect of an overwhelming number of great treats. The phrase begins to have the same magnetic pull as the slot machine bells ringing for gambling in Las Vegas. It doesn't always have to be a party of edible treats; if you have a toy-loving dog, announce that a Treat Party is coming before a game of tug, and repeat the phrase as you play. If you're doing it right, you should be out of breath by the end of each Treat Party.

4. Practice three times a day, gradually announcing the party when farther away from the dog or out of sight. If you have non-spicy, low-salt leftover foods, put them in the refrigerator as you wash dishes and then pull them out for a Treat Party after the meal. Practice indoors, outdoors, in front of the house, with distractions, and anywhere else you can think of.

Leslie Nelson's way of doing the Really Reliable Recall is to give a jackpot of rewards for the recall, presented one at a time. She calls that "fine dining." What I added to her protocol was the cue of "Treat Party," instead of just praising during the party, so that you get an emergency recall cue for free while you train your regular recall. I've had clients tell me that after only a few weeks, they've been able to use the "Treat Party" cue to rescue their dog from traffic, and that even then, they remembered to celebrate with a Treat Party for their dog.

I love using that goofy cue, because it reminds the students to keep the behavior strong by keeping up a fabulous rate of reinforcement. They don't say "Treat Party" unless they mean it. Saying "Treat Party" without handing out a lot of treats seems more like lying to their dog than not providing reinforcement for other cues. They also don't overuse the cue for everyday recalls, because it's sort of an embarrassing thing to shout. They even remember to avoid saying the cue at other times. My clients refer to it as a "T.P." or a "celebration" when talking about the cue, to make sure their dog isn't disappointed.

Bow

This is a fun addition to the dog's repertoire, but it's also really useful. I mostly teach it to dogs as a default way to get their human's attention. Bowing is a lot better than jumping up or barking at us for attention, and it's a lot more fun than sitting. It's also a nice way to stretch a dog before agility or other dog sports. Finally, a bow is also great for dogs that lack social skills. See the section on Frustration in Chapter 7 for more information. Special thanks to dog trainer Joey Iversen for letting me borrow her idea of teaching bows for attention.

Author and researcher Alexandra Horowitz observed that in the dog world, a dog tends to only do a bouncy bow if the other dog is paying attention first (see Resources). So, the bow is not exactly the first thing a dog does as an attention-getter, but it's a very obvious signal and it's a dog's way of signaling "Hey, I'm talking to you! Let's do something together" in a peaceful way.

I use the cue "Yoga" for the bow behavior, because it is a fun play on the "downward facing dog" pose and because Bow sounds too much like Down.

Teaching Yoga using capturing is ideal, because it gives the dogs a very natural stretch. Simply use a verbal marker like "Yes" or a clicker to mark the instant that the dog is in a deep, Play Bow stretch and then give a treat. This deep stretch often happens when they first wake up, so be ready to capture it then. Many dogs will bow if you stretch in your own version of a bow, so you can try that too. If you can feed while they're still bowing, do that! Be sure to give your regular release cue like OK or Free, so she knows that she can get up.

Once a dog catches on that you like the bow, she should begin to offer it more and more. Reward using treats, attention, or whatever the dog seems to want in the moment. You can either just leave it like that, or you can add the verbal cue, "Yoga." Simply say, "Yoga," when you first notice that the bowing has begun. Mark the behavior when the dog is fully bowing, and then reward.

APPENDIX 2

Other Techniques that Use Functional Reinforcers

This appendix is helpful if you are a training geek, like me, or if you know a lot of other techniques and want to fit BAT into the scheme of things. If you are new to training, this section may be overwhelming.

BAT is not new science, but rather, a better way to apply established principles. As an overall package, BAT was a new way of training when it first came out and BAT 2.0 is even more so. But like everything people do, BAT didn't come out of the blue; it was influenced by a variety of training tools, including some that use functional reinforcers. Several of those methods even use the functional reinforcer of distance from the trigger. I'll discuss those methods below.

Premack principle

The Premack principle (also known as "Premack's principle" in the literature) isn't a technique; it's a scientific principle that is the basis of a lot of common training techniques (see Resources). Discovered in 1959 by Dr. David Premack, this principle explores how the probability of a behavior in a given context, i.e., how likely it is to occur, is related to the probability of the behaviors that follow. His results were interesting, because they blew away the idea that an event is consistently reinforcing. For example, one study collected data on the duration of candy eating versus pinball playing in a class of first graders. When given the opportunity to choose freely, 61% spent more time playing and 39% spent more time eating.

- Gamers: playing game is high probability (more time spent playing than eating)
- Eaters: eating candy is high probability (more time spent eating than playing)

The gamers and eaters were broken into two subgroups, so there were four experimental groups. For one of the gamer groups and one of the eater groups, playing was contingent upon eating, i.e., if they ate a candy, they could play the game. For the other half, it was the reverse: if they played, they could eat a candy.

In both cases, if the low probability behavior came first, as a sort of price of admission, that behavior increased. The gamers who had to eat candy as the price of admission ended up eating a lot more candy: their average went from 5 to 26 pieces. The result was similar for the eaters who had to play in order to eat. They ended up playing more.

The other two groups were given the 'opportunity' to do a low probability event after they had already gotten to do the high probability event. Gamers were no more likely to eat after playing when gaming 'earned' them the chance to eat. Eaters were no more likely to play after eating when eating 'earned' them the chance to play. In other words, the opportunity to do a lower probability event is not reinforcing.

I see this when clients try to play with dogs in a way they don't like, or feed a treat when the dog isn't hungry. Playing that game or eating that treat are lower probability behaviors than whatever it is the dog would have chosen on her own.

Okay, so now we know that the opportunity to do a higher probability behavior can be reinforcing and the opportunity to do a lower probability behavior has no significant effect. That's interesting, but there's more. In another study with rats, Premack and John Terhune made the consequence not just the chance to do an activity, but the obligation to do so. The rats had three possible activities: drinking (highest probability), running on a wheel (middle probability) and pressing a lever (low probability).

The researchers made the running contingent upon drinking and on pressing a lever. In other words, the rat could not freely run on the wheel, but if it pressed the lever or drank, then a motor activated and the rat was forced to run on the wheel. Running was more probable than lever pressing, and they saw the same result as above: lever pressing went up in frequency. Drinking, which had the exact same consequence, went down in frequency. This indicates that being forced to do a lower probability activity is punishing. To summarize, *the probability of a behavior shifts up or down toward the probability of the consequence.*

One important thing to consider is that the punishment may come not from the activity the rat had to do, but the opportunity cost. When the rat was being forced to run on the wheel, the rat could not engage in the activity it was just doing. The drinking rat stopped drinking and ran, which means the high probability behavior had to stop. Losing the opportunity to choose a higher probability behavior could be the real punisher.

Let's think about that. The probability of a behavior shifts toward how frequently the animal would ordinarily do the behavioral options provided as a consequence. If doing X leads to the opportunity do a more likely behavior, then X is reinforced. In other words, in each context, the chance to do what we would normally do more reinforces the behavior we would normally do less. In the simplest of terms, freedom can be a reinforcer. If doing X limits the behavioral options to behaviors that are less likely in that context, then X is punished. Limiting our behavioral repertoire can be a punisher.

If your mother ever told you, "After you do your homework, you can go play with your friends," she was using the Premack principle. If the functional reinforcer of the behavior you're teaching is permission to do a particular behavior, like polite walking leading to squirrel chasing, you're using the Premack principle, too.

According to the Premack Principle, the *chance to do a high probability behavior reinforces the behavior it follows.* Being forced to do a less probable behavior punishes the behavior it follows. I like this description of reinforcement and punishment in terms of the Premack principle, directly from Dr. Premack: "What, then, is the difference between reward and punishment? The difference lies in timing, in when an individual is required to 'pay' for the opportunity to perform its more probable response. For reward, the individual 'pays' before; in punishment, the individual 'pays' after" (see Resources). So in essence, with reinforcement, we are in the dog's debt. With punishment, the dog is in our debt. Perhaps that is why people seem to irrationally prefer punishment.

Many functional reinforcers can be explained by the Premack principle. As I mentioned above, the frequencies calculated are situational, i.e., context-specific. In our BAT set-ups, we create situations where sniffing bushes and trees is very likely. Calmly taking in information about a trigger is harder, but still a pretty likely behavior (not normally, but in the set-ups it is relatively easy). If your dog were to make a list of Most Common to Least Common behaviors when hanging out in a field during your BAT session, sniffing would be way at the top of the list and calmly gathering info about a trigger would probably be lower down.

So when your dog calmly sniffs a trigger from a distance in a BAT set-up (low frequency), and then moves on to explore some odor on a tree, that opportunity to check out the tree is a naturally occurring reinforcer! *This is a good example of the Premack principle at work and why it is critical to provide an interesting environment for exploration.* In BAT, we use antecedent arrangements to create an environment in which the dog can take in information and relax, making our target behavior of polite interaction fairly likely. We also allow dogs to have access to their full behavioral repertoires, so appropriate behavior can be naturally reinforced by the opportunity to do even more likely behavior. (We do keep them from going in a straight line toward the trigger and recall if we have messed up and are seeing reactivity, so those are exceptions.)

However, not all functional reinforcers (in the sense that we use them in BAT) work because of the Premack principle. Functional reinforcers can also be something that happens around or to the dog, like the trigger moving away or becoming less active.

Furthermore, not all reinforcers using the Premack principle are functional for the social behavior we are trying to teach in BAT. Bonus rewards use the Premack principle by surprising a dog with some other high-probability behavior, like fetching a toy or eating a treat. Unlike walking away, bonus rewards are not functionally related to the disengagement behavior. In Mark and Move, I always encourage people to walk away first (functional reinforcer), and then give the bonus reward. In other words, the priority is to get the dog to safety and/or reduce arousal, rather than the treat. My experience has been that while we can build up strong, motivated behaviors by using surprising, powerful reinforcers, it's a problem to use bonus rewards exclusively. When we don't meet the dog's safety needs first, we may be reducing controllability and predictability. It's kind of like getting a surprise birthday party when you've had a stressful day and just need to relax. Controllability and predictability are important factors that BAT relies on to help dogs feel more comfortable around their triggers.

Treat and Retreat

I mentioned Treat and Retreat in Chaper 14 when I talked about getting dogs to like me quickly for private lessons. "Retreat n' Treat" was originally developed by Ian Dunbar in 1982 and the "Treat and Retreat" term was coined by Suzanne Clothier when she formalized the technique (see Resources). The idea is to play hard to get, so that the dog is the one who closes the distance to you: toss the treat to where the dog is and then walk away as he's eating. The dog will then follow you when you leave; repeat. You can also toss the treat behind the dog, so he's the one retreating. The functional reinforcer is the relief that the dog feels when he goes away from you to get the treat or when you back away from him. Dunbar says he used this to get himself out of a sticky situation with a big Akita who had already bitten four men. Suzanne Clothier has extended this method, which she now calls "Treat and Retreat." She elegantly explains how tossing treats to where the dog feels comfortable approaching, and then leaving, is infinitely better than luring a dog forward to you with treats, because it takes the social pressure off of the dog.

I use Treat and Retreat whenever I need to make fast friends. For long-term rehabilitation, I usually use BAT, not just Treat and Retreat. I find that BAT generalizes more readily and has some other perks, but Treat and Retreat is excellent for getting yourself into a dog's inner circle.

Two-Reward method

John Fisher developed the Two-Reward method to work with dog aggression, especially for 'Velcro' dogs who are quite attached to their owners (see Resources). As I describe it, you'll see how it is very different from BAT and much more stressful, but it does share a common thread of thinking about functional reinforcers, about why the dog might be reacting, and providing that as a reinforcer. The Two-Reward method first appeared in print in his posthumous work *Diary of a "Dotty Dog" Doctor* in 1997, but he had been using it for a while. The Two-Reward method used different reinforcers to teach dogs to offer calm behaviors, instead of barking and lunging. When working with a dog who was reactive to people, Fisher had the dog tethered, with the owner standing or sitting beside the dog. Then he would walk toward the dog until she barked at him. At that point, the owner would walk away as negative punishment and he would stay in position. When the dog relaxed fully, she would obtain two reinforcers: the return of the owner (who may also feed treats) and the exit of the stranger. He also mentioned that the dog could be reinforced for smaller amounts of relaxation, rather than waiting for her to lie all the way down. The Two-Reward method was one of the precursors of Trish King's Abandonment Training and also Constructional Aggression Treatment (see Resources).

Constructional Aggression Treatment

Constructional Aggression Treatment (or CAT) was developed from a series of research projects at University of North Texas under the supervision of Behavior Analyst Jesús Rosales-Ruiz. Eddie Fernandez researched the effectiveness of using the retreat of the person as a reward for sheep holding still in 2000, Melissa Morehead studied something similar for cows in 2005, and Kellie Snider studied the use of negative reinforcement in treating aggression in dogs in 2007 (see Resources). In the CAT protocol, the dogs are usually tethered, and the decoy approaches and retreats, as in the Two-Reward method, but they try to keep the dog from barking, lunging, or growling by having the decoy approach to a distance that does not cause the dog to react with aggression. When the dog starts barking, lunging, or growling, then the result is similar to the Two-Reward method in that the decoy stays in place as the dog barks himself out, i.e., until the aggression stops and the dog displays an acceptable alternative behavior.

In the original research, the dogs went through quite a few extinction bursts. One major downside to waiting for extinction with such emotionally laden behaviors is the stress it can cause to the dog you are working with, the helper, and even the caregiver. I'll talk more about that in Appendix 3. Additionally, in real life, the triggers are constantly in motion; standing still while the dog barks himself out is impractical and embarrassing for walks. Furthermore, I don't want to turn off the dog's built-in warning system by getting rid of growling or barking through extinction or punishment. CAT practitioners have begun to work to create set-ups that cause fewer outbursts, but as far as I know, this extinction process is considered to be an essential aspect of CAT.

My original interest in using functional reinforcers was inspired by what I had observed in CAT. I liked the concept of reinforcing with distance but was inspired to reduce the level of distress. When I tried CAT, I found that it was less stressful to lead the student dog toward the trigger and let him also be the one to move away. Leading the dog toward the trigger is something I have further changed in BAT 2.0. If the dog has the opportunity to move himself away reduces stress, it makes sense that he'd be even less stressed when moving forward is his own idea. It turns out it's actually more efficient that way, too. If you do BAT, look carefully at your video footage to see if you lead the dog toward the trigger in any way, by leaning, positioning your body, etc. I have also made other changes for controllability, including having the dog self-reinforce instead of the handler providing the reinforcer and encouraging movement. We now have the handler stay out of the way more; the functional reinforcer that the dog chooses is more likely to be right on target.

Horse training

Horse trainers, including Monty Roberts and Alexandra Kurland, have used walking away from the animal as their reward for decades, and Kurland also used a clicker and treats at the same time (see Resources). To my knowledge, Alexandra Kurland and Karen Pryor are the only authors to write about training with a marker signal along with the functional reinforcer of increased distance (see Resources).

A marker signal can come in very handy when you want to teach precise behavior or if the dog is having trouble disengaging from the trigger. As I described in Chapter 7, BAT uses a marker signal with Mark and Move; it may be a verbal marker or a clicker, depending on whether we are using treats or not. If you have a dog who has insufficient cut-off signals and social skills, even at a good distance, Mark and Move can be used to jump-start those behaviors through shaping. For example, some dogs' threshold distance is line of sight—if they can see another dog, they freeze and stare, or worse. In that case, you might have to use Mark and Move to shape disengagement, beginning with just marking for looking at the trigger or blinking. Just don't get too addicted to using Mark and Move when you don't need it, or you'll miss the full power of BAT. The original version of BAT used a marker signal each time the dog disengaged from the trigger, but I came to realize that it was distracting from the social situation when set-ups are going well. It was also reinforcing the dog's handler for going in toward the trigger.

The theory behind using walking away from a horse as a reinforcer for holding still or acting friendly is that they are prey animals, and that they would especially appreciate distance. I think that in any species, most aggressive displays are about proximity in some way—whether they are protecting their territory, themselves, or something else. Resource guarding can be interpreted to be about distance, too, as in, "Get away from my bone/bed/house/mom!" In other words, distance is a functional reinforcer for these behaviors. That is why we are careful to give dogs access to distance in BAT, as a naturally occurring reinforcer.

The evolution of BAT

In all but Ian Dunbar's Retreat n' Treat method (and Suzanne Clothier's version as well), the subject dog is stationary as the decoy approaches. In all of the other methods I am familiar with, it is the decoy that usually retreats, or the subject dog may be tossed a treat to prompt a retreat. I think there is great power in teaching the animal to retreat from a trigger and self-reward throughout this process, whether she is walking toward the trigger or is the one being approached. BAT reduces the dog's stress by allowing her to instigate approaches toward the trigger and move on or retreat from it whenever she wants. Furthermore, BAT 2.0 uses naturally occurring reinforcers, not just functional reinforcers provided by the trainer. This adds an extra layer of controllability for the dog, reduces distraction, and allows the animal to learn more from the 'conversation' with the trigger.

Until 2008, I had been using functional reinforcers as 'real life rewards' for a range of behavior problems, but not systematically for aggression. For aggressive dogs, I used classical counter-conditioning, along with methods similar to those used in *Control Unleashed* and other reward-based methods. Hearing about CAT got me started in using functional reinforcers to work with aggression and fear. I had been using counter-conditioning and systematic desensitization, as well as operant learning with positive reinforcement. I watched the CAT DVD and saw a lot of promise in it, although, like many other positive trainers, I was concerned that it would be too stressful for the dogs. I used the protocol and made some changes along the way.

As you may have noticed, I'm not a particularly good recipe-follower. This can probably be attributed to either my mother, who uses cookbooks only as a general guideline, or to my background in science. I like to learn and I like to fix things. I began to dig deeper, reading more about functional analysis and other methods that use functional reinforcers. By now, I had realized what I had operationalized was a separate entity that needed a name, although it was, of course, based on several existing techniques. The name, BAT, started as a joke, but it stuck.

As time went on, I ran my ideas for even more changes in BAT by my friend Lori Stevens, who is a TTouch practitioner. She asked insightful questions of the form "why do you do such and such" that were excellent food for thought! Over the years, I have had many such conversations and adjusted BAT accordingly. For example, in Germany, someone asked me, "Why is the leash so short?" It was a standard 6-foot (2 meter) leash and I hadn't even thought to question it. Now in BAT 2.0, the dogs can have a much more free experience on a long line, and the caregivers have the skills to handle it safely.

In conclusion, the other methods that use functional reinforcers for reactivity share common ground with BAT in the sense that they are operant counter-conditioning; they change the dog's emotional response to the trigger by teaching new behaviors. These methods teach the dog to offer appropriate behaviors without prompting from the human, and *can* teach dogs to be comfortable and even begin to like interacting with former triggers. But BAT is directly focused on creating a comfortable situation for interaction. The environment is engineered so that the dog is kept below threshold and can freely learn to change his behavior based on naturally occurring reinforcers. These factors and others create a positive and trusting relationship to make BAT a humane and low-stress process, which, according to research that I'll describe in the next appendix, makes it more effective. As I mentioned before, BAT teaches the animal to self-soothe (retreat when needed) versus teaching alternate ways to repel or ignore the intruder. I think that's a subtle but important difference between BAT and its many predecessors.

APPENDIX 3

For Trainers and Behaviorists:
Geek Speak on Terms and Quadrants

Note: Sources for cited works in Appendix 3 can be found in the Resources at the end of the book.

If you read this book and questions like, "Which quadrant does this use?" or "Isn't this just an application of behavior analysis?" or "How is this different from systematic desensitization?" pop into your head, then this appendix is for you. Or if you want to be one of the cool people who come up with such questions, then you might like this too. As dog trainers and behaviorists, it's important to understand the science behind our training techniques. If we can get our students to understand the principles, their dogs will benefit. That said, I have saved the bulk of the technical information for this appendix, because the jargon and technical arguments that professionals are fond of tend to just confuse and annoy most of the dog-loving world. Fair warning: I'll be using slightly more formal language in this section, so you might want to get some fresh air or a strong cup of coffee first!

Antecedent arrangements

I had this note in a Tip for Pros earlier in the book: "The strength of the dog's reactivity depends on her reinforcement history, but also on the context in which this history occurred. *Reinforcement selects behavior in context.*"

Let's take some time to dig into the idea of the behavior + context combination being reinforced. Reinforcement selects the stimulus-response pair, like the pairing of "see other dog" → "bark, growl, bite." The context matters. The reinforcement tells the dog that a specific behavior works in a specific situation. In other words, the consequence selects for the behavior in the presence of the antecedent and the whole context in which that behavior was emitted. For example, taking out bowls or toys to prepare your dog's meal signals that certain behavior will be reinforced with food. Sitting on the couch may signal that a different set of behavior will be reinforced and that the consequences will be something like attention or petting. Good training is about manipulating occasion setters, not just reinforcing behavior.

According to Donahoe, Palmer, and Burgos (1997), "reinforcers affect input–output relations and not output alone" and "context sets the occasion for responding, although its influence may not be apparent until the context is changed." Via the naturally occurring reinforcement that occurs in BAT, we can set the occasion for pro-social behavior by accounting for the context in which it is selected (reinforced). We begin with a context in which pro-social behavior is extremely likely and aggression/frustration/fear are extremely unlikely. Over time, we gradually change the context of our training set-ups to make them more realistic, i.e., similar to situations in which the aggression or other behaviors would have been emitted before BAT. In my experience, BAT changes the stimulus-response pairing in a wide variety of contexts:

OLD: "see other dog" → "bark, growl, bite"

NEW: "see other dog" → "wag and say hi" or "see other dog" → "sniff and move on"

With rehabilitation, BAT is basically about generalizing the Antecedent-Behavior pairing that already has a reinforcement history with a low-intensity version of the stimulus (the other dog is far away, for example). BAT relies heavily on careful antecedent arrangements, where the following is in place: 1) there are no antecedents that motivate or evoke the behavior you are trying to reduce; and 2) the learner is empowered to exercise and expand when they use the target behavior (polite cut-off signals, pro-social behavior, etc.). By doing BAT with people and other dogs, for example, the student dog gains confidence and fluency practicing an effective and appropriate social repertoire. If you look at Dr. Susan Friedman's Humane Hierarchy chart on page 241, you'll notice that antecedent arrangements are generally considered the least intrusive of interventions, i.e., change the environment to make the right behavior easy. Antecedent arrangements are even considered less intrusive than positive reinforcement. While we do still need to have administer positive reinforcement in certain situations, the primary focus in BAT is to rely on antecedent arrangement and naturally occurring reinforcers, rather than trainer-delivered reinforcement.

Behavior analysis: Functional behavior assessments

Behavior has a function: it serves some sort of purpose for the person or animal doing the behavior. Applied behavior analysis interventions focus on the function of the behavior whose probability you are trying to change. A functional behavior assessment determines the relationship between behaviors and environmental events to determine what has reinforced the behavior. When trainers consider antecedents, behaviors, and consequences, the consequence that maintains a particular behavior is considered that behavior's function. A functional behavior assessment can be done in different ways, including indirect functional behavior assessment, descriptive functional behavior assessment, and functional analysis. I'll explain each of those below in terms of a functional assessment of reactive dog behavior, but of course this applies to all species and behaviors.

Indirect functional behavior assessment. The behaviorist gathers information about what happens from people who have observed the dog's behavior in his regular environment. Interview the dog's guardians (in person or via a written questionnaire) on what happens before the dog reacts (setting events and triggers), how the dog reacts, what happens next, etc. This is very common for work with pet dogs.

Descriptive functional behavior assessment. The trainer collects data by observing the dog's behavior and situation directly without manipulating consequences, then analyzes that to determine the function of the behavior. For example, the trainer watches the dog and owner as they walk by a fake or real dog, looking for what triggers the reaction, what the specific behaviors are when the dog reacts, and what the consequences are from the environment and the owner. Another example is that the client brings in a video recording of the dog in a situation in which the reactivity occurs.

Functional analysis. The behaviorist sets up scenarios to measure whether changing the consequences of the reactivity has any effect on it. To test whether achieving Consequence A is the function of barking, for example, one would measure if the barking increases by systematically having Consequence A follow the barking. When working with a client, the ethics of this tactic are questionable, because if it is successful, then the dog is more reactive. If an opportunity to walk away from the triggering stimulus is hypothesized to be the function of the reactivity, then the trainer would test that hypothesis by setting up a situation where the subject dog would be over-threshold and react, followed by the subject dog walking away from the triggering stimulus. I am not really willing to test it that way, so I will just have to rely on more informal functional behavior assessments.

The answer to the question of "Isn't BAT just an application of behavior analysis?" is yes: if you want to look at BAT through that lens, it uses naturally occurring (functional) reinforcers to increase the frequency of replacement behaviors. However, the word "just" implies that there's something wrong with using science to develop treatment protocols. Theory and practice go hand in hand; this fosters continual growth and change. *Practitioners should base behavior modification techniques on sound scientific research, as I have done.* Applied work also feeds into science: researchers should be studying the effectiveness of individual interventions that are developed by trainers and animal behaviorists.

So what's really going on in BAT? More details for Geeks!

Note: This section was originally published in the Summer 2014 *APDT Chronicle of the Dog*. Cited works are listed in the Resources section at the end of the book.

The next section looks at some of the notable features of BAT through the lens of Applied Behavior Analysis and some other fields. BAT is a practical technique and relies heavily on natural processes, so it doesn't neatly fall under procedures or processes defined for research. That said, looking at the similarities to and differences between BAT and scientific results helps us describe what is happening. It's also critical to remember that we aren't working in a lab: real life is messy and that's okay. As Skinner wrote, "what we do is describe more than explain." Susan Friedman quotes this in her seminars and adds, "and that is usually enough."

One caveat is that explanations are based on my understanding of the science at this point in time. My specialty is practical, hands-on training. If any of you are behavior analyists, neuroscientists, ethologists, etc. and want to explore this further from your level of analysis, please do!

One notable feature of BAT is that it involves low-intensity exposure therapy adapted for non-human animals. Exposure therapy is an empirically supported intervention that has been successfully used with human clients for decades in various forms, including systematic desensitization with relaxation and shaping approach behavior with praise (Barlow, Agras, Leitenberg, and Wincze, 1970; Marks, 1975; Wolpe, 1961). The principle of **respondent extinction** was the inspiration for systematic desensitization and exposure therapy (Marks, 1975; Wolpe, 1961).

Respondent extinction is the weakening of an association created via classical conditioning. If one presents the conditional stimulus without pairing it with the unconditional stimulus or another conditional stimulus, then the conditional stimulus will lose the power to elicit the same response as the unconditional stimulus. In other words, the response is extinguished because it no longer predicts anything biologically important. There are arguments both for (Field, 2006) and against (Tryon, 2005) respondent extinction being the primary principle behind these therapies, but the arguments against it seem to apply primarily to humans and not to dogs.

BAT is based, in part, on the empirically supported principle of respondent extinction. Using careful antecedent arrangements, respondent extinction can be facilitated in a gradual, systematic way that does not elicit a fear response from the sympathetic nervous system. Keeping arousal low is important on several fronts, but here's one: research indicates that an asynchronously high heart rate during exposure therapy is a significant predictor of the return of fear after the therapy is fully completed (Rachman, 1989). In other words, when the heart rate was high, but other behavior indicated relaxation, the fear was likely to return.

Two common trainer sayings are: "dogs don't learn when they are over-threshold" and "dogs don't generalize well." But the truth is that when they are over-threshold, dogs are actually very efficient at learning. The problem is that what they learn is not what we are trying to teach: *dogs efficiently generalize what to be afraid of when they are over-threshold.* Inhibition of fear is much more challenging to learn and generalize (Vervlie,

Baeyens, Van den Bergh, and Hermans, 2013, Gunther et al., 1998). Fear conditioning is not very context dependent; it spreads like wildfire between different situations. If you learn that tigers are scary in the jungle, you had better still be afraid of them on the plains, or you will not pass on your genetic material. The bad news, then, is that the acquisition of fear generalizes more readily than reduction of fear. That is why it is critical to avoid using aversive training techniques and why it is important to train in multiple contexts when working to teach confidence.

Animal research indicates that respondent extinction silences fear neurons and remodels a specific type of inhibitory junction, called the perisomatic synapse (Trouche et al., 2013). In Trouche's study, two groups of mice received fear conditioning. The treament group went through a respondent extinction procedure and showed an increase in perisomatic inhibitory synapses in the amygdala compared to the control group, who did not receive that treatment. The increase of inhibitory synapses was found around fear neurons that were no longer firing in response to the stimulus after the procedure. What that likely means for BAT, which appears to function as low-intensity respondent extinction, is that the student dog's brain may now process signals about fearful stimuli in a different way; there could now be an increase of synapses that inhibit the fearful response. A change in brain structure makes sense, because, of course, change in behavior is only really possible with some sort of shift in the brain.

Another core mechanism at work with BAT is controllability. The older version of BAT used reinforcement given by the trainer to give the dog a sense of control, but the new version has the animal in control of more of the situation, with no need for reinforcement by the trainer. BAT is not an extinction procedure that is done to the animal. *A crucial aspect of BAT is the controllability of exposure to the trigger.* There are mountains of evidence that demonstrate that the degree of predictability and controllability modulates experience of the stimulus and the return of fear after extinction (Thomas et al., 2012; Yang, Wellman, Ambrozewicz, and Sanford, 2011; Maier and Watkins, 2010; Baratta et al., 2007; Mechiel Korte and De Boer, 2003). In fact, control over aversive events improves extinction, prevents the return of fear, and has a *protective effect when the animal is exposed to future stressors,* as if they expect the next stressor also to be controllable (Maier & Watkins, 2010; Maier, Amat, Baratta, Paul, & Watkins, 2006; Amat, Paul, Zarza, Watkins, & Maier, 2006). The effect of controllability on resilience applies to humans, too (Hartley, Gorun, Reddan, Ramirez, and Phelps, 2013).

Maier et al., (2006) posit that the perception of controllability actively inhibits the neural response to stressors in mammals. When animals underwent the same stressor with the only difference being controllability, the brain activity was very different:

(i) the presence of control is detected by regions of the ventral medial prefrontal cortex (mPFCv); and (ii) detection of control activates mPFCv output to stress-responsive brain stem and limbic structures that actively inhibit stress induced activation of these structures. Furthermore, an initial experience with control over

stress alters the mPFCv response to subsequent stressors so that mPFCv output is activated even if the subsequent stressor is uncontrollable, thereby making the organism resilient.

This increase in resilience due to controllability is one of the many reasons that I recommend using BAT with puppies as a way of life when introducing them to new situations. Let them really take things in and allow them to control their experience, so that in future circumstances where control isn't an option (i.e., emergency vet procedures), they will be more resilient. There are two exceptions to this rule: the handler must maintain physical and emotional safety for the puppy and those he interacts with and also may need to use positive reinforcement to teach impulse control.

One aspect of controllability is predictability that comes from knowing that one is safe due to one's own behavior. However, predictability is not the only reason controllability has great effects on resilience (Maier and Warren, 1988), so the controllability aspect of BAT is useful. Predictability alone is not as helpful as controllability, but adding more predictability reduces stress (Maier and Warren, 1988). If you want to add another element of predictability to the BAT protocol, you can teach a cue that signals the appearance of the trigger, such as "there's a dog." You can do this by calmly saying, "there's a dog" just before the dog sees another dog at sub-threshold levels. This is especially useful for dogs who startle easily or have trouble perceiving the trigger until it is too close. A practical downside to this is that you now have to be consistent about predicting the appearance of a trigger and whatever phrase you use is also one more context cue to fade later in your training. You also have to be careful not to put the dog into working mode. For these reasons, I do not include cueing the appearance of the trigger into the standard version of BAT.

I believe that the level of controllability, of *agency—the ability to control a situation based on one's own actions—is the active ingredient in BAT.* Controllability makes a significant difference in what the animal learns from BAT and how well it works.

In BAT, we work at a distance where the animals comfortably explore their environment and show some interest in the trigger with only sub-threshold behavior. This is important: by moving around in an environment with the stimulus, the animal has an opportunity to learn that the stimulus need not evoke fear and that the animal has control over exposure to that stimulus. In these set-ups, nature takes its course as the fear extinguishes and the animals learn to engage with stimuli in a less reactive way. For example, the dogs check out the trigger themselves; sometimes they are curious enough to go closer and sometimes they choose to move away. As they move, they are learning that they have agency in this situation. *They have choices; they can self-soothe or express curiosity.*

There may be times during where the dog feels more comfortable moving away after investigating the trigger. Situations inducing fear should be limited, but simply turning and walking away is not a problem and will not teach the dog that avoidance is the only option. In fact, being able to leave is likely to reduce the stress for the next attempt to approach. Say you were claustrophobic and just moved to a house with a walk-in closet. When you learn that there is no way for you to be locked inside, meaning that you can leave the closet at any time, you would probably be more willing to go into it. Getting that information is one thing, but personally experiencing that it is your choice to go in and that you can easily walk out would give you even more of a confidence boost. In human therapy, there has been much debate over whether engaging in 'safety behavior' (behavior that makes one feel safe) is productive for therapy. It turns out that engaging in safety behaviors does not necessarily interrupt the therapeutic process, and can even reduce stress and return of fear (Goetz, 2013; Milosevic and Radomsky, 2008; Parrish, Radomsky, and Dugas, 2008).

As we work with our dogs and sometimes even specifically train behaviors to deal with their fears, we should be conscious of which kinds of coping skills will lead to rehabilitation and which will not. Parrish, et al., (2008) wrote that clients' anxiety-control strategies may be less likely to become counter-productive when:

1. They promote increases in self-efficacy,

2. They do not demand excessive attentional resources,

3. They enable greater approach behavior and integration of corrective information (via 'disconfirmatory experiences'), and

4. They do not promote misattributions of safety.

The skills learned in BAT meet these criteria. If you are using another technique, take a look at the criteria above to assess whether it is a good fit. Does the behavior your dog is learning promote self-efficacy, meaning is it effective for meeting the dog's needs? Does it take a lot of your dog's attention away from the environment? Does it encourage approach behavior and gathering information about the trigger? Does it give a false sense of security because the goal is to teach them that all of the other dogs/kids/people are good and safe, when they really are not? If it does, you might want to consider if there's a way to modify the technique to teach behaviors that meet your dog's needs in a more effective, reliable way.

Goetz (2013) suggests two categories of safety behaviors: preventative safety behaviors are attempts to avoid or reduce the intensity of a situation and restorative safety behaviors are attempts to bring a situation back to its desired state. Avoidance would be in the preventative category and escape would be in the restorative category. *Preventative safety behaviors disrupted the therapeutic process, but restorative behaviors did not.* Restorative safety behaviors may be helpful for therapy and preventative safety behaviors tend to be detrimental. That means that if a dog has an experience with the trigger and moves on, you do not have to worry that this will teach the dog to be more afraid. By contrast, complete avoidance—for example, staring at the handler for treats, after gathering little to no information about the trigger, is a preventative safety behavior.

In your training sessions, reducing the stress level allows the dog to use more restorative safety behaviors. Work at enough distance so that there is no need for avoidance, so that the dog can comfortably engage with the trigger.

Why call it BAT and not just exposure therapy, desensitization with controllability, or low-intensity respondent extinction?

BAT is a specific technique that has been operationalized for non-human animals, so it needed its own name. It is a version of exposure therapy, a category of human anxiety therapies that can involve talking to the client, visualization, etc., done in a careful way to avoid stress beyond interest. In BAT, the dog desensitizes to his triggers, but it is done in a very particular way, with the dog in control of the experience. But BAT cannot just be called desensitization. BAT is a specific protocol that operationalizes one way to apply the principle of desensitization, just as clicker training is one way to apply the principle of positive reinforcement.

The same argument applies to extinction. I believe that a significant portion of the learning in BAT can be attributed to the *process* of respondent extinction. However, the actual *procedure* of extinction can be done in extremely stressful and intrusive ways, with no controllability by the learner. It can also be done carefully to avoid overt fear responses with a high amount of learner control, as with BAT. That means we cannot just call it respondent extinction, either. In addition to these distinctions between the principles and the protocols of extinction, it's important to clarify that BAT is not just about extinguishing a fear response—it applies to fear, yes, but also to frustration and aggression. Calling this technique BAT does not change the underlying empirically demonstrated processes of extinction and controllability, but it does help specify the operationalization and philosophy of the technique.

Dr. Susan Friedman (2009) created the Humane Hierarchy, illustrated on the next page, to help applied behavior analysts, behaviorist consultants, and trainers choose an intervention to modify behavior. This replaces the simple "is it effective?" way to assess a technique and gives us a way to consider ethics. The decision-making process follows the route of the car. At the bottom are the least intrusive ways to affect behavior change. Toward the top, notice that there are speed bumps that would make you stop to really consider whether the intervention is necessary. Before resorting to positive punishment, for example, you should collect and analyze data and consult with colleagues to be sure that, for this individual, less intrusive techniques are not effective. Taking that pause to really consider helps you find a less intrusive solution. Technically, this still leaves open the option of using force, but in practice, you can stay on the bottom of this hierarchy, because there are so many other great ways to change behavior.

Note that the Humane Hierarchy ranks the techniques that humans apply to change behavior, not environmental consequences that we are not providing. Naturally occurring reinforcement, punishment, extinction, etc. are not part of this chart. You don't have to worry about being an unethical trainer if you're just out walking and your dog learns to avoid stepping in a mud puddle to keep his feet dry.

Hierarchy of Behavior-Change Procedures
Most Positive, Least Intrusive Effective Intervention

Note that the concept of 'extinction' listed on the Humane Hierarchy is operant extinction, not the respondent (classical) learning process of the same name.

In terms of the hierarchy above, BAT focuses on antecedent arrangements. This is the second level of the hierarchy, after medical, nutritional, and physical changes, which should be considered before doing anything else to modify behavior. Changing antecedent arrangements means that we orchestrate experiences that avoid triggering the behavior and emotion that we are trying to change. This allows our learners to experience life in a new way. When we carefully arrange antecedents, respondent learning can take place, in the form of desensitization. Controllability is also an important aspect of BAT. The operant learning that happens during BAT is generally not due to reinforcement from the trainer, but from interaction with the environment. The trainer's main role is to maintain a safe space in which the dog can be comfortable to explore, limiting intrusion. The dog is free to move freely within that space, giving the dog control over naturally occurring reinforcers. When all is going well, that comes in the form of access to the trigger (R+). If the training set-up is sub-optimal and the dog feels the need to move away from the trigger, that is also allowed (R-) or intrusion is stepped up a notch to encourage movement away (redirection, R- of escape,

R+ of trainer treats). Finally, the handler's responses may be positive reinforcement. For example, the dog leads the 'dance' and when the dog moves on, the handler follows. This may be a positive social experience. If the dog solicits attention, the handler reinforces with attention and may suggest a direction of movement. The handler may also occasionally praise disengagement.

Differential reinforcement of an alternative behavior (DRA) is a procedure in which you extinguish behavior by withholding reinforcement for it, while reinforcing some other behavior instead. Because we are building up alternative behavior, BAT could be seen as a DRA procedure, but *the handler is not applying differential reinforcement.*

With BAT, we don't apply operant extinction, because it's not ethical (or useful, say the neuroscientists) to force a dog to stay in a stressful situation just because he's not offering the 'right' behavior to get out of it. If the dog growls, for example, move him away from the trigger. While that's only intended to help the dog calm down, it also may reinforce the growling. That's risky, but not as bad as it sounds. We can just arrange our set-ups so that growling or other such behaviors are very unlikely. That way, the dog gets lots of reinforcement for behavior we want, and not much reinforcement for the behavior we are trying to eliminate. That has a similar effect to differential reinforcement, without the added stress and disempowerment of extinction.

Thinking beyond quadrants

We shouldn't decide whether a method is ethical or not based purely on the learning theory quadrants. Frankly, I think doing so is the easy way out. As intelligent, empathetic beings, we can put more thought into it than that. Here are some factors that I propose you consider when deciding whether a training method that involves the presence of aversive stimuli humane.

1. Will the aversive stimulus remain aversive after treatment?

2. Do any other effective treatments avoid the aversive altogether?

3. If not, is the level of exposure to the aversive at the lowest amount possible for efficient learning?

4. Is exposure to the aversive active or passive?

5. Is the dog able to remove himself from the aversive at any time?

I'll address these questions one at a time with regard to BAT. If you use other kinds of training methods that involve any aversives (like leash walking, reactivity protocols, etc.), I suggest you walk through the list for those methods, too, even if you are 100% certain that what you are doing is humane. It's a good activity to repeat periodically, as new training methods are developed that can change your answers to the questions above.

Will the aversive stimulus remain aversive after treatment? No. The aversive stimulus does not remain aversive after BAT is finished. The whole point of BAT is to get the dog comfortable around the trigger. This is not the use of artificial aversives for the sake of changing unrelated behavior, like training a recall using a shock collar or using a head collar to lift a reactive dog's head and close his mouth until he calms down. The only aversive in BAT is the trigger: that stimulus is present in order to acclimate the dog to the stimulus itself, i.e., teach him that that particular environmental aversive stimulus is actually benign or pleasant. BAT and other reactivity rehabilitation methods like Control Unleashed and counter-conditioning with systematic desensitization all pass this test. I consider all of these methods to be 'dog-friendly' and criterion #1 is essential for that.

Do any other effective treatments avoid the aversive altogether? No. All methods that I know of to rehabilitate or prevent dog reactivity involve having the dog perceive the aversive triggering stimulus. We can't have them lie on a therapy couch to discuss their relationship with other dogs or people. We have to train experientially.

If not, is the level of exposure to the aversive at the lowest amount possible for efficient learning? Yes. In a BAT session, the level of arousal caused by the triggering stimulus should be just at the level of noticing and definitely not past the reactivity threshold. This is similar to other dog-friendly reactivity rehabilitation methods. However, since BAT doesn't usually use a lot of trainer-delivered food or toys during set-ups, more of the dog's attention is on the helper. In order to achieve the same level of non-reactivity without distractions present, the helper is usually further away at the beginning of a BAT session than with other dog-friendly methods.

Is exposure to the aversive active or passive? Exposure is incredibly active in BAT, except when specifically using passive exposure to the trigger that the trainer is getting the dog used to. The student dog leads the way toward the triggering stimulus, rather than having the stimulus presented to the dog. The handler's main role is to keep the dog from over-exposing herself to the trigger, i.e., walking too close to the trigger. In scenarios to specifically work on Sudden Environmental Contrast, the exposure is passive (i.e., a dog appears from behind a corner), but the dog can still move around and exposure is active whenever possible. I think this controllability is a strength of BAT over the way many other dog-friendly methods are practiced.

Is the dog able to remove himself from the aversive at any time? Yes! Allowing the dog to remove himself from the trigger at any time is essential for BAT. The dog is always allowed to move away from the triggering stimulus. This is a huge benefit of having the dog walking on a long leash versus being tethered or stationary with passive exposure. The handler is responsible for noticing when the dog is uncomfortable. Since the dog doesn't speak a human language, the communication is imperfect, but certainly the goal is to allow the dog to avoid anything she wants to avoid. Note: if a dog will not look at the helper or refuses to walk forward, you are working too close! The beauty of BAT is that the dog learns to make her own choices under your supervision, whether she is creating a buffer of extra space from the stimulus, or curiously moving closer to the stimulus while remaining below threshold. Controllability is an essential feature of humane care. Providing maximal opportunity to control her exposure to the trigger is required for a technique to be dog-friendly or humane. Having control over the level of stress is empowering and should be part of any protocol for reactivity, whether it's BAT or any of the other techniques. Having control over one's own safety creates learned optimism, the opposite of learned helplessness. Be aware that there is more than one way to force a dog into an uncomfortable situation. The obvious way would be to tether the dog or to pull him toward the aversive on a leash. But even if you use treats, or just your own movement, and never pull on the dog, you are still creating a conflict: even though you are not physically forcing the dog to be too close to the trigger, the value of the food or your presence may cause her to stay close, even though she really wants to go away.

Some useful ideas from social psychology

Social psychologists do research on how our species behaves as a whole. They look at general trends of what we do relative to one another, rather than looking at your childhood or personal situation like a therapist might do.

Social psychology studies how other humans (real or imagined) influence human behavior. I am including some concepts here that I think are relevant to this book because they might help you understand why clients or other trainers might be resistant to change.

Cognitive Dissonance. This is the feeling we get when we simultaneously believe two ideas that can't both be true. It is an uncomfortable feeling to hold onto conflicting opinions and the theories on cognitive dissonance in social psychology is that humans work hard to avoid this state of being. Here are some examples of conflicting ideas:

1. "I want to be thin," "I love chocolate," and "chocolate makes you fat."

2. "I have trained with choke chains," and "Training with choke chains is inhumane," and "I am a good person."

3. "Training without treats is inhumane" and "I like BAT!"

4. "If the dog moves away from the trigger, he was stressed" and "In humane training, there is never any stress."

The theory of cognitive dissonance proposes that people have an innate motivational drive to reduce dissonance. People get rid of cognitive dissonance in different ways. One way is to simply avoid thinking about the conflict. So the chocolate-loving person may just put the desire to be thin out of her head when eating chocolate. Or she may change behavior or add another belief, so there is no conflict, after all. For example, if you add on exercise: "My workout burns those chocolate calories," or wishful thinking: "Calories only count if you eat them while sitting, so I will eat my chocolate standing up!" then the dissonance is reduced. She could also remove one of the beliefs: "Being super thin doesn't matter" or edit one of them: "A small amount of chocolate in a balanced diet does not make you fat." We have a lot of creative ways to reduce dissonance. Some of them totally remove the dissonance and others just bring it down to a manageable level.

Taking a look at the second line, you'll see an example of the quandary that a trainer may have after her first exposure to positive training. Seeing that positive reinforcement training produces reliable results may have made her realize that choke chains are unnecessary. If they are not necessary and they are aversive, the trainer has been using inhumane training. But only bad people do inhumane things, and she is a good person! Her head threatens to spin off of her neck unless she can get rid of the cognitive dissonance. At this point, she has at least three choices in order to continue to believe she is a good person: become a "crossover trainer" and decide to stop using choke chains, become a "balanced trainer" by eliminating the belief that choke chains are unnecessary, or discount her learning of positive training altogether and go back to her old way of training. (If you're in this boat, I hope you choose the first option!)

Let's move on to the third set of inconsistent beliefs. One way that I have seen people fix this dissonance is to just feed a lot more treats in BAT. Unfortunately, that actually weakens the protocol, because the dog is not able to have the freedom to make his own choices based on naturally occurring reinforces. By reinforcing behavior yourself, you change the set of behaviors that are offered and the dog's motivation. If you look at the Humane Hierarchy, positive reinforcement is not at the pinnacle. The first ways to change behavior should rely on giving the animal behavioral control. Treats are great for jump-starting behavior, but they are not the only way to change behavior. In fact, sometimes feeding treats can get in the way. So another way to address this set of beliefs is to strike out the first statement. Treats are not a requirement of a humane training protocol. In fact, they are not always in the learner's best interest.

The cognitive dissonance in the fourth set of beliefs could be alleviated by asserting that the dog is not stressed, he only wanted to move away to go sniff something else. While that often looks like the case, that is not always true, either. What we do know is that the dog chose to approach and chose to move away, without visible signs of distress. In other words, he acted like any other dog. We can't remove all distress from an animal's life. We did not create the original fear or add an unnecessary aversive; we are teaching the dog how to integrate the trigger into his life. The *most* humane thing we can do is help dogs get over their fears, and that includes teaching them that their behavior can have a positive effect. Replacing the second statement with a quote by Dr. Susan Friedman takes care of that dissonance: "[Looking at] the degree to which a behavior reduction procedure preserves learner control is essential to developing a standard of humane, effective practice" (see Resources).

Ethics are very important to me. I hope that we can have a conversation in our community to see whether we, as a profession, have taken the easy way out and allowed learning theory quadrants, a construct, to replace a critical analysis to decide whether a technique is humane. Fortunately, I continue to see a shift in the way people are thinking about this. I think it's important to have criteria by which we judge the use of a training method in a particular situation, so that things like cognitive dissonance don't convince us that the training we do is humane (see below). However, I think it's also important to make sure those criteria are up to date, so that when we use them to judge a method, the result is consistent with our ethics.

My revised way to test whether the use of aversives is humane is in the section above. CC and other dog-friendly techniques use the same stimuli that we use in BAT, usually from a closer initial distance. BAT compares favorably to those other techniques on a test of whether it is humane, even though the Premack principle does tell us that we have some naturally occurring negative and positive reinforcement (when the dog moves on after gathering information). BAT uses the same stimulus level as other dog-friendly methods and gives the dog more control over their ability to engage or disengage with other dogs or people.

Fundamental Attribution Error. When we ourselves behave in some way, we tend to think of it as being justified, even if it turned out to be a mistake (unless we are depressed). When someone else makes a mistake, we tend to attribute it to a character flaw. That's the fundamental attribution error at work.

For example, let's say you're on a walk and your dog poops in someone's yard. Suddenly, you realize you have no bags, so you make a mental note to come back later to scoop it up. You know the whole situation and you know that your decision to walk away was based on what just happened. But the neighbor sees you walking away without scooping and calls you a lazy, inconsiderate dog walker. You knew that your behavior happened for a reason, but the other guy assumed there was something inherently wrong with you.

According to the research of social psychologists, people have a tendency to look for character flaws to explain bad behavior, rather than looking for a situational explanation. It's kind of like the opposite of functional analysis and it's the reason why dogs are labeled as "dominant" or "stubborn" rather than "under-socialized" or "under-motivated." In ourselves and those close to us, we tend to create situational explanations of behavior (unless we are in a conflict with them over the behavior in question). With others, we tend to just write them off entirely as being fundamentally flawed. As another example, you probably have some explanation for why your dog may lunge on a walk, but if another dog does that, you might think of that dog as a bad dog, or that the dog's handler is a jerk for walking too close to your dog.

The fundamental attribution error also comes out when we use the label of "aggressive dogs," versus the behavioral description of "dogs who bark, growl, and bare teeth in response to triggers X, Y, and Z." The former is a personality assessment and the latter is a more helpful description, which is behavioral and situational. I am just as guilty as the next person of using the phrase "reactive dogs," "aggressive dogs," "fearful dogs," etc., because those phrases are a whole lot shorter and easier to say. But be aware of what it means when you use this kind of shorthand. Dr. Susan Friedman, Chirag Patel, and Ken Ramirez have great discussions in their seminars as to why we want to "unlabel" our dogs. Susan provides downloadable images in many languages on her site for her Unlabel Me campaign (see Resources).

www.behaviorworks.org

I'm writing about this here for two reasons. First, make sure that you remember to look for situational explanations of your dog's behavior (and then use those to train alternative behaviors). This empowers you and your dog: you can change the environment, and thus the behavior. Character flaws have a fixed property, so we just give up. Second, the fundamental attribution error applies to other trainers, too. "Positive" trainers tend to see a character flaw in "traditional" trainers who use physical punishment, thinking of them as inhumane or cruel, too stupid to learn good, modern training. Conversely, traditional trainers tend to see character flaws in "cookie pushers," thinking that we are weak people who don't have the stomach for real training. Both sides think that the other does harm and that their own behavior is justified, so we don't empathize, look for common ground, or use our well-honed behavior modification skills. While I don't always agree with the explanations that other people have for their behavior, remembering that they do not necessarily have character flaws, gives me the empathy to reach out. Every one of us has some justification that may be hard to overcome, due to the cognitive dissonance problem that I mentioned before. Knowing that lets us empathize with one another and gives us a chance to create a better world together.

APPENDIX 4

Trainers and Clients Share Their Experiences with BAT

I'm leaving the last paragraphs to some of the forward-thinking trainers and devoted dog lovers who have used BAT. I think it is only fitting, because without the interest my students, I wouldn't have been inspired to write this book! The articles are different interpretations of my deliberately vague call for short write-ups on their experiences with BAT. These letters came in from all over the world, so you'll note British English as well as our Americanized form.

I am very grateful that so many people took time out of their busy lives to share their experiences of BAT for this book. As far as I know, the people who submitted articles for this appendix are great trainers. However, since I haven't vetted them 100% or seen them work with clients personally, this is not necessarily a list of referrals. Certified BAT Instructors (CBATIs) are trainers and behaviorists who have been thoroughly tested, so you can confidently work with any CBATI mentioned below or in the CBATI directory at GrishaStewart.com.

Think of this appendix as feedback on the BAT method itself and an example of the many ways people have used BAT successfully.

Emmy's BAT progress was a team effort
Dennis Fehling, CBATI, CPDT-KA, TTouch1, Redmond, Oregon, USA, friendsforlifedogtraining.com

Giving her control of movement has made all the difference. Emmy is a very large female longhaired German shepherd. My clients moved here from Olympia Washington last year and immediately started working with me for Emmy's dog reactivity and my wife Pam Bigoni for K9 Nosework. Since we started, Emmy has made amazing progress on both fronts. She has earned her nose work 2 title and has worked with several different dogs for her reactivity. In the last few months, Emmy is has been able to help others clients and their dogs by playing the role of the helper dog. Each time I see Emmy, I am told that her interactions with other dogs get better and better. She actually had three encounters with off-leash dogs that have run up to her and she has just turned and walked away. My clients have been the best to work with and have been very open to the entire process. I can honestly say in all of the months we have worked together we have had only one outburst from Emmy which I give all of the credit to my clients for the time they have invested and their willingness to make sure Emmy's needs are met.

I am also very proud of the fact that when Emmy goes to her nose work trials, all of the people that know her are saying how much calmer she is around all of the other dogs and how much more focused she is when working. During the BAT sessions we have made sure that we have practiced in many different areas with many differ-

Emmy has made great progress with BAT.

ent sizes and shapes of dogs, we also make sure that Emmy is in full charge of her sessions as far as when she has had enough. In my honest opinion, this is what has made all of the difference for Emmy. I have so many people and dogs to thank for Emmy's progress and continued healing. I have to thank Gina and Dan Suomi for being the best clients in the world, Pam Bigoni for her amazing nose work teaching. I also want to say a huge thanks to Andrea Martin for her great coaching during the sessions with Gina and Emmy and to her dogs Levi and Summer for being great neutral dogs for the sessions. Emmy has become a BAT success story for many reasons and continues to make huge improvements. And last but certainly not least a huge thanks to Grisha Stewart who has brought BAT to the world and given all of us a new set of skills which is helping dogs and people all over the world.

A note from Gina: We had a beautiful BAT moment while camping. As we have discussed so many dog owners think their dogs are under voice control but when it comes to something that is too tempting, the humans lose!

The four of us were walking and a man unzipped his tent and let his Shar Pei out charging full speed toward Emmy and Travis. Travis encountered the dog first and Emmy chose to keep going. The owner followed with a lame excuse...couldn't find his leash! The Shar Pei decided to move on to Emmy. Emmy stopped, a little fluffed up, but had a brief sniff with the dog, no barking or growling. The owner made his way over and finally took his dog home and Emmy moved on. One year ago, I am sure her reaction would have included end of the leash barking and growling! I was so proud.

Harmony and communication
Katie Grillaert CBCC-KA, CPDT-KA, CBATI, Fetch Dog Training and Behavior Minneapolis, MN, USA, fetchmpls.com

It's hard for me now to remember a time that I didn't teach Behavior Adjustment Training to my students. Our reactive dog rehabilitation program is transformed, and provides even better support to our students. We also use BAT as a preventative tool in our puppy training, wallflower classes, and even basic manners training. It would be easy to say that BAT is now part of our culture, with fabulous benefits for both our human and our canine learners.

I have a favorite moment when using BAT with students. There's always a particular time where the dog and handler share a beautiful "Aha!" The dog realizes that he is empowered to make choices about his environment—if he is feeling confident today, or if he would like extra time or space today. And his handler learns that she is able to recognize and understand even the subtlest suggestion from her dog. There is harmony, there is communication—the shared joy is tangible.

Career-saving techniques for competition dogs
Molly Sumner CDBC, CPDT-KSA, CBATI, CWRI, Frenchtown, NJ, USA, kindredcompanions.com

I was first introduced to BAT when my competition obedience dog—a Shiba Inu named Mashi—became reactive around other dogs. He had been attacked multiple times and was highly nervous in competition environments. Even when other dogs were not around his nerves would get the better of him and he would ring run or ground sniff until we were excused from the ring. At his worst he would lunge at other dogs who stared at him or growled.

Fast-forward three years and Mashi is a different dog. He is up beat, engaged, and relaxed. He is confident and can comfortably sit or lie down in a line of upwards of 12 dogs while I hide out of sight for the duration of a stays exercise. What made this miracle turn around was BAT.

Because many behavior modification protocols use markers, or operant techniques, Mashi would go into 'training mode' and not reap the benefits of any kind of relaxation or redirection. It would also amp up his stress, being in 'training' mode around triggers. Instead of fixing the problem, it seemed to make it worse. This is when we turned to BAT.

BAT uses natural desensitization, which allowed Mashi to observe his triggers, on his own time and emotional state and empowered him by giving him control over his interactions. Over time he was comfortable observing and disengaging from triggers and eventually even sought them out with curiosity and confidence. Since using BAT my dog doesn't just enjoy the competition ring again, he also enjoys the company of calm, well-mannered dogs. More than I could have ever hoped for.

Mashi is an obedience champion, thanks to BAT.

BAT has been miraculous for Sam

Sally A. Bushwaller, CPDT-KSA, CNWI, Chicago, Illinois, USA, bushwaller.com

I have had great success using BAT and other functional reinforcers for helping heal some broken dogs. One dog in particular is a Pit mix or Heinz 57 dog I've been working with. We'll call him Sam.

In February 2011, we began working together. Sam had spent some significant time at a no kill shelter and had bitten (with punctures) a shelter worker. Another shelter volunteer developed a relationship with Sam and adopted him, determined to fix him. In addition to reactivity to people, Sam was also reactive to dogs.

Initially, Sam couldn't look at a dog from more than ½ block away without reacting. He also reacted to most people he encountered on walks, especially 'odd-looking' people. I began doing BAT sessions with Sam and his owner, using my dog as a decoy. Each session Sam continued to improve greatly. After just four sessions our dogs were able to parallel walk, then meet with a fence between them and then without the fence.

Improvement really snowballed after that. In a short period of time, Sam was walking side-by-side on daily walks with one or two other dog "buddies" and his owner was allowing him occasional off-lead play with a neighbor's dog.

We have now done 11 BAT [1.0] sessions. The last four sessions have been at dog parks. We don't go inside, we work outside at the fence. Sam can sniff just about any dog who comes up to him without reacting, even if the dog inside the park is a little barky. We are still working on surprise dog appearances, but even that is improving. The owner says BAT has been miraculous for Sam, he is truly a different dog than he was just a few short months ago. He hardly pulls on walks anymore, because he's so much calmer and relaxed. Everyone is thrilled with his progress.

During this process, Sam's reactivity to people has mostly disappeared because the owner worked the BAT process each time Sam began to focus on anyone while on walks. Sam's owner is the ideal client. He keeps great notes on Sam's interactions with other dogs and has embraced BAT, using it on all his walks for every dog they encounter. Thanks to his owner's loving heart and dedication to BAT training, an impossible-to-place dog has been rehabilitated.

These days, I continue to use BAT on an almost daily basis, and prefer to use the more "organic" approach of BAT 2.0 when I have room to do so.

Proud and satisfied clients
Katrien Lismont, TTouch Practitioner, CumCane Trainer, CBATI Bretzfeld, Germany.

BAT is dotting the "i" for me in positively training dogs that show leash reactivity. It is teaching the dogs to drive home without GPS. No big signs, no big interventions, just smoothly moving on in the environment, perfecting the gentle leash handlings skills, becoming less and less visible and less and less essential as a guard. I have never found a more empathic and empowering training to teach dogs to handle encounters with their triggers. It teaches the human to read his dog from the back of her head and changes emotions bit by bit, in the dog as well as in the human end of the leash.

Ever since I offer practical BAT Trainings in my Training center, reactivity has been reduced dramatically, resulting in proud and satisfied clients, just because the dogs feel they are understood.

Thank you Grisha!

Saved my dog's life
Yvonne and Stan, California, USA

This is to say thank you, from a layperson who had an out-of-control dog. Almost five years ago, my husband and I got a rescue puppy, four months old. If we had been experienced with dogs in any way, we likely would have noticed the early signs of discomfort and anxiety on walks. (And maybe experience would have helped me with subtle cues from a neighbor's dog who bit our puppy in the face, instead of trusting the owner who said the dog was friendly and asked if they could greet in front of our house on leash.) Instead we wound up with a disaster. He would go ballistic for other dogs (and also silently, with no warning, jump at people who got too close).

Off-leash he has always been a dream; on-leash he became Cujo. A neighbor gave us a reference for an expensive trainer who taught us to use a choke chain; needless to say that only exacerbated our dog's anxiety to the extreme. He learned that he was right to be scared and I couldn't even control him with the choke chain. He just wound up gagging and rasping and I was scared we were damaging his trachea. It was awful, and we did it for months. My husband started hating our dog, and I was flooded with adrenaline and sometimes in tears walking him. And our poor dog was miserable. In desperation I searched for a solution online and found you.

To say that your work has helped our dog and us enormously is a huge understatement. I honestly feel like it has saved his life (and ours.) We live in a neighborhood full of dogs where he was always in the red zone. I was at my wits end. I couldn't imagine giving him to a shelter where he would be put down, but he is so strong (a pit mix) that I didn't know what to do. If we had a yard, I probably would have stopped walking him altogether. I had to figure something out, and you saved us, so thank you!!

I can't tell you how grateful I am for your work. Your approach went against everything I had learned and been taught, and yet it instantly made intuitive sense. From the first time we tried it, when we walked outside and let him sniff the air for as long as he liked (several minutes) and get the lay of the land and decide which direction felt most comfortable for him, we knew we were on the right path. Thank you for figuring this out. We are forever grateful.

A former Cujo

Mikey has learned to make decisions for himself
Anita and Mikey, Bend, Oregon, USA

Mikey is a toy Australian Shepherd about 12 years old. He was a rescue who came with no background information other than he had been at the Dallas Humane Society for about one month. He was totally shut down at the time, but as he opened up, we found out that he had a strong herding instinct and was reactive to other dogs. He would get upset and run up to them and bark in their face. I was afraid that someday another dog would take offense at this and take his face off!

Before we found BAT, we worked with a Veterinary Behaviorist who tried the latest and greatest in dog training. We gave treats for looking at other dogs and attended a class with other reactive dogs. During one session Mikey was visciously attacked (unprovoked), and badly injured by a medium sized dog when the owner dropped the leash. We stopped training, Mikey healed and several months later we moved to Bend and were introduced to Dennis Fehling and BAT. At our first session, Mikey's threshold to another dog was about 1000 ft. He had no idea what to do and just stood—no sniffing, no walking, nothing, while waiting for me to tell him what to do. Over time Mikey has learned it's ok to sniff and make decisions for himself. In fact, he loves sniffing so much he also takes classes in nose work where they call him the "energizer bunny" because he never stops searching. But that's another story.

Mikey's life has improved greatly with BAT techniques. He is more relaxed easily managed when we go for walks. He's calmer and no longer hyper-vigilant watching for other dogs. We've learned techniques to use that can help distract, or escape from unforeseen situations that previously would have caused a melt down for Mikey. Last week during our session, Mikey was relaxed enough that we could all sit calmly, enjoying the day, about 75 feet from the neutral dog. Mikey is a work in progress.

Walking on clouds
Laura Monaco Torelli CPDT-KA, KPACTP, Director of Training at Animal Behavior Training Concepts Chicago, Illinois, USA, abtconcepts.com Posted to the FunctionalRewards Yahoo group and reprinted with permission.

Note: This case used BAT 1.0.

Today marked one of those many wonderful days that remind me of why we love what we do to help families and their pups be successful. I am walking on clouds, and want to share the significance of what today's training session means to me and one of my dog teams here in Chicago. This team is a member of this list, and she gave permission for me to post. Out of confidentiality, I will not disclose her or her dog's name. But she can choose to introduce herself should she like.

We met 1.5 years ago after she rescued a male Ridgeback mix from an abusive home. There was the calm before the storm: the period that occurs after a dog has been placed into a safe home, can sleep soundly, eat healthy food, have access to clean water, receive gentle affection, patience and kind interactions in the presence of a new family. Not living in an unpredictable and volatile environment that has put him into survival mode for who knows how long. As time went by, his behavioral concerns became more evident, and they were referred to me for additional help.

The baseline video of his developing reactivity toward other people was heart breaking. He has (until today) always been wearing equipment and carefully managed due to his quick arousal time and lunging in my presence. More about today in a bit!

The owner is, for lack of better verbiage, one of the most magnificent natural teachers. Her patience and dedication toward her rescued dog are beyond admirable, and the patience and empathy that she has for herself and this journey has me at a loss for words at times. She is the reason her pup is where he is today with our progress.

My initial assessment referred her to our Veterinary Behaviorist here in Chicago, Dr. John Ciribassi. He immediately came on board to help build our collaboration. With his expertise, the support of her referring veterinarian, and myself, we moved forward with the slow and steady process to help her and her dog.

After some trials, my client shared a critical thread of information about her dog and what seems to make him more comfortable in the presence of a new person—if that person is walking one of his favorite dog friends around the neighborhood. So in complement with medication management, clicker training, foundation training and the help of a sweet female black mix, I was able to get closer to her dog than I ever had before.

The process of having this female dog help me help her dog was also slow going. I am a very conservative trainer based on my zoo and aquarium background and working with large animals that require extensive safety protocols. And I am truly grateful that my client respected and understood why we were focused on keeping him below threshold in my presence as much as we could. We would set up our trials in controlled settings outside at a local park, have "pre-session" and "post-session" meetings, arrange for a friend of my client's to videotape the process that her dog was relaxed and felt safe with, and would ensure that we were all safe.

Combining and integrating Behavior Adjustment Training into our overall treatment plan proved critical toward this client and dog's success, and toward our success as a collaborative team helping them move forward.

This post could go on and on, but we are where we are today because of so many critical and appreciated variables.

Today (after three months of not seeing each other) we set up another session and trials. We met at the local park (no black lab mix friend needed!) and started our sessions. It was magnificent to watch. My client has approached our plan like an art form. She has been teaching him how to offer excellent canine communication below his threshold, how to make relaxed choices that he can now control, and how to offer beautiful default behaviors that keep him from escalating up the canine communication pyramid.

So at the end of our session, he allowed me to come into his home, while he was off leash, and decided that playing with his favorite ball while lying on his couch was just the ticket for him. He made the choice to let me into his home. He made the choice to walk away from me and play with a favorite toy. He made excellent choices with minimal social pressure from me. He was relaxed.

I always share with my puppy and dog teams that our goals need to be fun so we are having a good time so we repeat the behaviors of teaching and positively managing our dogs. Some families are emotionally exhausted because their attempts to walk their dog have been effectively punishing them due to their dog's behavioral concerns. So they stop trying and nothing changes to swing the pendulum in a positive direction.

Today was a great session for me, our client, and her dog on so many levels. The beauty of the basics, foundation training, and veterinary collaborations all came together.

A practical program for the pet owner

Teoti Anderson, CPDT-KA, KPA-CTP, Trainer and Owner of Pawsitive Results, LLC, APDT Past President, author of DogFancy Ultimate Guide to Dog Training, Animal Planet Dogs 101 Dog Training, Puppy Care and Training, and Super Simple Guide to Housetraining Lexington, South Carolina, USA, getpawsitiveresults.com

Note: This case used BAT 1.0.

I had been hearing about BAT and reading about other trainers having success with it for reactive dogs. I got Grisha's DVD and really enjoyed learning more about the program. I also immediately thought of an excellent candidate for me to try this technique with—an adolescent, insecure Doberman client of mine.

This dog had gone through several of my Family Manners classes and did very well with obedience, but he was insecure at heart. His triggers were strangers, exacerbated by new environments. He also reacted to other dogs but would warm up to them and play with them once introduced. When the Doberman saw a stranger he would growl and lunge at the end of the leash, but then retreat. He often would put his owner in between him and the stranger. He also growled at the family's young daughters and had nipped one.

Detailed interviews revealed the dog had been fearful as a puppy, and that the girls would often corner him in an attempt to engage him in play. I also learned the dog had, time after time, made great choices in trying to avoid confrontations, but the owners had not recognized this. It seemed the dog had a low threshold for close contact and when it was breached, he would growl a warning and try to get away. If escape was not possible, that's when he would lunge and nip.

While the owner was embarrassed and frustrated by the dog's behavior, he was one of those clients you just love to work with—he truly loved his dog and was willing to work! I thought this combination was a great opportunity to try BAT.

For our first session, I gave my client instruction on how to use the clicker. We warmed up with clicking for the dog giving eye contact. Then for our first scenario, we had my assistant come down the family's stairs in the house. This had proven to be a trigger in the past with guests and visiting family. Once the dog noticed the assistant and looked at his owner, the owner clicked and walked briskly with the dog down the hall, away from the stairs into the kitchen. In just a few minutes, the dog was able to approach my assistant without reacting.

This was repeated over several different sessions, with different assistants serving as 'scary strangers,' some scenarios inside the house and some outside. With each session the dog improved faster and faster. In between our sessions the client worked with his dog at home and in the neighborhood, and reported considerable improvement. Our last session was at a park, with considerable distractions. While we did cross threshold a few times due to an inability to completely control the environment, each episode was brief, with a quick recovery. I was extremely proud of this team's progress! While the owner realized that this was still a work in progress, he was very pleased with the results.

BAT proved to be an excellent program for this team:

- I really liked the use of the clicker as a marker to specifically identify to the dog what behavior we wanted. It made it much easier for my client to identify desired behavior, and helped redirect his focus from his frustration at the dog's aggressive behaviors.

- By allowing the dog to move away from the 'scary strangers' it offered the dog an additional reward for desired behavior, as the distance was more of a comfort than proximity to 'danger.'

- By moving briskly, sometimes even running, it also allowed this athletic, adolescent bundle of nerves to expend his energy in a more desirable manner. He was happy to run away! He began to look forward to the running, and as a result his body language considerably relaxed and he sometimes even offered play behaviors. We did use treats at the beginning of the program, but found that the running was a more desired reward for this particular dog.

- While I understand the science behind this program, my client didn't have to in order to practice at home and see results. This is critical to me—it doesn't do the client any good if I'm the only one who can perform the treatment. It's true that as a professional I am more aware of environments and able to set scenarios up more efficiently, but this is still a very practical program for the pet owner.

Before we began BAT, the owner was considering possibly rehoming this dog. After our sessions the owner realized his dog's aggression was based in fear, he learned how to recognize when his dog was uncomfortable, and BAT gave him a way to teach his dog more desirable behaviors. They continue to be a great team!

Primary protocol for reactivity

Andre Yeu, Trainer and Owner of When Hounds Fly Toronto, Ontario, Canada, whenhoundsfly.com

I use BAT 2.0 all the time. I first learned about Behavior Adjustment Training in the fall of 2009. At that point, I had been working on Duke's (my rescue Beagle) on-leash reactivity for over three years.

Prior to being introduced to Behavior Adjustment Training, I had primarily been using operant methods with food reinforcement—exercises like "Watch me" and "Look at that," and reinforcing Duke for polite greetings with dogs. These methods had produced good results over those three years for Duke. During that period, Duke even attended group classes at busy indoor training halls and he was fine, although he was heavily managed.

As I started up own my training business, I taught others with reactive dogs the same exercises that I was taught—operant methods with food reinforcement. For most dogs, the owners were thrilled with the results they saw. Some dogs improved miraculously in a matter of weeks—so much so that their owners could take them anywhere again and no longer worry about their reactivity. While I was thrilled for them, it left me wondering why I had been unable to achieve that sort of change with Duke. So, my quest for an answer continued.

That quest led me serendipitously to Behavior Adjustment Training. It was on a lunch break at a Karen Pryor Academy workshop that I was introduced to it briefly. Searching for it online took me to Grisha's resource page, and the rest is history. Since incorporating Behavior Adjustment Training into my toolbox, I have found it to be the primary protocol I use and prescribe for treating reactivity. I've achieved the greatest breakthroughs in helping reactive dogs through its use. I believe that those dogs that struggle with pure classical counter-conditioning, or operant methods using food reinforcement find their salvation in Behavior Adjustment Training.

What I find most compelling about Behavior Adjustment Training is it allows a dog to relearn natural distance increasing behaviors. After years of training with food reinforcement, a reactive dog can end up heeling past rows and rows of triggers. Certainly that is incredibly liberating for the owner, but to me, it always seemed kind of mechanical for the dog. In contrast, in just one or two sessions of Behavior Adjustment Training, we see dogs offer an amazing array of behaviors—head turns, lip kicks, sniffs, yawns, scratches, sits, downs, and many more. Also, the absence of food forces handlers to be honest about what a dog's true threshold is, and begin work at that point, instead of starting at an artificial threshold that can be supported by the presence of food.

In the last several years, my clients and I have celebrated a lot of successes thanks to Behavior Adjustment Training—one Mini Schnauzer that had not met another dog in over two years, that can now visit the nearby dog run and make friends, a Maltese-cross that used to spin in the air at the sight of another dog that can now walk right past another barking, snarling dog, to my boy Duke, who can happily resume sniffing the ground as dogs that used to bother him pass by.

BAT creates an atmosphere of trust between the dog and the handler

Casey Lomonaco, KPA CTP, Rewarding Behaviors Dog Training, rewardingbehaviors.com Endicott, New York, USA

This was first written for BAT 1.0 but applies to BAT 2.0 as well. Why exactly do I like Behavior Adjustment Training so much? I thought about this question when Grisha informed me she was releasing a new book. There are a number of reasons I really enjoy using this technique both with my own dogs and my client dogs. These include:

It gives dog owners incentive to learn to read their dog's body language. Any trainer will tell you that this critical skill is the foundation of creating both empathy toward and a relationship with an animal of any other species. While many of my clients have said, "I wish my dog would just talk to me," BAT teaches them that dogs actually do talk to them in a language they can learn to understand and use to their training advantage.

It creates a relationship and atmosphere of trust between the dog and handler. Like other dog-friendly behavior modification techniques, it removes the oppositional barriers created by traditional training while empowering both the dog and the owner. The owner is empowered by having tangible skills to immediately reduce her dog's stress, arousal, and frustration levels. The dog is empowered because she learns that she has the ability to control her environment through communicating her needs to her owner. It's a win/win!

No more waiting to start on critical behavior modification. It's not uncommon for me to get a severely obese and very reactive dog in my practice. Often, it is extremely difficult to motivate these dogs with food initially, and I never want to tell a handler, "We can start work once you get the weight off your dog." BAT allows us to begin training right away, using the rewards the dog is already receiving or desiring from the environment. This is helpful to the dog's emotional health (through stress reduction), and physical health (once the owner has the tools needed to walk/live with the dog successfully, the dog will get more exercise and the weight will begin coming off)!

It provides handlers with a tangible, effective, and thorough introduction to the critical concept of the Premack principle. Many novice handlers have a hard time identifying environmental reinforcers and using them effectively along with primary reinforcement (often, food) in the development and maintenance of behaviors. BAT helps dog owners become better dog handlers—the lessons learned in BAT apply directly toward other aspects of living with dogs, including refining manners and other behaviors in "every day" life situations.

BAT is flexible. I've used BAT with both reactive dogs who would like to increase distance from their triggers as well as with frustrated dogs that want to decrease the distance to the trigger but don't yet know how to retain their composure to earn that opportunity.

BAT plays well with others! BAT is not exclusive—I have a number of clients who use BAT techniques in conjunction with Look at That and other Control Unleashed games in addition to simple "Open Bar, Closed Bar" counter-conditioning techniques—sometimes all of these techniques will be used within a single session!

It's fun! Last of all, Behavior Adjustment Training is fun for dogs and their people. Above and beyond anything else, trainers know that the only way owners follow through with training protocols consistently and reliably is if doing so is enjoyable for them and gives them results. BAT offers both to harried clients and owners of reactive dogs!

Shelter dog trainer BAT experience
Alice Tong, CPDT-KA, KPA CTP, Choose Positive Dog Training, choosepositivedog-training.com, Oakland, California, USA

As a Shelter Dog Trainer, I saw a lot of dogs with reactivity to and fear of other dogs, children, or men. With limited space and time in a shelter environment and high noise and stress levels, shelter dogs needed to gain progress with these issues to become more adoptable as quickly as possible. Using Grisha's BAT, I have not only seen dogs gain progress with these issues quickly and effectively, they have simultaneously become more confident and sociable by learning they are safe and can make calm choices instead of over-reacting. In the shelter environment we were able to have access to multiple 'neutral dogs' to use for BAT sessions, and thus could have consistency to work with a dog more than just once a week. I have worked with many shelter dogs that tended to become immediately overly stimulated when exiting their confined living spaces, and yet were still able to respond well to BAT sessions.

BAT also strengthened my ability as a shelter dog trainer to build a deeper relationship with individual dogs by becoming even more adept at observing the subtleties of their body and facial movements to make sure they are truly under threshold when training. Even the slightest turn of the head, an eyebrow muscle lifting a bit, or an increase in rate of respiration, could be an important signal for the trainer to read, and may determine how fast or slow the dog progresses. With so many dogs in the shelter who need help and attention, it is a wonderful way to naturally get to know each dog's personality by 'listening' to their body language through their preferred cut-off signals. If I am reading the dog well enough, the dog can begin to work his/her own program without the micro-management that often occurs with on-cue handler work. BAT succeeds in increasing a reactive shelter dog's confidence and decreasing feelings of fear and insecurity, resulting in a dog that no longer needs to act out through reactive/aggressive behaviors. I am excited for BAT to reach not only more trainers and shelter workers, but the average owner as well. By learning BAT, owners can learn to 'hear' what their dogs are saying, and their dogs can feel understood and empowered.

Thomas: A cautionary tale

Dani Weinberg, Ph.D., Certified Dog Behavior Consultant at Dogs & Their People, Karen Pryor Academy Faculty, Author of "Teaching People Teaching Dogs" Albuquerque, New Mexico, USA http://home.earthlink.net/~hardpretzel/DaniDogPage.html

Note: All names of dogs and people have been changed. This case used BAT 1.0.

This is the story of Thomas, a neutered Pit Bull/Blue Heeler mix, owned by a busy professional woman. More importantly, it's the story of how a successful BAT intervention can go wrong—not for lack of skill on the part of the trainer, nor for poor response on the part of the dog, but because the owners are not committed to the process. I have used BAT with other dogs and their supportive and grateful owners. It has always helped the dog to learn better coping strategies to deal with Scary Things, and it's easy to teach to owners as well so that they can use it immediately. That's why the Thomas case stands out for me as a cautionary tale.

When I first met Thomas, he was 19 months old, adopted from our local private shelter at about six months. All that his owner, Delia, knew about him was that he was a transfer from another shelter.

He was free-fed a "sensitive-stomach" food until I recommended a better quality food that he did well on. He had a good exercise schedule, walking daily and hiking on Sundays. Delia had been taking him to a traditional training school. What she learned there, she said, had made it possible for her to walk him. He wore a choke chain so she could "control him better."

Thomas is a high-energy young dog who fits Jean Donaldson's description of the Tarzan type in her book *Fight! A Practical Guide to the Treatment of Dog-Dog Aggression* (see Resources). She writes on page 12: "Dogs that come on too strong [to other dogs]. They appear hyper-motivated and have coarse social skills."

When Delia first adopted Thomas, she would take him to the dog park. That soon stopped when she saw him hyper-aroused and tipping over from play to aggression. He now has occasional play dates with a female dog but wears a muzzle so he does not injure her in his over-the-top play style.

Delia's main concern was Thomas' reactivity to people who came to the house. He would bark, growl, pull on the leash (he was always on-leash when visitors arrived), whine, shake, and, if he could, nip the visitor. Delia would 'introduce' him to visitors in the front yard, with Thomas leashed, on his choke chain and muzzle. She would 'make' him sit and then lie down. Then she would wait until he 'calmed down'—at which point she would either put him in the back yard, out of the way, if the visitor was staying, or take him out so that they could take a walk with the visitor. Once on the walk, Thomas was fine and even allowed the visitor to pet him.

First session

I had asked that Thomas be in the back yard when I arrived so as to avoid an over-threshold introduction. Delia and I sat in the kitchen talking for a while, and then she brought him in. At my request, he was on leash but not muzzled. He reacted in his usual aggressive manner upon seeing me. I wanted to learn more about him, so I did a few simple training exercises. When I tried to reinforce voluntary eye contact, he remained agitated, so I went back to simply clicking and treating him. He was very interested in the food. As long as I kept it flowing, he was relatively calm, but when I paused for a moment, he resumed his barking and lunging. Next, I tried to teach him to target my hand, and he learned that very quickly—but still reverted to aggressive behaviors when I paused.

I showed Delia how to play Look At That. Thomas learned the game quickly. I asked her to practice the game often but only when there were no triggers present. My plan for our next session was to use Look At That as a first step into BAT.

Second session

At my request, Delia had invited a friend, Ruth, to come and help. Ruth was someone Thomas had previously been reactive to in the front yard but not away from home on walks. Because he knew her and she was a frequent visitor, I decided to use her as our first helper.

We started with Bar Open/Bar Closed, with Ruth and me alternately appearing from behind a wall about 15 feet away. This simple counter-conditioning technique seemed like a good foundation before starting BAT. Thomas soon began to give the desired response: see person and immediately turn to handler for his treat. He seemed impervious to Delia's very rough handling—jerking his leash and harshly asking him to sit every few seconds.

We gave Thomas another break outdoors while we discussed what had happened. In our next training period and after I had made a few appearances in a row, I decided to move a little closer. I appeared and took a few steps towards him, reducing the distance quickly to within about five feet. On my next appearance, I walked right up to him and offered him a handful of treats. He took them calmly. I repeated that on my next appearance, and he took the treats again. And then suddenly, he started barking, lunging, and trying to nip me. I had exceeded his tolerance for my proximity and inadvertently put him over his threshold. That can happen when the dog suddenly realizes how close the person is. He becomes anxious and reverts to his old behavior.

We gave Thomas another rest outdoors while I explained the objectives and method of BAT. The front yard was not very big, but we managed to plot out a path for BAT. Delia would handle Thomas, while Ruth and I, hidden around the corner of the house, would take turns appearing for the Look At That game. Our starting distance was about 35 feet. When that was going well, Delia and Thomas would gradually shorten the distance from us with each repetition.

To my delight, Thomas did very well. He remained calm and relaxed up to a distance of about ten feet away. I decided to leave well enough alone and not push him beyond his threshold. We stopped, put him in the back yard to rest, and went indoors to discuss what had happened.

I left Delia that day with instructions to practice Bar Open/Bar Closed and Look At That on their walks, but only in the absence of triggers. Our plan for our next session was to invite Paul, a neighbor, and use him as a helper.

Before leaving, I suggested that Delia talk to her veterinarian about possibly doing a complete thyroid panel, on the chance that hypothyroidism might be contributing to the aggression. I also suggested that she give Thomas Suntheanine, a natural calming supplement. I learned later that she had done neither. I also doubt that she practiced any of the techniques I had shown her.

We scheduled another session which Delia had to reschedule because of her work commitments. After that, we were unable to schedule any more sessions, ostensibly because Delia's work was just too demanding.

In spite of the good results we had seen in Thomas using BAT, it seemed to me that Delia had decided this was not going to work. Delia's force-based "training" of Thomas was, in her mind, the only way to modify his aggressive behavior. She had been skeptical about my methods from the start but expressed willingness to try them. I had taken her at her word.

It's also worth noting what her goals were for Thomas, as expressed in the behavior questionnaire she had filled out before our first meeting: "I want Thomas to be able to play and socialize with other animals, fully and joyfully. I want my friends and family to be able to sit with him and see the beautiful, sweet soul that I experience....I am confident that Thomas will grow into being a perfect dog."

The combination of unrealistic goals and force-based training are deadly to BAT work. BAT requires the full participation of the dog as he learns to make better choices. It also requires commitment and compliance from the owner. The saddest part of this story is knowing that Thomas was ready and willing to do this, if only his owner had let him.

An exciting exploration I share with my dogs
Debi Carpenter with Emsie and Harry USA

It's been four years since I first began to use BAT with Harry and Emsie, in response to Harry's issues of shyness, and Emsie's fears around many triggers such as certain types of dogs and people. Since I first began working with them in this way, I have taken note that there are innumerable dog personalities, and endless dog owner assertions made out there in the world and to be encountered on virtually each and every walk; with my continued application of BAT, and heightened awareness from utilizing BAT techniques, I am able to see these encounters more as an exciting exploration that I share with my dogs, rather than experiences to avoid or shy away from.

Emsie and Harry on an adventure.

With the terrain of dogs and dog owners comes an understanding of dog behavior, and the varying viewpoints of that understanding, which can be vastly complex. I think on just about every walk I am assured by the owner of an off-leash dog "don't worry, my dog is friendly," as an out of control, sometimes accurately depicted as friendly and often times not, dog races toward Harry or Emsie, each presenting the need to interpret the situation with the best of Harry and Emsie's interests at heart. I have learned that BAT is not just for Harry, Emsie and I; it is all of that, but it also is an intuitive method to interact in a world where decisions around our dogs need to be made quickly and in as positive a light as possible.

Harry and Emsie enjoy a life that includes kayaking, riding in a bike trailer, swimming and boogie boarding, just to name a few of their favorite activities. As you might imagine, these activities also bring chance encounters with other dogs and people in a wide array of settings, and with it the need to navigate thru those chance meetings in a way that allows them to feel safe, confident and secure. Over these past few years both Harry and Emsie have grown in their ability to feel at home in these situations, and to more quickly move beyond an encounter that might push their limits.

I am grateful to have two wonderful dogs and a technique that allows for enjoyable outings in a way that respects and builds upon the magical relationship between dogs and their owners.

BAT for fear of traffic

Beverley Courtney, BA(Hons), CBATI, MAPDT(UK), Trainer and Owner of Good for Dogs! Worcestershire, UK, goodfordogs.co.uk, brilliantfamilydog.com

Meg, a Border Collie, aged one, arrived at my classes very anxious and uncomfortable about the other dogs in the small class, and manifested this discomfort through barking ferociously and lunging on the end of her lead.

Her dedicated owner Linsey, who had only adopted Meg from a farm two months before, asked for further help. Meg had a huge and potentially dangerous fear of traffic. Here's what Linsey said: "On the road Meg's ears are always back. She crawls, keeping as close as she can to bushes, walls, fences. If a car passes she puts her brakes on, digs her back legs into the ground, tucks herself in and starts to panic. Then she bolts forward and tries to get somewhere—anywhere—at 100 miles an hour, no rational thought involved."

BAT changed all that. Her attitude and posture changed dramatically for the better even in her first session. With sensitive lead-handling, Meg was soon able to cope with the presence of traffic.

Linsey used the same techniques for Meg's fear of dogs, and recently sent me this update:

"We are up in Scotland now where Meg has quickly become a full time member of the family pack and is having a great time. We're in week 2 of beginners' agility, where her good behaviour has been amazing.

"There are lots of noisy strange dogs, three of them very reactive, and Meg is a perfect angel. Sits and waits her turn, does not react to the aggressive dogs and focuses 100% on me when she is off her lead in the class. A different dog to the one in your Hereford class eight months ago.

"Traffic walking is greatly improved. She is still a bit edgy but nowhere near as bad as she was. Her confidence is growing and I think walking with the others is helping."

Determined to succeed

Shiley Soh and Bambi, Singapore

3 years ago:

1. The distance between Bambi and her trigger (kids) was the size of almost half a football field;

2. The sound of a kid running foot steps, freaks her out. She growls.

3 years later:

1. A kid can be within 5 to 10 meters from her. She stops, look at trigger, look at me and carries on with her walk. Continues with her sniffing.

2. The sound of running footsteps no longer freaks her out. She doesn't growl like before. She looks at the running kid. He or she can be playing and screaming or talking loudly. She looks then disengages herself by continuing her ground sniffing.

Previously on our walks when she spots kids, she would stop walking. Now when she spot kids on our walk (e.g. in the middle of a bridge), she continues to walk past without growling. Though her panting increases but that's gone once the trigger passes by. She has also learnt to create space between herself and the trigger by using mommy as the human barrier!

Thank you & Peanut so much. I never dreamed I could make it with Bambi. Three years ago I cried buckets when I saw how damaged she was. She went from a second prize winner at her first ON competition to three failures after the incident. I was very very very determined to succeed in helping Bambi. I was a nervous wreck. I remembered you taught me to remember to Breathe. A lot of trials

Shirley and Bambi

& errors along the way in the three years. Today, I am a much better handler, more confident in my walk & absolutely handle my leash a whole lot better! Bambi has taught me when she is ready and when she is not.

Thank you & Peanut so very much for BAT. I was like a headless lost soul before I came to know about BAT. However, I see hope & possibilities when I learnt about BAT. Even watch your website like a hawk! Haaaaa. When BAT was held in Singapore this past November, I encouraged my hubby to sign up. Unfortunately, he had a heart attack one day before the seminar. Nevertheless, he cheered me on to go ahead to assist Andy with the logistics as I had agreed. With a heavy heart, on first day seminar, I was on site. It was then that I told myself for my hubby and for Bambi, I will and I must make good this opportunity to learn and grasp much more than I did before.

True enough, a lot of key take-home for me being a participant as well as a helper to Carly. I saw my walks and work with Bambi get so much better. I could even share briefly about BAT with strangers on the walk. One owner was holding her dog's leash so tightly when her dog was eager to meet Bambi. The more she pull, the harder she lunge. I explained loose leash. She gave it a go. Instantly she saw the change in her dog and expressed "wow, it works. I didn't know, I am a first time owner."

Turning point
Jude Azaren and Dusty, USA

Note: This case used BAT 1.0.

Two years of working various aggression protocols had not put much of a dent in Dusty's human aggression, but in August of 2009, Dusty had his first BAT session shortly after Grisha introduced BAT to an aggression e-list in which I participated. A friend and I drove to the home of an acquaintance (the decoy). When Dusty got out of the car and saw the decoy in the street, he was very fearful. He tucked his tail and tried to jump back in the car. This surprised me because the decoy wasn't even near us and Dusty was usually not fearful at that particular distance. So I walked him around the street a bit until his tail untucked and he seemed interested in his surroundings.

When Dusty seemed better, we started to work. We did several BAT variations and mixed them all up. The decoy walked towards us; we walked towards the decoy; we did parallel walking; we did pass-bys. Sometimes, my friend walked with the decoy. Most of the time, the decoy walked alone. Each trial showed improved demeanor on Dusty's part.

Distance was the main reinforcer: Dusty and I walked away, ran away, or the decoy moved away. Sometimes Dusty got treats, and I often praised him for making good decisions. Behaviors that were rewarded included every visible degree of relaxation: unfurrowing his forehead, relaxing the jaw, soft eyes, relaxed blinking, eye contact with me, watching the decoy move without stiffening, air scenting in the decoy's direction, passing the decoy without any sign of lunging.

What I loved about this entire session was that Dusty was totally engaged in the work and was happy to try to figure out the right responses to get to run away, to get the decoy moving, to get a treat, etc. This whole experience was so obviously a very good one for him. We stopped to walk at a park on the way home. Suddenly two teenagers ran straight for us from only about 30 feet away. I braced myself for Dusty to lunge and bark and was about to do a fast about turn and run away. But Dusty looked at them and calmly looked at me as they were VERY quickly approaching. His look said, "Can we run away now, Mom?" and we did just that. I was shocked that he figured this out and remained calm with just the single BAT session we had done an hour earlier.

We weren't done training after just one session, of course, but it had a powerful impact and led to Dusty generalizing his new confidence to numerous other fears he had. BAT has been the turning point in Dusty's aggression treatment. He is a much more relaxed, happy dog. I can't express my enthusiasm for this protocol and my gratitude to Grisha for sharing it.

Ninja BAT helped my dog on and off lead

Deborah Campbell, CBATI, with her own dog Flossy, UK

Flossy, a working-type Border Collie, was around 14 months old (in 2011) when I started applying the BAT principles (after attending Grisha's first UK BAT presentation/workshop) to her walks and encounters with people. She was highly reactive (bark lunging) towards people on walks, around the neighbourhood and in the garden/home. Flossy was in fact to become the catalyst to later becoming a Certified BAT Instructor in 2014.

When I gave a home to Flossy, I wanted to learn as much as possible about how I could help her and so I purchased the original BAT/Organic Socialization Book & DVD. No one was really doing set ups or had 'assistant' dogs available for me to work with so I began doing 'stealth' or 'undercover' BAT in the local high street on lead, all the while attempting to remain below threshold—which is imperative for the welfare of the dog. There were marked improvements towards her ability to switch off from people who were doing their own thing and walking around, within about a month of 2 to 3 short sessions a week in the high street. These improvements transferred quickly to off lead walks. Most of Flossy's walks are off lead in the forests/woods and it is here when strangers could have been walking down the same path or could have been appearing seemingly from nowhere which would have caused Flossy concern. With continual, but steady improvement, Flossy learnt to acknowledge and disengage from the stranger walking towards her. Finally, because Flossy has learnt she can keep herself safe and calm, she has learnt she can remove herself (extricate) from a situation if she feels any slight discomfort—as would happen with any well socialised dog meeting and greeting. Intriguingly I found (at the time), this meant she discovered her confidence and inner social self and started being able to show interest in people talking to her.

Watching Flossy independently learning has been a wonderful thing. I do not need nor expect Flossy to love everyone or not do I want to micromanage her every encounter/experience. The aim of BAT is to engineer the environment to allow her to make good, natural choices in normal social situations.

Simple enough for everyday use
Jonas Valancius, Reksas Dog Training School Kaunas City, Lithuania, reksas.lt

I am a dog trainer in Lithuania. Now here's the time when dog training culture is raising quickly in my country and in all the World. More people like to be responsible owners and are searching for positive ways of communication with their dogs even when they have hard behavior problems. I found Grisha's BAT as one of the most innovative ways.

In my practice BAT techniques are useful in several aspects:

- It teaches the owner non aversive ways of behavior modification
- It makes the owner deepen his knowledge into his dog's body language
- It is simple enough for everyday use (like Mac plug and play), easy to learn, dynamic and very practical
- It is healthy: the owners must move.

I am happy that I've found BAT.

The perfect way to preserve homeless dogs' positive behaviour
Ryan Neile, Senior Animal Behaviourist at Blue Cross Burford, Oxfordshire, UK, bluecross.org.uk

At Blue Cross, we take the behavioural rehabilitation of our animals very seriously, and BAT 2.0 is an essential tool without which we could not transform as many dogs as we do. It's practice helps us to strip away a reactive dogs stress, confusion and frustration clearing the way for their social skills to flourish, and for true and meaningful change to occur! Even dogs without behaviour problems are at risk when in rescue kennels, so BAT is the perfect way to preserve homeless dogs' positive behaviour whilst they are waiting to find their next home. What's perfect about BAT is its simplicity, and the speed at which it can work in all situations. It's application improves your powers of observation and timing, but above all, it teaches you train in the moment and to be conscious of the part you play during the dogs journey!

GLOSSARY

5-Second Rule: A way to pet a dog that gives the dog a chance to communicate when to start and stop. Wait to pet until the dog is asks for contact by nuzzling or some other behavior. Pet for no more than 5 seconds, remove your hands, and then wait for the dog to ask for more. Modify to less time for puppies or dogs who prefer less contact.

Agency: The ability to control a situation based on one's own actions. The phrase "sense of agency" is applied to humans in the literature, but there are arguments that agency or "mammalian agency" could also be applied to non-human animals as well (Panksepp, Asma, Curran, Gabriel, and Greif, 2012; Steward, 2009).

Agonistic display: According to Wikipedia, an agonistic display is "The combative or territorial behavior of an animal that feels threatened by or intends to threaten another animal, usually of the same species." In other words, agonistic displays are what most people, including me, call "aggression" although that's not technically correct. Agonistic displays in dogs can include barking, growling, lip curling, snarling, leaning forward, hackles up, lunging, air snapping, biting, and other negative reactions. Those behaviors are not always agonistic displays, but reading the whole picture can help you determine the dog's intentions.

Airlock: A buffer in front of exits so that the dog must go through two or more doors/gates in order to escape.

Antecedent Arrangements: Also called "management." Antecedents are stimuli that come before behavior in time. The environment and experience of the learner can be specifically choreographed. Setting up the situation so that the target behavior is unlikely or that other specific behavior is more likely. Antecedents can be distant (diet, physical health) or proximal (distance to another dog, presence of treats, etc.).

Applied Behavior Analysis: The process of applying and studying protocols that are systematically based on the scientific field of behavior analysis. ABA protocols are designed to improve socially significant behaviors and research studies the effectiveness of the protocol on the change in behavior. This often involves a functional assessment to discover the consequences that maintain the current behavior. See Behavior Analysis.

Behavior Adjustment Training (BAT): A philosophy and set of techniques to teach dogs to meet their needs in socially acceptable ways. Can also be applied to other species.

Behavior Analysis: The scientific study of behavior (any measurable thing that a person or other animal does), which looks for environmental and biological factors that influence behavior. The term was coined by B.F. Skinner.

Bite Threshold: Level of stress or stimulation at which the dog resorts to biting.

Body Block: Using your body to back a dog away from something, like getting a loose dog to back away from your dog. You don't actually touch the dog, but you basically walk through them to make them back off of something. Body blocking is aversive and should be used only rarely.

Braking Hand: The hand that is holding the middle part of the leash, i.e., the part closest to the dog.

Choice Point: A situation in which the animal's environment prompts her to respond with a behavior. Choice points in BAT are skewed so that the dog is likely to choose to do the behavior you prefer.

Classical Conditioning: See Respondent Learning.

Counter-conditioning (CC): A procedure that changes the emotional charge (valence) of a stimulus. For example, if a dog is afraid of children, the standard Counter-Conditioning/Systematic Desensitization procedure would be to pair up the appearance of children with food. Every sight of a child would be followed by treat. With backwards conditioning (treat leads to appearance of child), the dog can be accidentally classically counter-conditioned to avoid treats. Counter-conditioning can be done without taking behavior into account, but operant procedures, which empower dogs to affect the environment with their behavior, can also change the valence of the emotional association. The valence would likely go from negative to positive when the experience is pleasant and the animal's behavior leads to desired outcomes. BAT is an example of an operant counter-conditioning procedure.

Cut-off Signals: When two dogs meet, cut-off signals are behaviors that are requests for additional space or a reduction in the stress level of the meeting. Used to avoid conflict.

Default Behaviors: The set of behaviors a specific dog normally performs in response to an environmental stimulus. For example, many dogs have a default behavior of jumping and barking at the door or sitting on a rug in the kitchen to receive their meals. Default behaviors are what the dog does on his own without a human explicitly cueing him to do a particular behavior.

Differential reinforcement of an alternative behavior (DRA): A procedure in which one behavior is under extinction (not reinforced) and a replacement behavior is reinforced.

Discrimination: The process by which an animal learns to offer a behavior in response to certain stimuli and not others. For example, a dog may discriminate between children and adults, i.e., learn to not bark at adults, but may still bark at children. The sight of children and adults elicits different behaviors because they are perceived as different stimuli to the dog. A drug detection dog may discriminate between the drug he is looking for and the smell of food in a person's luggage. Discrimination is the opposite of generalization.

Empowerment: Behavior has an effect on significant events, i.e., behavior changes the environment in a way that meets the individual's needs. Opposite of disempowerment, where there is little to no behavioral control over important events.

Event Marker: Signal that indicates the dog's behavior is what you want and has earned reinforcement. Examples are clicker, verbal "Yes," visual hand-flash, or vibration collar for deaf dogs. You are "marking" the behavior when you use an event marker. Delay between event marker and treats is usually no more than about two seconds. Also called a "marker" or "marker signal."

Functional Behavior Assessment: A formal analysis of the relationship between a target behavior and environmental events to discover the reason, purpose, or motivation of a behavior.

Functional Reinforcer: If a behavior is done to achieve a particular consequence, that consequence is a functional reinforcer for the behavior. Dogs do what works, i.e., dogs do whatever best earns a functional reinforcer. With BAT, we set up situations in which desired behavior naturally earns the functional reinforcer that is normally achieved by reactivity. We may also have the trainer provide a functional reinforcer, but the emphasis on BAT 2.0 is to create opportunities for naturally occurring reinforcers.

Generalization: The process of learning that two events or stimuli are both cues for the same behavior, or that a cue in a different setting is still the same cue. This is a critical process in any training, but especially when working with reactivity. Generalization is what makes the dog more predictable—situations that we consider similar are not necessarily similar to the dog, without generalization training.

Graduated Prompting: Series of prompts to help the dog make a good choice in the smallest, least intrusive way that works. If a smaller prompt doesn't work, use a more obvious one.

Handle Hand: The hand that is holding the handle end of the leash.

Helpers: People and dogs who have been arranged to help you with training. Their distance to the student dog, motion, and other movements can be controlled so that your dog can experience these triggers in a pleasant or low-stress way. Also known as "decoys" or "stooges."

Lazy Bones BAT: Method to passively train the dog using the principles of BAT. Ideal for fence fighting and guarding territory.

(BAT) Leash Skills: A collection of handling techniques meant to provide a sense of freedom while still maintaining safety and the ability to keep the dog from getting too close to the trigger.

Management: Changing your dog's environment to make it impossible or unlikely that he'll do behavior you do not want him to do. See also antecedent arrangements.

Magnet Effect: There is a certain distance from the trigger at which the dog is forced to deal with it. This is analogous to a magnetic field, where a magnet and a piece of metal can remain apart until they are close enough, at which point they are quickly drawn together. Even if they really want to just get away, many dogs are 'magnetically' drawn in and pull or run toward the trigger, barking and growling. We want to avoid the magnet effect.

Mark and Move: A technique of BAT 2.0 that is used in situations when the "follow your dog" version would be too much freedom. Specifically, the handler marks a behavior, moves away, and gives a reinforcer. Always use the least intrusive version of Mark and Move that you can, so that the dog can pay more attention to the social situation and naturally occurring reinforcers.

Mime Pulling: A BAT leash skill in which the handler looks a bit like she is pulling on the leash, but is really just sliding her hands along the leash away from the dog, making eye contact, and stepping away to encourage the dog to follow.

More Please Signal: A behavior that gives the dog a more active role in counter-conditioning. When the dog does the More Please Signal, the counter-conditioning can begin. If the dog ceases doing the More Please Signal, the counter-conditioning stops. The trainer should try to stop before a More Please Signal or signs of stress, so that the process is as pleasant as possible.

Naturally Occurring Reinforcer: A reinforcer that is not directly provided by the trainer as a consequence of behavior. For example, a dog turns away from the trigger and sniffs a bush, which has an odor the dog finds appealing. Having the odor of the bush get into the dog's nose is a naturally occurring reinforcer for the sniffing behavior. If the dog were to turn and sniff the bush, but a trainer presented a treat or even pressed a button on some device to produce an odor, that would not be naturally occurring. If the trainer just put some objects into the area for the dog to encounter, that would be considered naturally occurring reinforcer (if interacting with it reinforced behavior) because the trainer did not cause a certain event in response to the dog's behavior. See Reinforcement for the definition of "reinforcer."

Operant Learning: Type of learning in which a person or non-human animal changes behavior because of the environmental consequences of that behavior. Also known as "operant conditioning," although there are good arguments to fade out the use of the term "conditioning" when speaking of learning in non-human animals, as it is no longer used to apply to humans.

Premack Principle: This principle states that activities can be reinforcers or punishers based on their relative probabilities. In particular, a behavior can be reinforced by the opportunity to do a more likely behavior. That is, if the animal gets to do a certain behavior right after doing a lower probability behavior, the lower probability behavior will be reinforced.

Prosocial Behaviors: Behaviors used as communication to another dog (bow, approach, etc.) that generally result in the other dog walking closer and engaging in social activity (sniffing, play, etc.). Prosocial behaviors are a type of social courtship.

Proprioception: A sense of where one's own body parts are in relation to one another as well as how much effort is involved to move the body. The cerebellum is responsible for most unconscious proprioception.

Problem Behavior: Behavior you want to see less frequently. This term is being faded out of use, as we focus on what we want the learner to do. See Target Behavior.

Quadrant: Short-hand developed by trainers to understand operant learning. Learning can be thought of as split into four quadrants: positive and negative reinforcement and positive and negative punishment. Positive and negative are indications of whether the learning took place because a stimulus was added (positive) or removed (negative).

Raise Criteria: Increase expectations on reinforceable behavior. For example, you might reward a dog for looking at you after looking at the trigger, but then you might raise criteria by waiting until your dog offered something more difficult, like sniffing the ground or a full-body turn. The trick with raising criteria is to only make it a little harder, so that your expectations are still easily met.

Reactivity: Technically over-reactivity. Fear, aggression, or frustration responses that are over the level that dog-savvy humans consider 'normal.'

Reinforcement: The strengthening of the behavior via consequences to that behavior. The consequence itself, i.e., the event following a behavior that causes that behavior to be more likely in the future, is called a reinforcer. Can be positive (think addition, like getting something the dog wants) or negative (think subtraction, like relief from stress or social pressure).

Replacement Behavior: Dog behavior that you can live with that can reasonably have the same functional reinforcer as the behavior you are trying to reduce or eliminate. See also Target Behavior.

Respondent Extinction: The weakening of an association created by classical conditioning, for example, by presenting the conditional stimulus without the unconditional stimulus.

Respondent Learning: A process that pairs two stimuli together in such a way that the "conditioned" stimulus begin to elicit the same physiological response as an unconditional stimulus or another conditioned stimulus. This can give an emotional charge to a neutral stimulus through association. Here's an example of delay conditioning: the conditioned stimulus is consistently followed by another stimulus (click leads to treat). In this way, a dog who doesn't have any initial response to the clicker can develop one through respondent learning. If she hears a click and then gets a tasty treat many times, she will begin to elicit the biological response of drooling after hearing a click. She may also demonstrate other behavior that we associate with being 'happy,' like wagging loosely, etc. Also known as "Pavlovian conditioning" or "classical conditioning," although there are good arguments to fade out the use of the term "conditioning" when speaking of learning in non-human animals, as it is no longer used to apply to humans.

Setting Event: Context clues from the internal and external physical environment that predict possible consequences of behavior. For example, if loud noises are aversive for the dog and there is a party going on, the presence of extra people and loud sounds are setting events. A child then reaching into the dog's food dish may lead to a bite, whereas the dog may have just growled in a different context. We can improve behavior almost immediately by changing setting events, such as covering street-view windows with opaque film.

Set-up: Training session in which you have arranged for the presence of a predictable and/or controllable trigger, so that your dog may interact at a safe distance, with little to no distress. With BAT, set-ups are usually done in a large area that will encourage exploration.

Systematic Desensitization: Gradual exposure to a trigger with relaxation before the intensity of the trigger is increased. Humans doing systematic desensitization for phobias are taught relaxation exercises to self-soothe. In dog training, systematic desensitization usually means the progressive exposure aspect of systematic desensitization, and it is generally combined with classical counter-conditioning in lieu of self-relaxation techniques. Also called "graduated exposure therapy."

Sub-threshold: Dog is able to cope and self-soothe without panic or aggression. If you were to ask the dog about how stressed she was, she'd say, "not at all" or "just a little."

Sudden Environmental Contrast (SEC): An unexpected, startling change in the level of stimulation. Examples include a seated person at a dinner party standing up and encountering a box that was not in the room before. Also known as "sudden environmental change."

Target Behavior for an Intervention: Observable action (behavior) that is selected to be changed by a behavior modification protocol. This is generally an increase in the frequency or a change in the topology of the behavior (how it looks). For example, instead an aggressive display, we might prefer that the dog approach in a curve, sniff the rear, turn head away, and walk away, then that's our definition of the target behavior of "polite greeting."

Threshold: The line between levels of stimulation, "dividing where the dog is able to cope and self-soothe without panic or aggression from where the dog is not able to cope without panic or aggression." I think of it as a line between a calm, happy dog and a freaked out, stressed dog.

Trigger: An event, person, animal, noise, or other factor that leads to an undesired or abnormally large reaction. If your dog barks at black dogs, then black dogs would be considered to be triggers for your dog's reactivity. A trigger is also known as the "triggering stimulus."

Trigger Stacking: Stress accumulation due to exposure to multiple triggers, either simultaneously or close enough in time that the dog's reactivity has not returned to normal. For example, if a sound-sensitive dog who is afraid of children hears a loud crash before he sees a child, he is more likely to bite than if he had met the child under calmer circumstances.

ABOUT THE AUTHOR

Grisha Stewart, MA, CPDT-KA is a dog trainer and international seminar presenter who specializes in empowerment and dog reactivity. She has two books, several DVDs, and runs an online dog training school from Alaska. Grisha also founded Ahimsa Dog Training in Seattle. Ahimsa has earned many awards, including Best of Western Washington. "Ahimsa" is a Buddhist doctrine of nonviolence to all

It's important to be able to cue behavior...

living things, which reflects Grisha's focus on empowerment training for all animals, including people.

Grisha has a Master's degree in Mathematics from Bryn Mawr College and postgraduate training in psychology with an emphasis on animal behavior from Antioch University. Her first career as a theoretical mathematician and college instructor serves her well in dog training and behavior consultations, because she relies heavily on the problem solving, critical thinking, and teaching skills she gained in that field.

Canine behavior fascinates Grisha and she is highly motivated to help improve our techniques for rehabilitating and training dogs. Her professional interest in reactivity and the need to find an efficient rehabilitation technique for her own dog's fears led Grisha to develop BAT. To see the BAT seminar schedule, learn more about BAT, purchase streaming videos, arrange an online video consultation, participate in BAT

Chats, or register for online courses, visit GrishaStewart.com. Grisha is an avid hiker, a mediocre but enthusiastic rock climber, and a passionate advocate for the humane care and training of animals.

But having fun is part of the point of being alive!

RESOURCES

Books

Nan Arthur, *Chill Out Fido: How to Calm Your Dog*

Ali Brown, *Focus not Fear: Training Insights from a Reactive Dog Class*

Jean Donaldson, *Fight! A Practical Guide to the Treatment of Dog-Dog Aggression*

John Fisher, *Diary of a 'Dotty Dog' Doctor*

Barbara Handelman, *Canine Behavior: A Photo Illustrated Handbook.*

Anders Hallgren, Ph.D., *Stress, Anxiety, and Aggression in Dogs*

Alexandra Horowitz, Ph.D., *Inside of a Dog: What Dogs See, Smell, and Know*

Alexandra Kurland, *The Click that Teaches: A Step-By-Step Guide in Pictures*

Patricia McConnell, Ph.D., *Feisty Fido*

Leslie McDevitt, *Control Unleashed: Creating a Focused and Confident Dog*

Pat Miller, *Do Over Dogs: Give Your Dog a Second Chance at a First Class Life*

Karen Pryor, *Don't Shoot the Dog*

Kathy Sdao, *Plenty in Life is Free: Reflections on Dogs, Training and Finding Grace*

Cheryl Smith, *Dog Friendly Gardens; Garden Friendly Dogs*

Grisha Stewart, *Ahimsa Dog Training Manual: A Practical, Force-Free Guide to Problem Solving and Manners*

Andrew Weil, *Breathing: The Master Key to Self-Healing* (audio book)

DVDs

Trish King, *Abandonment Training*

Patricia McConnell, *Lassie, Come!*

Leslie Nelson, *Really Reliable Recall*

Kathy Sdao, *Improve Your I-Cue*

Grisha Stewart, *BAT 2.0 Empowered Animals Series* (also streaming at GrishaStewart. com)

1. *Talk with Me: Simple Steps for 2-Way Understanding Between Dogs and People*

2. *Walk with Me: Safety, Fun, & Freedom with Leash Training for You and Your Dog*

3. *Problem Prevention: An Empowered Approach to Life with Dogs*

4. *Survival Skills: Coping with Dog Reactivity in Real Life*

5. *BAT 2.0 Set-Ups: How to Orchestrate BAT Set-Ups and Variations with Dogs*

6. *BAT for Geeks: A Technical Perspective on Behavior Adjustment Training 2.0*

Cited works and other sources

Note: these are sources cited in this book, not necessarily recommendations. See the text for more information on what I've written about these sources.

Amat, J., Paul, E., Zarza, C., Watkins, L. R., and Maier, S. F. (2006). Previous experience with behavioral control over stress blocks the behavioral and dorsal raphe nucleus activating effects of later uncontrollable stress: role of the ventral medial prefrontal cortex. *The Journal of Neuroscience*, 26(51), 13264-13272.

Baratta, M. V., Christianson, J. P., Gomez, D. M., Zarza, C. M., Amat, J., Masini, C. V., Watkins, L.R., and Maier, S. F. (2007). Controllable versus uncontrollable stressors bi-directionally modulate conditioned but not innate fear. *Neuroscience*, 146(4), 1495-1503.

Barlow, D. H., Agras, W. S., Leitenberg, H., and Wincze, J. P. (1970). An experimental analysis of the effectiveness of "shaping" in reducing maladaptive avoidance behavior: An analogue study. *Behaviour Research and Therapy*, 8(2), 165-173.

Capaldi, E. D., Viveiros, D. M., and Campbell, D. H. (1983). Food as a contextual cue in counterconditioning experiments: Is there a counterconditioning process? *Animal Learning & Behavior,* 11(2), 213-222.

Field, A. P. (2006). Is conditioning a useful framework for understanding the development and treatment of phobias? *Clinical Psychology Review,* 26(7), 857-875.

Friedman, S. G. (2009). What's wrong with this picture? Effectiveness is not enough. *Journal of Applied Companion Animal Behavior,* 3(1), 41-45. (also available at http://behaviorworks.org/files/articles/What's%20Wrong%20with%20this%20Picture.pdf)

Goetz, A.R. *The Effects of Preventative and Restorative Safety Behaviors on Contamination Fear.* MS thesis University of Wisconsin Milwaukee, 2013. Retrieved from http://dc.uwm.edu/etd/251/

Gunther, L. M., Denniston, J. C., and Miller, R. R. (1998). Conducting exposure treatment in multiple contexts can prevent relapse. *Behaviour Research and Therapy,* 36(1), 75-91.

Hartley, C. A., Gorun, A., Reddan, M. C., Ramirez, F., and Phelps, E. A. (2013). Stressor controllability modulates fear extinction in humans. *Neurobiology of Learning and Memory.*

Haw, J., and Dickerson, M. (1998). The effects of distraction on desensitization and reprocessing. *Behaviour research and therapy,* 36(7), 765-769.

Maier, S. F., Amat, J., Baratta, M. V., Paul, E., & Watkins, L. R. (2006). Behavioral control, the medial prefrontal cortex, and resilience. *Dialogues in Clinical Neuroscience,* 8(4), 397.

Maier, S. F., and Warren, D. A. (1988). Controllability and safety signals exert dissimilar proactive effects on nociception and escape performance. Journal of Experimental Psychology: *Animal Behavior Processes,* 14(1), 18.

Maier, S. F., and Watkins, L. R. (2010). Role of the medial prefrontal cortex in coping and resilience. *Brain Research,* 1355, 52-60.

Marks, I. (1975). Behavioral treatments of phobic and obsessive compulsive disorders: A critical appraisal. In M. Hersen, R. M. Eisler, & P. M. Miller (Eds.), *Progress in Behavior Modification,* Vol. 1. New York. Academic Press.

Mechiel Korte, S., & De Boer, S. F. (2003). A robust animal model of state anxiety: fear-potentiated behaviour in the elevated plus-maze. *European Journal of Pharmacology,* 463(1), 163-175.

Milosevic, I., and Radomsky, A. S. (2008). Safety behaviour does not necessarily interfere with exposure therapy. *Behaviour Research and Therapy,* 46(10), 1111-1118.

Mohlman, J., and Zinbarg, R. E. (2001). What kind of attention is necessary for fear reduction? An empirical test of the emotional processing model. *Behavior Therapy,* 31(1), 113-133.

Panksepp, J., Asma, S., Curran, G., Gabriel, R., and Greif, T. (2012). The philosophical implications of affective neuroscience. *Journal of Consciousness Studies,* 19(3), 6.

Parrish, C. L., Radomsky, A. S., and Dugas, M. J. (2008). Anxiety-control strategies: Is there room for neutralization in successful exposure treatment? *Clinical Psychology Review,* 28(8), 1400-1412.

Premack, D. (2009) Reward and Punishment versus Freedom. *Essays.* Retrieved from http://www.psych.upenn.edu/~premack/Essays/Entries/2009/5/15_Reward_and_Punishment_versus_Freedom.html

Rachman, S. (1989). The return of fear: Review and prospect. *Clinical Psychology Review,* 9(2), 147-168.

Smith, R. G., and Churchill, R. M. (2002). Identification of environmental determinants of behavior disorders through functional analysis of precursor behaviors. *Journal of Applied Behavior Analysis,* 35(2), 125-136.

Snider, K.S. (2007). "A constructional canine aggression treatment: Using a negative reinforcement shaping procedure with dogs in home and community settings." Retrieved from ProQuest Digital Dissertations. (AAT 1452030)

Telch, M. J., Valentiner, D. P., Ilai, D., Young, P. R., Powers, M. B., and Smits, J. A. (2004). Fear activation and distraction during the emotional processing of claustrophobic fear. *Journal of Behavior Therapy and Experimental Psychiatry,* 35(3), 219-232.

Thomas, B. L., Cutler, M., and Novak, C. (2012). A modified counterconditioning procedure prevents the renewal of conditioned fear in rats. *Learning and Motivation,* 43(1), 24-34.

Trouche, S., Sasaki, J. M., Tu, T., and Reijmers, L. G. (2013). Fear Extinction Causes Target-Specific Remodeling of Perisomatic Inhibitory Synapses. *Neuron.*

Tryon, W. W. (2005). Possible mechanisms for why desensitization and exposure therapy work. *Clinical Psychology Review,* 25(1), 67-95. Chicago.

Wolpe, J. (1961). The systematic desensitization treatment of neurosis. *Journal of Nervous Mental Disorders,* 132, 189–203.

Yang, L., Wellman, L. L., Ambrozewicz, M. A., and Sanford, L. D. (2011). Effects of stressor predictability and controllability on sleep, temperature, and fear behavior in mice. *Sleep,* 34(6), 759.

Websites

Grisha's online resources, including BAT, training gear, and other dog training and behavior topics. http://GrishaStewart.com

Canine Noise Phobia Series by Victoria Stilwell: https://positively.com/dog-wellness/dog-enrichment/music-for-dogs/canine-noise-phobia-series/

Dog Decoder mobile app with Lili Chin illustrations: http://www.dogdecoder.com/

Ian Dunbar on "Retreat & Treat." http://www.dogstardaily.com/training/retreat-amp-treat

Sprinkles information by Sally Hopkins http://www.dog-games.co.uk/sprinkles.htm

Shirley Chong on "Loose Lead Walking." http://www.shirleychong.com/keepers/LLW

Unlabel Me Campaign by Susan Friedman. http://www.behaviorworks.org/htm/downloads_art.html

Washington State Animal Codes. http://www.animal-lawyer.com/html/wa_state_animal_codes.html Virginia Broitman on "Two-Reward System." http://www.cappdt.ca/public/ jpage/1/p/Article2RewardSystem/content.do

INDEX

Also available from Dogwise Publishing

Go to www.dogwise.com for more books and ebooks.

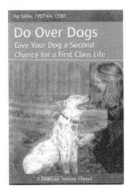

Do Over Dogs
Give Your Dog a Second Chance for a First Class Life
Pat Miller

What exactly is a Do-Over Dog? It might be a shelter dog you're working with to help her become more adoptable. Perhaps it's the dog you've adopted, rescued, or even found running stray who is now yours to live with and love...forever. Or it could be the dog you've lived with for years but you realize he still has "issues" that make him a challenging canine companion. A Do-Over Dog is any dog that you think needs—make that deserves—a second chance in life.

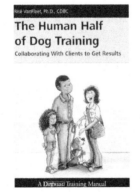

The Human Half of Dog Training
Collaborating with Clients to Get Results
Risë VanFleet

One challenge for many trainers is that their success with dogs ultimately depends on the cooperation, understanding and follow-through of the people whose dogs are being trained. In The Human Half of Dog Training, author Risë VanFleet draws upon her experience as a child and family psychologist to teach dog trainers how to take a collaborative approach with clients to help insure the best possible outcomes for their dogs.

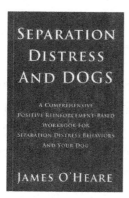

Separation Distress and Dogs
James O'Heare

Separation Distress and Dogs is a positive reinforcement based workbook for understanding, assessing and changing separation distress related behaviors in dogs. Written for guardians of dogs who exhibit distress behaviors when left alone, it presents an easy to follow, yet comprehensive, behavior change program. Includes systematic desensitization and behavior shaping, as well as empowerment training and relationship rehabilitation. It also includes sections for professional behavior consultants.

Canine Body Language
A Photographic Guide
Brenda Aloff

Canine Body Language by Brenda Aloff is a guide to canine body language. Never before has the body language of dogs been so thoroughly documented with photographs and text. Hundreds of images in this almost 400 page book illustrate the incredible variety of postures, behaviors and situations that the typical dog either manifests or encounters in his day-to-day life.

Dogwise.com is your source for quality books, ebooks, DVDs, training tools and treats.

We've been selling to the dog fancier for more than 25 years and we carefully screen our products for quality information, safety, durability and FUN! You'll find something for every level of dog enthusiast on our website www.dogwise.com or drop by our store in Wenatchee, Washington.

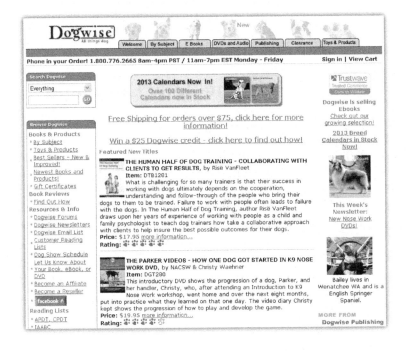